MW01292961

MULTIPLE PERSPECTIVES ON COLLEGE STUDENTS

This edited collection explores diverse perspectives about today's college students from a variety of higher education stakeholders – including faculty, researchers, policymakers, administrators, parents, and students themselves. All too often, those concerned with higher education make assumptions based on outdated information; the voices in this volume provide a grounded and real understanding of college students and explore how we might better support them in our colleges and universities. Each section includes a series of essays, with a culminating chapter written by scholars who analyze, contextualize, and ground these perspectives in theory. *Multiple Perspectives on College Students* brings current data and experience to light in a way that helps readers understand the needs and opportunities for supporting all college students for success.

Needham Yancey Gulley (he/him/his) is an associate professor of Higher Education Student Affairs at Western Carolina University, USA. He has a long history of advocating for social justice within the educational context through his scholarship, teaching, publications, presentations, trainings, and volunteer endeavors. His first book was a co-edited text published in 2017; an edited volume entitled *Using the CAS Professional Standards: Diverse Examples of Practice*; the first book ever jointly published by NASPA, ACPA, & CAS. In 2019 he was honored as a Diamond Honoree by ACPA College Student Educators International.

MULTIPLE PERSPECTIVES ON COLLEGE STUDENTS

Needs, Challenges, and Opportunities

Edited by Needham Yancey Gulley

Routledge
Taylor & Francis Group

NEW YORK AND LONDON

Cover image: © Getty Images

First published 2023
by Routledge
605 Third Avenue, New York, NY 10158

and by Routledge
4 Park Square, Milton Park, Abingdon, Oxon, OX14 4RN

Routledge is an imprint of the Taylor & Francis Group, an informa business

© 2023 Taylor & Francis

The right of Needham Yancey Gulley to be identified as the authors of the editorial material, and of the authors for their individual chapters, has been asserted in accordance with sections 77 and 78 of the Copyright, Designs and Patents Act 1988.

All rights reserved. No part of this book may be reprinted or reproduced or utilised in any form or by any electronic, mechanical, or other means, now known or hereafter invented, including photocopying and recording, or in any information storage or retrieval system, without permission in writing from the publishers.

Trademark notice: Product or corporate names may be trademarks or registered trademarks, and are used only for identification and explanation without intent to infringe.

Library of Congress Cataloging-in-Publication Data
Names: Gulley, Needham Yancey, editor.
Title: Multiple perspectives on college students : needs, challenges, and opportunities / edited by Needham Yancey Gulley.
Description: New York, NY : Routledge, 2022. | Includes bibliographical references and index. | Identifiers: LCCN 2021061715 (print) | LCCN 2021061716 (ebook) | ISBN 9780367333737 (hardback) | ISBN 9780367333744 (paperback) | ISBN 9780429319471 (ebook)
Subjects: LCSH: College students--United States. | Universities and colleges--United States. | Education, Higher--United States.
Classification: LCC LA229 .M787 2022 (print) | LCC LA229 (ebook) | DDC 378.1/980973--dc23/eng/20220419
LC record available at https://lccn.loc.gov/2021061715
LC ebook record available at https://lccn.loc.gov/2021061716

ISBN: 978-0-367-33373-7 (hbk)
ISBN: 978-0-367-33374-4 (pbk)
ISBN: 978-0-429-31947-1 (ebk)

DOI: 10.4324/9780429319471

Typeset in Bembo
by SPi Technologies India Pvt Ltd (Straive)

CONTENTS

QUESTION 5
What Can You Do to Support Today's College Students? **165**

FOREWORD

Kristen A. Renn

Although a shrinking segment of commercial media may still depict college students as a curated-for-diversity group of carefree young adults on an ivy-covered neo-Gothic campus, that image is fading even in the popular imagination. A collective $1.7 trillion student loan debt (Friedman, 2021) hangs over the United States and has been the subject of substantial attention during the pandemic, the 2020 presidential election, and subsequent rounds of federal policymaking. Thirty percent of all adults have incurred educational debt (Federal Reserve, 2021). The pandemic forced millions of students and instructors off campus and into "Zoom U," or as one of my students described it, "All of the hard parts of college and none of the fun." Even before the pandemic, reports of food and housing insecurity among students (Strauss, 2020) provided evidence that being a college student does not provide protection against the realities of economic precarity. The pandemic, by nearly all accounts, exacerbated economic, academic, and psychological challenges to students' well-being and success. Anyone who in 2020 still thought college life was one big party interrupted by occasional homework was not paying attention; anyone who still thinks so is even more out of sync with reality.

Still, higher education retains massive appeal to high school graduates or those students returning as adults. As noted in Chapter 2, undergraduate enrollments peaked at 17.10 million in 2017 and have declined slightly since then. With graduate student enrollments included, the numbers have stayed around 20 million for several years. In spite of all of the criticism, widespread awareness of the potential for leaving college with student debt, and a global pandemic, higher education remains a desirable endeavor. Whether place-based or online, non-profit or for-profit, higher education continues to be a destination in which students and families are willing to invest. The investment is not a sure bet.

Thirty-eight percent of students who begin a four-year degree do not complete one (U.S. Department of Education, National Center for Education Statistics 2020), potentially leaving them with student debt and no degree to assist them in getting a job that will help them pay off that debt. And even for those who do complete, economic outcomes and social mobility are not equally assured due to racial and gender-based inequities in employment and compensation.

With so many people willing to continue to put their trust in higher education, and such uncertain outcomes, there is an urgent need to pay attention to the people Needham Yancey Gulley has defined in this book as stakeholders. What is it that makes so many people – students, families, communities, government, the public – continue to believe in the possibilities of higher education to contribute to the personal and the public good? And what do these stakeholders themselves point to as the problems and potential solutions? Because I rarely stop to ask the kinds of questions asked in this book to people like the ones featured in it, I was eager to find out what the writers had to say about students, their needs, challenges, and opportunities.

Without risking any spoilers, I can say that the writers here made me think more deeply about some of my assumptions about some stakeholders. I do talk with and listen to current students a great deal. Without question, the students featured throughout this book offer important insight into student life today. They do so with honesty, transparency, and generosity.

Honest, too, are the off-campus stakeholders featured here, including a state legislator and a set of parents of four college graduates. The legislator's writing reminded me of the trust that is bestowed on institutions by the governing bodies that provide substantial funding for higher education. The parents' writing reminded me of the trust that families place in us to be not *in loco parentis*, but alongside parents as partners in the growth and learning of their children. I have been socialized not to call college students "children," and certainly they are not in the abstract, but in the context of their families, they are the children, no matter how old they are. The parent-child bond is not the same as the college student relationship, but there are elements of parental care and personalization that are worth emulating as we aim to provide the best education for each of our students. Not every student comes directly to college from a childhood home, but every student deserves to be treated with care and personalization.

The institutional actors of various levels and roles hold up the third leg of this book's stool. From varied perspectives they offer insight garnered from careers long or not-so-long, reminding the reader that higher education is worth investing in and worth fighting for. From these writers, I gained hope that it is not too late to correct our course, to keep adjusting our sails, to keep adapting to changing student populations, to identify and meet the challenges today and ahead.

Taken in sequence, the stakeholders' ideas in the book layer on top of one another to form a kaleidoscope, in which the image shifts slightly and becomes more colorful depending on the perspective of the writer. But taken as a whole, the effect is more like one of those "magic eye" images that pops up into three dimensions to create a 360-degree perspective on college students, their needs and challenges, and opportunities to serve them better. Ultimately the book is an invitation to take seriously this multidimensional perspective, to honor the reality of college students' lives, and to evolve higher education to meet their needs.

References

Federal Reserve. (2021, May). Report on the economic well-being of US households in 2020. Board of Governors of the Federal Reserve System. Retrieved on April 15, 2022 from https://www.federalreserve.gov/publications/2021-economic-well-being-of-us-households-in-2020-student-loans.htm

Friedman, Z. (2021, February 20). Student loan debt statistics in 2021: A record $1.7 trillion. *Forbes*. Retrieved on April 15, 2022 from https://www.forbes.com/sites/zackfriedman/2021/02/20/student-loan-debt-statistics-in-2021-a-record-17-trillion

Strauss, V. (2020, February 20). Housing and food insecurity affecting many college students, new data says. *The Washington Post*. Retrieved on April 15, 2022, from https://www.washingtonpost.com/education/2020/02/20/housing-food-insecurity-affecting-many-college-students-new-data-says/

U.S. Department of Education, National Center for Education Statistics. (2020). *The Condition of Education 2020* (NCES 2020-144), Undergraduate Retention and Graduation Rates. Retrieved on April 15, 2022 from https://nces.ed.gov/fastfacts/display.asp?id=40

ACKNOWLEDGEMENTS

The writing of this book has been one of the more difficult undertakings of my professional career. This has been true partly because of my own foolishness in taking on such an endeavor without coeditors. Partly due to the intersection of this project with personal struggles related to professional balance and personal mental health. Partly due to a global pandemic that interrupted the very ways we all see the world and operate in it. The completion of this book is a long time coming, and I have several folx to thank for the support through the process.

I had the idea for this book many years ago when having dinner with Laura A. Dean at our favorite Italian restaurant in Athens, Georgia. We actually discussed two books that night and made the first one a reality with the partnership of our friend Shannon Dean-Scott several years ago. So, to Laura, thank you for all of the many wonderful conversations where we engage in the problems and the solutions of our field through laughter, wine, and whiskey.

Part of the challenge in putting this text together is the sheer volume of contributors. There are very few carrots or sticks to get stakeholders outside of the academy to write essays for a mainly academic text, but many did. Contributors to this book took time out of their lives to write when they might not normally do so and when they had little to gain individually. To the employed academics who contributed, they also balanced their contributions with all other things they have going on – which is always too much. All of them did so along an extended time line with patience. I thank everyone for contributing parts of themselves.

Patience is a theme here, and I thank the publishers for theirs as personal, professional, and COVID delays continued to extend the time line for the project. Among the most patient folx who have supported this project is my husband, Corey Johnson. A prolific scholar who is disciplined in his academic pursuits, he is also supportive in his private ones. He has balanced personal support with professional challenges as I have worked (and some days not worked) on this project. We have navigated living in two countries, both teaching in a small space during a pandemic, moving twice, and renovating a home during the process of writing this book. Thank you, Corey, for staying the course at my pace, even when it is slower than we both would have liked.

Finally, thank you to my students who, daily, remind me of the role that perspective and place play in our ways of knowing. You check my assumptions and question my realities as I try to show you what exists behind the curtain that is the system of higher education. I do not have all of the answers, but I love getting to be in community with you as we wrestle with the questions. The solutions come from the collective conversations and not from the silencing of voices.

1

INTRODUCTION

Needham Yancey Gulley

> **Yancey Gulley** (he/him/his) is an associate professor in the Higher Education Student Affairs program at Western Carolina University. His first co-edited book is *Using the CAS Professional Standards: Diverse Examples of Practice.* He is focused on scholarship that highlights diversity in higher education regarding both students and institutions.

Years of social media and pop culture messaging highlight the American college student with characteristics such as being between 18–24 years old; attending full time; living in a residence hall or campus-adjacent housing; loves partying, going to student club meetings, or playing intramural sports; and has no outside commitments to interfere with their studies. Yet, a report from the Higher Learning Advocates published in 2018 indicates that "while the pop culture archetype still holds sway with many in the general public, policymakers are attuned to demographic shifts" (Higher Learning Advocates, 2018, para. 1). But I am not sure that this is true. I question whether any of our higher education stakeholders are actually attuned to shifts in who is being served or who could potentially be served by the system of higher education. And, I am not the only one who questions what those inside and outside of the academy think about higher education and who we serve, and whether or not these views are supported by the facts. Many are asking these questions, including groups like New America, the Higher Learning Advocates, the Lumina Foundation, and other think tanks. Articles exploring who college students are today often show up in the media, such as the *Wall Street Journal* and NPR. The basis for much of these discussions is the fact that many have a misconception about who college students are. If we

DOI: 10.4324/9780429319471-1

do not know who our students are, how are we expected to provide appropriate educational environments to fulfill the purported educational mission of higher education? The Lumina Foundation (2021) puts it quite simply, "Today's students are vastly different from those decades ago, but colleges are still structured as if 18- to 21-old, full-time students are in the majority."

If colleges and universities do not know who our students are, how can we create institutions for their success? If colleges and universities do not know who our students are, how can we expect other stakeholders to? Colleges and universities are not the only ones who make decisions about the structure of higher education. Many others do as well. A few examples of other stakeholders who influence higher education include the following:

- Legislators who make huge financial and policy decisions that particularly impact public institutions. Take for example the passing of NC Promise in North Carolina that capped tuition at three institutions to $500/semester. Not only does the legislature appropriate budgets to public colleges in the state, in passing NC Promise, they also took control of the decision-making of the institutions.
- The Department of Education, which creates policies impacting any institutions of higher education in the United States that receive any public funds. Consider that the way institutions must interpret and operationalize many aspects of Title IX legislation comes directly to institutions from the Department of Education through directives known as "Dear Colleague Letters." These directives often change with the political affiliations of those in the executive branch.
- Alumni who leverage their financial contributions to influence the direction of institutional culture. Consider that when Jerry Falwell Jr. was President of Liberty University and was embroiled in a very public scandal, it was the demand of alumni that led the board to remove him from his position. That is quite a significant feat given that the power he and his family swayed over the institution began in the 1970s.

The question becomes – when they are using their power to change higher education, are they doing so with the same information and based on the same data? The answer is unequivocally no. There is constant conflict between key players in higher education regarding a variety of aspects of higher education, from policies in residence halls, to the number of credit hours necessary to earn an associate's degree, and everything in between. These conflicts lead to frustration, lawsuits, protests, and more, and we enter the debates with passion and frequently with resolution of our own opinions but not a willingness to really understand the position of others.

The purpose of this edited text is to explore the diverse perspectives that a variety of higher education stakeholders have on the college student. In this text,

I have engaged a wide range of people to unpack who today's college students are and why multiple people and groups have their own ideas on what those students offer and need. Those who have a vested interest in and/or exert influence over higher education share their perspectives so that readers can get a sense of the various points of view present in conversations and decision-making around college students and higher education. There are so many types of people who have a vested interest in college students and higher education, from lobbyists to parents, from politicians to career coaches, from researchers to the students themselves, and many more in between, and some of these voices are weighted more heavily than others when decision-making around higher education. The difference in weight is largely related to the positional authority or influence they have within higher education. A college president is going to have more authority than a career coach, for example, though both care and have a stake in the system of higher education. With so many folx having unique perspectives on higher education, it is no wonder that there are misunderstandings and miscommunications among stakeholders when discussing college students and the system of higher education in which they engage. By asking everyday people from significant stakeholder groups to contribute to this book and thoughtfully and reflectively considering their perspectives, we can better understand where others are coming from when influencing systems of higher education within their locus of control or larger locus of influence. By asking contributors to answer questions specifically about college students versus the system of higher education itself, I aim to put students and student outcomes at the forefront of the conversation that is ever evolving into one about the neoliberal system that is becoming (maybe has become) higher education.

Many misconceptions about who college students are in large part due to the diversity of voices present in conversations related to them. These misconceptions are perpetuated in media representations of college students (think about movies from *Animal House* to *Pitch Perfect* being set in liberal arts, residential institutions), a penchant for equating collegiate sports as representative of all collegiate institutions (think about the airing of collegiate sport being how many Americans access any views of college students), romanticized ideas of grass-filled quads where undergrads through frisbees and lounge on blankets discussing Proust, and much more. We use terms like "traditional college student" and "nontraditional college student" in many types of discourse about higher education. The assumption being that the "traditional college student" is 18–24 years old, white, and attending a four-year, residentially focused institution full time. The further implicit assumption here is that this is the "majority" of students currently engaged in higher education in the United States. I argue that these distinctions are not just outdated but extremely harmful (see Gulley, 2016; Gulley, 2021). And, to be clear, these are the students for whom higher education was designed in the United States dating back to when the modern system of higher education took shape in the 1910s and 1920s. These students are also those for which the system is being maintained. Yet, the majority of college students actually are not in this demographic category, as student identities and enrollment trends have changed over time. Renn and Reason (2013) noted, "Enrollment trends suggest that students are diverse in manifold sociodemographic categories, including sex, race, ethnicity, sexuality, and socioeconomic status. Students also bring with them experiences, attitudes, and beliefs that further complicate the landscape of higher education" (p. 24). Students are also of varying ages and enroll in higher education with a myriad of different life experiences and responsibilities. This increasingly diverse student body also attends a wider variety of institutional types than in the past, including community colleges, for-profit institutions, professional schools, and online universities, just to name a few. Yet, our systems of managing, funding, legislating, accrediting, and operating higher education have not had the same evolution, and many stakeholders are not aware of the shift or the future predictions related to college student enrollment trends or demographic projections related to student identities. For example, it surprises many that from 1999 to 2015, community colleges enrolled the majority of college students, and the average age of the college student continues to rise and is projected to do so into the future (see Chapter 2). So, in this book, some contributors give us the numbers to shed light on the demographic realities and trends of who today's college students are and who they might be in the future, while others provide theoretical framing of diversity in higher education. Having a clear picture of who college students in the United States are can help those who have a vested interest in higher education have more fruitful conversations about higher education and the direction it should be taking in the future.

Engaging the Text

There are several ways in which this text can assist readers in understanding college students, as well as the perspectives and motivations of various higher education stakeholders. These include

1. amplify voices of a variety of stakeholders,
2. provide frameworks for understanding student diversity and enrollment trends based on current and predictive data and relevant theoretical perspectives,
3. share a framework for understanding diversity in higher education as an ever-growing reality, and
4. have scholars analyze and make meaning across the contributors representing stakeholder groups.

To gain the stakeholder voices, representatives from various categories of folx with a vested interest in and influence on higher education were asked to write brief essays in response to one of a specific set of questions about college students.

Questions were intentionally framed to be about students and not about educational systems in hopes of garnering understandings that are student centric versus system bound. While these might seem (and are) contingent on each other in a reciprocal way, centering students as the primary way to consider higher education allows us to have a humanistic and developmental approach to understanding the purposes and impacts of our colleges and universities. By asking a diverse group of stakeholders about college students, we have an additional opportunity to understand the diversity of the college student makeup itself as stakeholders highlight various aspects of the student body from their perspectives. The benefits of understanding the college students from these various perspectives are

1. we can get a better sense of who college students are and what needs and opportunities they bring with them when enrolling in our institutions, and
2. we can better understand the ways that different stakeholders think about college students so that we might have more fruitful conversations across stakeholder groups.

This book also provides commentary from higher education scholars in order to assist readers in making sense of the diverse perspectives from the myriad of stakeholders. While all stakeholder's ideas and insights are valid, they are likely not all equally informed or recognized equally across decision-making bodies or in relation to the theories that underpin higher education and student development. In fact, some stakeholders have more authority than others, as they have the power to make structural decisions about higher education and must "prioritize among them and how they become involved in decision-making (directly or indirectly)" (Gross, Godwin, & Solomon, 2019, para. 2). Consider the Department of Education representatives who create policies that impact Title X regulations, for example, as opposed to the parent who has no direct policy control. The higher education student affairs scholars included in this text offer analysis of contributor responses in direct relation to each other and the larger body of literature about higher education to highlight some of this knowledge differential.

There are five questions about college students that frame this text:

1. Who Are Today's College Students?
2. What Are the Needs of Today's College Students?
3. What Are the Most Significant Challenges for Today's College Students?
4. What Are the Most Significant Opportunities for Today's College Students?
5. What Can You Do to Support Today's College Students?

Four different higher education stakeholders respond to each question with brief essays. These essayists were chosen after a thorough review of literature on who has a vested interest in higher education and then brainstorming people from these categories. I used my networks from 20+ years in the field to help identify potential essayists, with special attention to gaining diversity of roles, length of time in such positions, geographic orientation, educational background, race, gender, etc. Invitations for contributors were sent and more than 60 essayists were invited before arriving at the 20 final essays. In an effort to have as many voices present as possible, each stakeholder group is only represented in one essay throughout the text, except for students who are represented in a response to all questions, though variation in the types of institutions they attended and their own demographic backgrounds were intentional. As Kezar and Dizon (2020) note, we must give power and weight to the student voice to create positive change within the academy. Responses to each of the questions posed are grouped in sections, followed by a summative/critical analytic chapter in which a higher education scholar analyzes and contextualizes those essays. These analysis and discussion chapters are written by higher education student affairs scholars who present themes found in the responses and unpack them in light of relevant literature, theory, and stakeholder positionality. The goal of the analysis chapters is twofold:

1. address how respondents collectively answered the prompt, and
2. address why various stakeholders have differing views on the answer.

Book Outline

The opening chapters of this text offer context for who the contemporary college students are, how to understand the diversity in higher education, and ways to consider the variety of stakeholder roles that influence higher education. In Chapter 2, Biddix, Gabourel, and Cuevas provide a quantitatively driven look at student enrollment data, offering statistics related to student demographics. In doing so, they allow readers to see who we are currently serving in higher education, through what types of institutions, and in what ways while also looking toward the future student body through analysis of trend data. One important illustration of the data is that students in higher education are more diverse and nuanced than many stakeholders seem to realize. Reviewing disaggregated data within particular classrooms, institutions, systems allows stakeholders to see inequities in students, student success, student enrollment, and more so that we can make sense of the data in critical ways and examine how our systems contribute to those inequities (Byon & Roberson, 2020; Kodama & Dugan, 2013; McNair, Bensimon, & Malcom-Piqueux, 2020). In Chapter 3, Torrez offers a more theoretical exploration of who today's college students are by highlighting diversity within the student population and how stakeholders should consider the topic of student diversity in the practice of higher education. Readers should take special note of the difference in the tone of these two chapters as they offer a stark contrast in the ways we think about and discuss college students. This difference in representation is core to the point of this book – highlighting the various ways in which different people address the topic of college students and higher education.

In Chapter 4, Davis and Barnes provide a look into the variety of stakeholders who have a vested interest in or influence on higher education in the United States. Their introduction to stakeholder categories and analysis of their varied perspectives shows us how diverse the players are who make decisions about higher education, from who attends to how it is funded and everything in between. This analysis sets readers up to explore the essays written by some of these representatives with a nuanced and critical lens, taking into account things like stakeholder motivations, experiences, and potential blinders.

The rest of this text sheds light on the actual perspectives that various stakeholders have on the college student. There is a tendency among those who have a vested interest in higher education to talk more than we listen and to talk about policy, budgets, and institutional survival more than about students. This is, at least, a common occurrence among what I will call professionalized stakeholders in higher education. Professionalized stakeholders are those whose incomes and careers are in any directly significant way related to higher education, examples include college/university administrators, staff and faculty, higher education think-tank employees, Department of Education officials, and the like. Even outside of the United States, researchers are discussing stakeholder groupings by identifying those who have an active role versus a seemingly more passive role in institutions of higher education or the systems that underpin them, though this distinction is likely based on power and direct versus indirect influence (Beerkens & Udam, 2017). By asking stakeholders from both categories (hopefully even more) to respond to prompts directly about students, we might better understand what informs various ways of making decisions when conversations rise to the level of structural support, maintenance, and change in higher education. How frequently do we hear a member of the state legislature talk about the needs of college students or an education think-tank researcher talk about the best way they can support college students? How often are these ideas congruent and how often are they in direct competition? Knowing how each of the stakeholders feels about and thinks about college students (who are – or should be – the core of our higher education system), we can better understand each other's perspectives. We might also find that some stakeholders think less about centering students in the decision-making process and more about the institutions or the overall system.

There is a great amount of theorizing about the cognitive, psychosocial, and personal development of college students, as well as the place of higher education in the larger societal context of the United States. Through the various theories, we try to make sense of the foundations of our system of higher education, how students learn and grow, and how best to support student success. While not all who have a stake in or influence upon higher education are familiar with these theories and while many of these theories are challenged for a variety of reasons (including a lack of diversity in the research that led to their formulation), these theories can help us understand the perspectives different folx bring when considering higher education and college students. In order to allow for a variety of voices to be heard and understood, this text takes no particular theoretical stance from the outset but allows for those to be explored when analyzing stakeholder responses. For current and future higher education and student affairs practitioners and faculty, these analytic chapters are ripe opportunities to address what Pendakur, Quaye, and Harper (2020) call the "clarion call for all in staff, faculty, and administrator roles in higher education to do better by students, particularly those who experience the range of exclusion and harm embedded in their collegiate environments" (p. 1).

(Inevitable) COVID-19 Impact Statement

While I want to avoid terms like *unprecedented* and *new normal*, it is necessary to address the impact that the COVID-19 pandemic (and our national response – or lack thereof to it) has had on this book. This project has been some time in the making, and while engaging many potential stakeholders and solidifying essayists and then having scholars respond was going to be a lengthy process in the best of times, the pandemic added to the difficulty in accomplishing the task. The reality is that most of the essays presented in this book were written prior to the COVID-19 outbreak that so drastically altered our world in 2020, yet a few were written after that. Given that the analysis chapters were written after the essays were collected, those chapters were mainly written at some point during the COVID-19-drenched reality. When any contributor was writing after the start of the COVID-19 pandemic, I encouraged them to acknowledge it but not dwell solely on it. This decision was made for the sake of some continuity in one's ability to read across essays while not denying the changed world in which we live (after all, a reality check is part of the point of this text). Books represent the time in which they are written, and books are written in months and years and not days (generally speaking) and I ask readers to acknowledge the timing of this project and the span of time it represents. After all, one of the very points of this book is to acknowledge that "today's" college student is ever evolving, and it is almost impossible to stay current. My hope is that we can all, as stakeholders, be less behind than we have been. Today is virtually tomorrow and tomorrow is basically today and in the grand scheme of things, it is all history anyway. To this end, should I be fortunate enough to revisit this text in a second edition, I commit to making the process more concise as to avoid such lapses across contributions.

Conclusion

As you will see throughout this book, it is difficult to think about college students without thinking about student success. As McNair, Bensimon, and Malcom-Piqueux (2020) point out,

> [S]uccess requires reciprocal engagement from students as well as from educators. Students must fully engage in the pursuit of their educational goals, but the institution must also create a learning environment that promotes equity and inclusion by understanding the diversity of the students that it seeks to educate.
>
> *(p. 4)*

I expand this notion to say that legislators, think-tank experts, parents, career/college coaches, and other valued stakeholders must also understand this diversity in order to do their part to support and encourage student success. This book is one attempt to have us all get on the same page or, at least, be able to improve our communication with and understanding of each other. We must stay attuned to our students in terms of who they are, what they offer, and what they need if we, as stakeholders, are to continually (re)invent systems within higher education that promote the success of who we serve instead of who the systems were built to serve.

In this book, you will find high school students sharing their anticipation of going to college and what they hope to find when they get there. A state legislator talks about stopping college only to return again years later to finish his degree and what it felt like to be older than most of his classmates, as well as how he perceives the changing role of technology in education. Parents of four college graduates discuss the struggles they had with some children when encouraging them to pursue and complete higher education while other children were more self-motivated. A college president discusses the difficulty in really defining college students in a way that makes it easy to support them. Multiple college students talk about their success and their struggles while providing recommendations to others on how best to support college student success. These are real insights from real people who frequently do not speak the same lingo or come together in dialogue. Are your experiences captured in this text? Are those of others that you know who care about higher education? What perspectives will be new for you? Which will affirm your beliefs. To find out, read on with an open mind and a listening heart and then join the conversation.

Suggested Activity/Self-Check

Readers of this text are encouraged to reflect on their own understandings of and beliefs about today's college students before further engaging in the content presented here. It would be advantageous for you to answer, for yourself, the five prompts framing stakeholder contributions to this book. In the conclusion, you will find a guided reflection activity that will call on you to reflect on your own conceptualizations of college students prior to reading this book and after you have consumed the information found within it. To trace your own perspective in relation to others who impact and are impacted by higher education, answer the following questions for yourself and put the responses aside for later reflection.

1. Who Are Today's College Students?
2. What Are the Needs of Today's College Students?
3. What Are the Most Significant Challenges for Today's College Students?
4. What Are the Most Significant Opportunities for Today's College Students?
5. What Can You Do to Support Today's College Students?

References

Beerkens, M., & Udam, M. (2017). Stakeholders in higher education quality assurance: Richness in diversity? *Higher Education Policy, 30*(3), 341–359.

Byon, A., & Roberson, A. J. (2020). *Everyone deserves to be seen.* Institute for Higher Education Policy. https://www.ihep.org/wpcontent/uploads/2020/11/ihep_aapi_brief.pdf

Gross, K., Godwin, P., & Solomon, J. D. (2019). *UB op-ed: Education's many stakeholders (An article revisited).* University Business. Retrieved September 23, 2021, from https://universitybusiness.com/ub-op-ed-educations-many-stakeholders-an-article-revisited/

Gulley, N. Y. (2016, August 5). The myth of the nontraditional student. *Inside Higher Ed.* Retrieved from https://www.insidehighered.com/views/2016/08/05/defining-students-nontraditional-inaccurate-and-damaging-essay

Gulley, N. Y. (2021). Challenging assumptions: 'Contemporary students', 'non-traditional students', adult learners', post-traditional', 'new traditional'. *Schole: A Journal of Leisure Studies and Recreation Education, 36*(1–2), 4–10.

Higher Learning Advocates (2018, October 31). *Survey reveals gap between public and policymakers when it comes to understanding today's college students* [press release]. https://higherlearningadvocates.org/news/survey-reveals-gap-between-public-and-policy-makers-when-it-comes-to-understanding-todays-college-students-2/

Kezar, A., & Dizon, J. P. M. (2020). Renewing and revitalizing shared governance: A social justice and equity framework. In A. Kezar & J. Posselt (Eds.), *Higher education administration for social justice and equity: Critical perspectives for leadership* (pp. 21–42). Routledge.

Kodama, C. M., & Dugan, J. P. (2013). Leveraging leadership efficacy for college students; Disaggregating data to examine unique predictors by race. *Equity & Excellence in Education, 46*(2), 184–201.

The Lumina Foundation (2021, October 26). *Today's students.* https://www.luminafoundation.org/campaign/todays-student/

McNair, T. B., Bensimon, E. M., & Malcom-Piqueux, L. (2020). *From equity walk to equity talk: Expanding practitioner knowledge for racial justice in higher education.* Jossey-Bass.

Pendakur, S. L., Quaye, S. J., & Harper S. R. (2020). The heart of the work: Equitable engagement for students in US higher education. In S. J. Quaye, S. R. Harper, & S. L. Pendakur (Eds.), Student engagement in higher education: *Theoretical perspectives and practical approaches for diverse populations* (3rd ed.) (pp. 1–16). Routledge.

Renn, K. A., & Reason, R. D. (2013). *College students in the United States: Characteristics, experiences, and outcomes.* Jossey-Bass.

2

TODAY'S U.S. COLLEGE STUDENTS BY THE NUMBERS

J. Patrick Biddix, Kriss G. Gabourel and Frank Cuevas

J. Patrick Biddix (he/him/his) is professor Higher Education, Coordinator of the Higher Education Administration PhD program, and Associate Director of the Postsecondary Education Research Center (PERC) at the University of Tennessee. His research and teaching expertise includes research design and assessment, student success and engagement, and higher education policy. Dr. Biddix is the author of *Research Methods and Applications for Student Affairs (Jossey-Bass, 2018) and co-authored the 2nd edition textbook of Assessment in Student Affairs* (Jossey-Bass, 2016) and the 2nd edition of *Frameworks for Assessing Learning and Development Outcomes* (CAS, 2021). He serves currently as faculty fellow with the Division of Student Success, where his work is focused on student assessment initiatives. In 2015, he received a Fulbright Scholar Award to study student engagement and learning in Montreal, Canada.

Kriss Gabourel (she/her/hers) is a PhD Candidate pursuing a degree in Data Science and Engineering at the University of Tennessee in Knoxville. She is a Bredesen Center Fellow and graduate research assistant for the Postsecondary Education Research Center (PERC). Her research emphasis is in learning analytics for higher education, and her research interests include improvement of intelligent tutoring systems and the role of community colleges in higher education.

DOI: 10.4324/9780429319471-2

Dr. Frank Cuevas (he/him/his) serves as Vice Chancellor for Student Life at the University of Tennessee, Knoxville. Dr. Cuevas also serves as Adjunct Assistant Professor for the Department of Educational Leadership & Policy Studies in the College of Education, Health, and Human Sciences. Dr. Cuevas began his Student Affairs career at The Ohio State University. He returned to his alma mater (FSU) in 1995 and served in various leadership roles over his fifteen-year tenure. In 2010, Dr. Cuevas joined the University of Tennessee, administration as Executive Director of University Housing and has served in several leadership roles within Student Life. In 2020, Dr. Cuevas was appointed as the Vice Chancellor for Student Life. He has co-authored a chapter, *Navigating Your Career as a Mid-Level Manager*, for special issue of New Directions for Student Services. Dr. Cuevas is involved in a number of professional organizations.

In 1995, the American Council on Education published a report painting a portrait of the college students of the day. They rooted their publication in the reality that "it is difficult for those outside of higher education to imagine the complex mosaic that is the U.S. college student population. The diversity of these students is startling, even to those who work on college campuses" (p. 2). The "complex mosaic" of today's student population can be characterized by differences in race and ethnicity, gender and gender identity, age, socioeconomic status, immigration status, and sexual orientation, as well as many other factors. Their attitudes, values, and beliefs are as complex as their demographics. Any number of combinations of these characteristics intersect to comprise the complexity of individuals enrolled in postsecondary education today (Patton, Renn, Guido, & Quaye, 2016).

To contextualize this contemporary changing landscape, we begin this chapter with a population summary to highlight key demographic trends in the pipeline for future students. We continue with a broad contextual overview of current enrollment trends in higher education. The largest section of this chapter gives an outline of enrollment characteristics, focusing on gender and ethnicity shifts in the past two decades. We include snapshot trends for other demographics, a comparison of student intentions and plans, and a view of student attitudes, values, and beliefs from 2007 to 2017. The final data section focuses on degree attainment. We close the chapter with a summary and considerations based on these trends.

Population Overview

Between 1997 and 2017, the U.S. population grew by almost 22%, from approximately 266.5 to 324.3 million. Concurrent with this growth, the racial and ethnic makeup of the nation changed substantially. Although whites continued to represent the largest racial and ethnic group in the United States, their share of the overall population decreased from about 72% in 1997 to 61% in 2017. Among children under 18, whites currently represent slightly less than 50% of the population. Much of the progression in racial and ethnic diversity comes from the growing Hispanic[1] population, which increased from about 11% to 18% in the given time frame. This was followed by Asians,[2] who increased from about 4% to 6% over the same period. Blacks remained relatively constant as a share of the total population, declining slightly from 12.5% to 12.3%.

Postsecondary Education Overview

The Higher Education Act of 1965 empowered the U.S. government to provide financial assistance to students seeking to attain a postsecondary education. Today, there are more than 6,400 institutions of higher education in the United States authorized to administer federal financial aid. The following contextual information is drawn primarily from data collected and analyzed by the National Center for Education Statistics (NCES); most can be referenced in McFarland et al. (2019).

Title IV institutions (referring to the specific Title within the Higher Education Act that authorizes federal financial aid) can be classified in many ways. Table 2.1 is a broad overview of the major categorizations.

In the fall of 2017, there were about 20 million students enrolled across all sectors of higher education. More than 80% of these students were undergraduates, more than half were female, and more than a third were Students of Color.

TABLE 2.1 Institutions by sector

Institution sector	Count	Percentage%
Four-Year Institution	**2,807**	**43.5**
Public	748	11.6
Private, nonprofit	1,595	24.7
Private, for-profit	464	7.2
Two-Year Institution	**1,896**	**29.4**
Public	969	15.0
Private, nonprofit	152	2.4
Private, for-profit	775	12.0
Less than Two-Year Institution	**1,747**	**27.1**
Public	236	3.7
Private, nonprofit	72	1.1
Private, for-profit	1,439	22.3
Total	**6,450**	**100**

Overall enrollment in higher education increased steadily from the late 1990s through 2010. This increase was most dramatic among full-time students, as full-time enrollment grew about 45% between 2000 and 2010. During that same time frame, part-time enrollment increased by about 27%. Since 2010, overall enrollment has seen a slight decline. Again, that decrease is most evidenced in full-time enrollment, which decreased by 9% between 2010 and 2017. Part-time enrollment decreased by about 4% in the same time frame. In the next decade, undergraduate enrollment is projected to increase only slightly (McFarland et al., 2019). Enrollment projections indicate that future growth in enrollment will be driven more by part-time students. By 2029, projections estimate that part-time enrollment will have increased by about 4%, whereas full-time enrollment is estimated to have only a 1% increase.

Postsecondary Enrollment Characteristics

Enrollment by Institution Type and Sector

From 1997 to 2017, community colleges (two-year schools) and doctoral universities were the most popular destination for postsecondary students (Figure 2.1). From 1999 to 2015, community colleges enrolled the majority of college students. However, this trend peaked in 2010 and declined steadily until 2016, while the number of students attending doctoral universities continued to rise.

Enrollment in both undergraduate and graduate programs has risen from 1997 to 2017 (Figure 2.2). Total undergraduate enrollment in all degree-granting institutions increased by 37% from 2000 to 2010. However, since 2010, undergraduate enrollment has been on a slight decline, while graduate and professional enrollment has consistently risen over the past decade, by nearly 53%.

Trends in enrollment for these same two decades can also be observed by sector. Though they make up a small percentage of total enrollment, there has

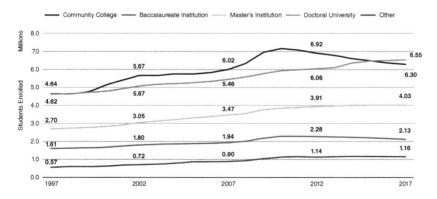

FIGURE 2.1 Postsecondary enrollment by institution type (1997–2017)

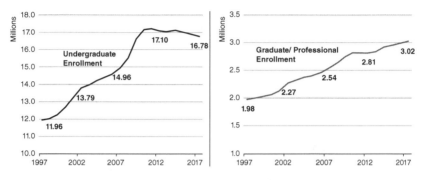

FIGURE 2.2 Undergraduate and graduate enrollment (1997–2017)

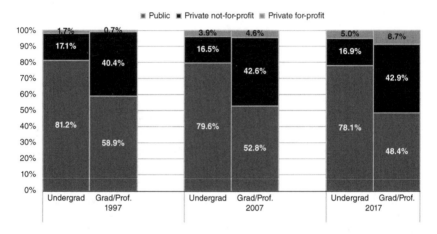

FIGURE 2.3 Proportion of undergraduate and graduate enrollment by sector (1997–2017)

been a significant shift in the private for-profit sector (Figure 2.3). Enrollment at for-profit institutions, as a percent of total undergraduates enrolled, has increased fivefold over the past two decades. A substantial portion of the rise in graduate enrollment has come from the for-profit sector.

Enrollment by Gender

Throughout most of higher education history, men have enrolled in college at higher rates than women.[3] This trend shifted in the late 1980s when for the first time in the United States, more women enrolled than men. In the past several decades, the enrollment gap has slowly increased. In 2017, about 57% of enrolled students were female and 43% were male (a difference of 14%). As Figure 2.4 represents, there are 12.5% more women than men enrolled at the undergraduate level. At that graduate level, that gap is 19.0%.

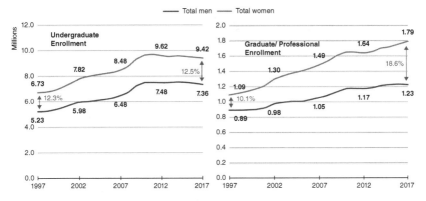

FIGURE 2.4 Undergraduate and graduate postsecondary enrollment by gender, 1997–2017

Enrollment by Race/Ethnicity

With regard to race and ethnicity,[4] the total percentage of nonwhite undergraduates has increased in the past two decades from 28% to about 45%. This growth is largely attributed to the increasing number of Hispanic students, which has almost tripled in the past 20 years. Figure 2.5 shows changes in race and ethnicity among undergraduates, demonstrating relatively modest growth among all groups except for Hispanic students. Similar changes occurred in graduate enrollment. While the white graduate student population shows a modest increase, populations of nonwhite graduate students have more than doubled in each racial or ethnic group.

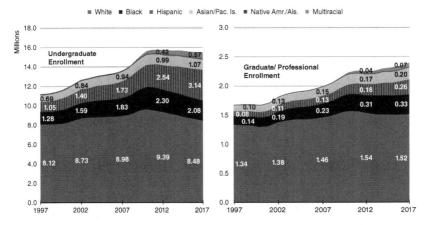

FIGURE 2.5 Undergraduate and graduate postsecondary enrollment race/ethnicity, 1997–2017

TABLE 2.2 Postsecondary enrollment by age

	Undergraduate			Graduate		
	1995–1996	*2007–2008*	*2015–2016*	*1995–1996*	*2007–2008*	*2015–2016*
Mean (Average)	22.28	26.03	25.73	32.38	32.51	32.38
Standard Deviation	(7.60)	(9.37)	(9.06)	(8.85)	(9.38)	(9.66)
% 15–23	NA	58.26%	58.96%	NA	11.2%	13.12%
% 24–29	NA	17.93%	18.28%	NA	39.3%	39.17%
% 30+	NA	23.81%	22.76%	NA	49.5%	47.72%

Source: National Postsecondary Student Aid Study (NPSAS): 1996a, 1996b, 2008a, 2008b, 2016a, 2016b

Enrollment by Age

Overall, the average student age has risen since 1996 (Table 2.2). In 2016, while the average age of the undergraduate student was about 26, there was considerable variation. A closer look shows most students are in the 15–23 range. Among graduate students, the average age has stayed relatively stable at about 32. Almost half of all graduate students are over 30, but there has been a slight rise in the percentage of younger graduate students in the past decade.

Enrollment by First-Generation Status

"First-generation" status has received considerable attention in the past decade as researchers have identified multiple links between college success and having a parent who graduated. According to the most recent large-scale data from NCES, 24% of college students were classified as first-generation (neither parent had attended college), 34% were considered continuing generation (at least one parent had some postsecondary education experience but did not have a bachelor's degree), and 42% had at least one parent with a bachelor's degree or higher (Redford & Hoyer, 2017, Figure 2.1, p. 5). In an analysis of literature from several sources prepared for an NCES data brief on first-generation student outcomes, Cataldi, Bennett, and Chen (2018) noted that the percentage of first-generation students had declined in the past two decades from 37% in 2000 to 33% in 2012.

Redford and Hoyer (2017) also identified that the highest percentage of first-generation college students were white, followed by Hispanic, Black, students of other races, and Asian. When comparing race/ethnicity between first-generation and continuing-generation students, white students make up about 49% of first-generation students vs. 70% of continuing-generation students.

Among Students of Color, however, this pattern is reversed; Black and Hispanic students make up a larger percentage of first-generation students than continuing-generation students.

Enrollment by Sexual Orientation and/or Gender Identity

Data with regard to sexual orientation and/or gender identity has not been included in most large-scale surveys until the past five to ten years. The National College Health Assessment (NCHA) was the first to ask about sexual identity and gender identity in 2008. The most recent and comprehensive demographic study was published as part of a large partnership coordinated by the Tyler Clementi Foundation at Rutgers University. Researchers identified common terminology and coding to categorize and examine queer-spectrum and trans-spectrum undergraduate student experiences in four-year institutions across a variety of measures from seven national surveys. The authors noted that the work "demonstrate[s] the complexities that arise when attempting to operationalize sexual identity and gender identity in survey research" (Greathouse et al., 2018, p. 10).

The team identified queer-spectrum populations as bisexual, gay, lesbian, queer, pansexual, same-gender loving, etc., and/or trans-spectrum populations as androgynous, gender nonconforming, genderqueer, transfeminine, transmasculine, transgender, etc. As noted in Table 2.3, students who identified as queer-spectrum ranged between 5.3% and just under 14% of the student population. Students who identified as trans-spectrum represented between less than 1% and up to 3.8% of the undergraduate population.

TABLE 2.3 Postsecondary enrollment by sexual orientation and/or gender identity by survey data source

	Queer-spectrum	Trans-spectrum
2016 Student Experience in the Research Institution	11.4% (*n* = 9,879)	1.7% (*n* = 1,526)
2016 Diverse Learning Environments Survey	<14%*' (*n* = 2,764)	<1% (*n* = 225)
2017 National Survey of Student Engagement (NSSE)	5.3% (*n* = 27,487)	<1% (*n* = 1,571)
2016 The Freshman Survey (TFS)	about 8.5% (*n* = 12,872)	<1% (*n* = 675)
2016 Your First Year of College (YFCY)	12.7% (*n* = 2,022)	<1% (*n* = 156)
2016 American College Health Association NCHA	12.7% (*n* = 9,331)	3.8% (*n* = 2,294)
2017 College Senior Survey	9.7% (*n* = 1,853)	<1% (*n* = 160)

Source: Greathouse, et al. (2018)
* decimal percentage not reported

Enrollment by Disability Status

Among undergraduate students, 5.3% reported some type of disability in 1996. This increased to 10.9% in 2008 and to 19.5% in 2016. A similar rate of increase is present among graduate students. In 1996, just 3.2% of graduate students reported some type of disability. This increased to 7.3% in 2008 and to 12.0% in 2016. An important consideration for these differences is that the definition changed in each iteration. By 2016, the definition had expanded to include learning disabilities, depression, attention deficit disorder, and attention deficit hyperactivity disorder, which were not previously calculated.

Enrollment by Dependency Status and Marital Status

About 25% of college undergraduates and about 35% of graduate students have legal dependents other than a spouse (Table 2.4). This has been consistent for the past two decades. Among the undergraduates with dependents, about half were married in 1995. That percentage has dropped to about 43% by 2016. About two-thirds of the graduate students with dependents are married. Consistently, about 50% of undergraduate students are classified as dependents.

Enrollment Dependency Status and Income Level

Table 2.5 displays income categories for graduate and undergraduate students based on their dependency status. For undergraduates, consistently half of the students qualify as dependents. An increase is noted in the $100,000 percentage, which tripled in the 20-year span. It is worth noting that "middle-income"

TABLE 2.4 Dependency status and marital status

	Undergraduate			Graduate		
	1995–1996	2007–2008	2015–2016	1995–1996	2007–2008	2015–2016
Dependent	49.41%	51.30%	50.70%	–	–	–
Independent	50.59%	48.70%	49.30%	–	–	–
Unmarried – No Dependents	17.33%	16.15%	20.55%	–	49.90%	53.90%
Married – No Dependents	8.76%	6.14%	4.90%	–	16.40%	14.14%
Unmarried – with Dependents	12.42%	13.83%	13.62%	–	9.40%	8.83%
Married – with Dependents	12.08%	12.57%	10.23%	–	24.20%	23.44%

Source: NPSAS: 1996a, 1996b, 2008a, 2008b, 2016a, 2016b

TABLE 2.5 Dependency status and income level

	Undergraduate			Graduate		
	1995–1996	2007–2008	2015–2016	1995–1996	2007–2008	2015–2016
Dependent students						
Less than $20,000	9.29%	6.09%	9.14%	N/A	N/A	N/A
$20,000–$39,999	11.25%	8.84%	8.57%	N/A	N/A	N/A
$40,000–$59,999	11.39%	8.63%	6.64%	N/A	N/A	N/A
$60,000–$79,999	8.26%	7.55%	5.95%	N/A	N/A	N/A
$80,000–$99,999	4.08%	6.36%	4.86%	N/A	N/A	N/A
$100,000 or more	5.14%	13.84%	15.55%	N/A	N/A	N/A
Independent students						
Less than $10,000	14.78%	11.28%	15.2%	25.58%	20.7%	27.16%
$10,000–$19,999	11.46%	8.43%	9.22%	17.68%	10.9%	11.06%
$20,000–$29,999	8.29%	7.36%	7.05%	14.46%	9.9%	9.62%
$30,000–$49,999	8.90%	9.87%	7.54%	19.91%	17.6%	15.33%
$50,000 or more	7.15%	11.76%	10.29%	22.12%	40.8%	36.83%

Source: NPSAS: 1996a, 1996b, 2008a, 2008b, 2016a, 2016b

households between $40,000–$80,000 have shrunk considerably, indicating that while incomes have increased among the higher-income households, the lower-income households have not experienced a similar shift. This is consistent with the long-term U.S. trend toward increasing inequality.

There also has been considerable change in graduate student income levels in the past two decades. The rate of students earning less than $10,000 has remained consistent, while the rates for students from $10,000–$49,000 have declined. The percentage of those earning over $50,000 rose considerably during this period.

Enrollment by Work Intensity while Enrolled

As noted in Table 2.6, fewer students are working while enrolled than a decade ago. In 2008, 75% of undergraduate students worked at least part time. By 2016, that number had fallen to about 61%. Graduate students experienced similar trends, at about 74% and 63%, respectively.

Freshmen Class Plans and Expectations

The Higher Education Research Institute (HERI) at the University of California, Los Angeles, administers The Freshman Survey (TFS) and Your First Year of College (YFYC), which are useful sources of information about the incoming and outgoing undergraduate freshman classes enrolling in four-year institutions.

TABLE 2.6 Work intensity while enrolled

	Undergraduate			Graduate		
	1995–1996	2007–2008	2015–2016	1995–1996	2007–2008	2015–2016
Did not work	N/A	24.97%	39.11%	N/A	25.8%	33.66%
Part time	N/A	42.06%	35.71%	N/A	21.4%	19.96%
Full time (35+ hours/ week)	N/A	32.97%	25.17%	N/A	52.8%	46.38%

Source: NPSAS: 1996a, 1996b, 2008a, 2008b, 2016a, 2016b

Following are insights including reasons for attending, major and career plans, expectations and involvement, and a closer look at wellness.

Majors and Careers

While majors were relatively distributed across academic fields, only three intended majors were selected by more than 5% of incoming students in 2017: biology (8.2%), undecided (7.8%), and nursing (5.4%). That health fields were most popular is less surprising, given that nearly one-quarter (20.7%) of students described themselves as premed, while 6.6% were pre-law. With regard to intended careers, many planned to become business executives (4.8%), but this was a decrease from a decade ago (8.4%). Intend to become a physician went up (10.9%) from 2007 (6.7%), while being an engineer (6.9% in 2017) was relatively stable from 2007 (6.2%). With the exception of undecided (10%), all other possible occupations were distributed across a wide variety of fields (Pryor et al., 2008; Stolzenberg et al., 2019).

Expectations and Involvement Plans

There were few shifts from the 2007 to the 2017 incoming class in terms of expectations and plans for their first year. Table 2.7 shows a comparison between plans and expectations of the two classes. In 2017, just over half of the incoming class planned to be involved in a student club or organization, a slight increase from a decade ago. Of this, the most notable change was in the increase in students intending to participate in volunteer or community service work (up 24.5%).

Health and Well-Being

In 2007, students frequently or occasionally were worried about their health (45.4%) or felt unsafe on campus (20.6%). At the end of their first year, half

TABLE 2.7 Expectations and plans of the incoming class, 2007 and 2017

Student estimates "very good chance" that they will:	2007	2017	% Change
Change career choice	13.6%	12.3%	−10.6%
Change major field	13.9%	11.7%	−18.8%
Get a job to help pay for college expenses	47.4%	50.7%	+6.5%
Participate in volunteer or community service work	27.7%	36.7%	+24.5%
Seek personal counseling	7.5%	14.4%	+47.9%
Participate in student clubs/groups	45.4%	51.2%	+11.3%
Join a fraternity or sorority	10.4%	11.4%	+8.8%
Participate in a study abroad program	28.8%	32.1%	+10.3%

Source: 2007 and 2017 CIRP Freshman Survey Weighted Norms

(50.1%) of the freshman class rated feeling isolated from campus life frequently or occasionally. A large percentage also frequently felt overwhelmed (41.7%) and depressed (11.7%; Liu, Sharkness, & Pryor, 2008). The largest percent change in expectations during this time was among students who expect to seek personal counseling, up almost 50% from 2007 to 2017 (Pryor et al., 2008; Stolzenberg et al., 2019).

In 2017, wellness continued to be a concern for students after the first year. Only 25.2% of students reported they maintained a healthy diet, although this was moderated by finance, as only 16.8% of those with financial concerns about college maintained a healthy diet versus 31.5% of those with no concerns. Nearly 20% (19.1%) said they did not get adequate sleep during their first year. Also, about 23.1% reported below average or extremely below average emotional health; only 41% sought counseling since entering college. In 2017, anxiety was problematic for first-year students, with 38.6% reporting they frequently felt anxious. Transgender students were most anxious (68.6%), with 45.3% of females compared to 26.6% of males feeling anxious. Students who are biracial/multiracial or Hispanic report the highest rates of frequent anxiety at over 40%. Asian students report the lowest levels of frequent anxiety at 33.5% (Couch, 2018).

Student Engagement, Learning, and Experiences

Several major survey programs produce annual highlight reports useful for understanding engagement, learning, and related experiences of postsecondary students in four-year institutions. Following are insights from recently available reports, including some prior findings for comparison. Data sources include TFS, YFYC, and the College Senior Survey from HERI; the National Survey of Student Engagement (NSSE) from the Center for Postsecondary Research at Indiana University, and the Community College Survey of Student Engagement (CCSSE) from the Center for Community College Student Engagement at the

University of Texas at Austin. The samples are broadly representative of post-secondary institutions in the United States and reports are based on weighted national norms.

Student Engagement and Learning

In 2007, NSSE results focused on several high-impact practices that were associated with learning and developmental gains for undergraduate students. These included learning communities, research with faculty, study abroad, and culminating senior experiences. Factors supporting student success included interactions with their academic advisors, which overall resulted in greater self-reported gains in personal and social development, practical competence, general education, and more frequent use of deep approaches to learning. Disappointing insights included that first-generation and transfer students were much less likely to participate in high-impact practices, such as learning communities, research projects with faculty, study abroad, or a culminating senior experience (National Survey of Student Engagement, 2007).

In 2017, NSSE results focused on college environments inside and outside the classroom. Findings indicated that when campus spaces are inclusive and welcoming, students feel a stronger sense of belonging, develop intercultural competence, and have greater cognitive development gains. Notably, Hispanic/Latino and white students had more positive views regarding institutional support for diversity, while gender-variant students, as well as students with disabilities and STEM (science, technology, engineering, and mathematics) majors, had a less positive view. Although first-year, gender-variant students rated their interactions with students, advisors, and faculty highly, their ratings for student services and administrative staff and offices, as well as perceived support from their institutions, were lower. This was especially the case for helping manage nonacademic responsibilities and providing support for their overall well-being (National Survey of Student Engagement, 2017).

Community College Students

The 2018 national report for the CCSSE focused on academic advising in community colleges. Students who met with advisors were more likely to be engaged in active and collaborative learning, exhibit higher levels of effort, report gains in academic challenge, describe higher levels of faculty interaction, and feel more supported as learners. After a semester of enrollment, most students enrolled in community colleges (78%) reported meeting with an advisor at least once. Almost all of those students (92%) were satisfied with their advising experience. While the majority of students received advice about registration (86%), many discussed support services (76%), set career goals (73%), made an academic plan (65%), considered commitments outside of school (53%), and considered employment

TABLE 2.8 Support for community college learners

	Very little	*Some*	*Quite a bit*	*Very much*
Encouraging contact among students from different backgrounds	14.4%	29.4%	31.4%	24.8%
Helping cope with nonacademic responsibilities (work, family, etc.)	35.5%	33.9%	19.3%	11.3%
Providing support to thrive socially	24.8%	37.5%	24.4%	13.4%
Providing the financial support to afford your education	21.2%	26.3%	26.2%	26.3%

Source: CCSSE 2019 Benchmark Frequency Distributions (Weighted)

opportunities based on career interests (39%; Center for Community College Student Engagement, 2018).

A closer look at the 2019 cohort data[5] shows that most community college students (75.6%) felt they received the support they needed to succeed "quite a bit" or "very much" during the course of the year (Community College Survey of Student Engagement, 2019). As shown in Table 2.8, there were notable differences with regard to specific types of support.

Postsecondary Degree Completion

In 1997, about 2.9 million postsecondary credentials were awarded by Title IV institutions in the United States. By 2017, that number had increased to almost four million. The largest gains came from associates degrees awarded, which almost doubled in the 20-year time frame, and master's degrees, which increased by about 85%.

Degrees Awarded by Gender

In 1997, about 1.3 million degrees were earned by females. The rate of increase was stable from 1997 to 2002, at about 2% a year. The next 15 years saw a sharp increase in the rate of awards earned, averaging about a 3.5% increase each year. By 2017, females earned 75% more degrees than they did 20 years ago. The rate of increase for males paralleled the females in the early years, as men also averaged a stable increase of about 2% a year from 1997 to 2002. The next 15 years saw an increase in male awards, but at a lesser rate of increase than females, averaging about 3.3% increase each year. By 2017, the split in the percentage of degrees earned by males and females was about 42% to 58%, respectively (Figure 2.6).

With regard to degree type, data for male and female students show some interesting trends (Figure 2.7). In 1997, women earned more associate's, bachelor's, and master's degrees; however, men earned more doctoral and professional

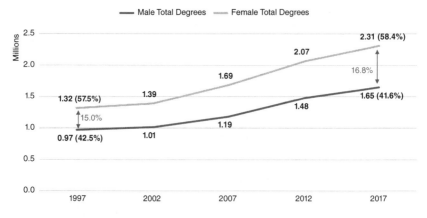

FIGURE 2.6 Degree attainment by gender, 1997–2017

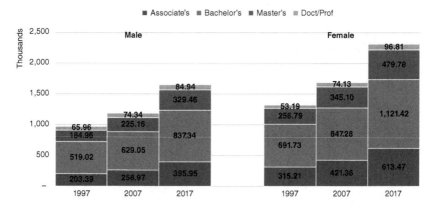

FIGURE 2.7 Postsecondary attainment by gender and degree type, 1997–2017

degrees (65,960 to 53,190). A decade later, the trends remained the same across all types of degrees, except for terminal degrees, where females (74,130) nearly matched males (74,340). By 2017, more females (96,810) earned doctoral and professional degrees than males (84.940).

Degrees Awarded by Race and Ethnicity

Although the largest percentage of degrees awarded in the United States are bachelor's, there have been some notable shifts. As displayed in Figure 2.8, across all groups, approximately 50% of all graduates earn bachelor's degrees. However, the proportion of associate degrees earned has increased in all groups, most notably among Hispanics and Native Americans. Another shift worth noting is the decrease in the proportion of bachelor's degrees awarded to Black or African American students. This shift from bachelor's degrees can be observed in the

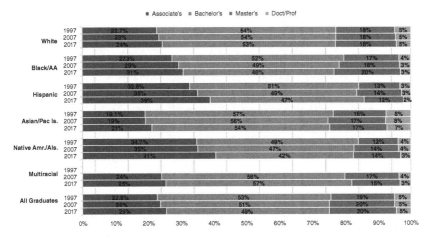

FIGURE 2.8 Proportion of degree attainment by race/ethnicity and degree type, 1997–2017

proportional increases in both associate's and master's degrees. Black graduates are the only group who have shown a sustained increase in the proportion of graduate degrees awarded over the time period examined.

Degrees Awarded by Age

As of 2017, 44.4% of adults aged 25 and older had attained a postsecondary degree (associate's or higher). This was an increase from 31.1% in 1997. The rise in degrees has led to a steady decline of adults at all age levels who have no postsecondary degree. Figure 2.9 shows the increase of adults at specific age levels with postsecondary degrees from 1997 to 2017.

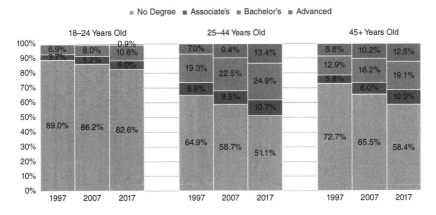

FIGURE 2.9 Educational attainment by age, 1997–2017

Summary

Data presented in this chapter portray the population of U.S. college students as increasingly diverse in many aspects. Table 2.9 summarizes data from this chapter on college student characteristics for the past two decades. Campuses are becoming more heterogeneous in terms of race and ethnicity. Regarding age, the typical age of a first-time freshman continues to be 18–19 years old. The average age of students is, nevertheless, on the rise as nontraditional students return to college at increasing rates.[6] Female students have been the majority over the past two decades; however, as gender identity becomes a more visible population classifier, references to nonconforming gender identities continue to grow and be reflected in the data.

The growing diversity in today's college student population has been fueled by an increasingly diverse college pipeline in the nation. While race and ethnicity

TABLE 2.9 College student enrollment trends overview, 1997, 2007, 2017

Majority characteristics of undergraduate college students			
Enrolled	*1997*	*2007*	*2017*
Gender	Female (56.4%)	Female (56.7%)	Female (56.3%)
Ethnicity	White (72.1%)	White (65.9%)	White (54.7%)
Age	18–19 (24.1%)	18–19 (25.9%)	18–19 (26.3%)
Institution Type	Community College (32.8%)	Community College (33.8%)	Doctoral University (32.5%)
Household Income	$37,005	$50,740	$61,372
Pell Student Loan Student?	No (73.1%)	No (68.9%)	No (63.9%)
Average Pell Amount	$2,630	$3070	$4,045
Average Loan Amount Other	$3,599	$4967	$7,093
SAT Verbal Score	505	502	533
SAT Math Score	511	515	527
Intended Major	Health Professions	Health Professions	Health Professions
Bachelor's Degree Graduate	**1997**	**2007**	**2017**
Student Debt?	Not Available	Yes (58%)	Yes (59%)
Average Debt	$14,000	$22,000	$28,500
Major	Business (37%)	Business (22%)	Business (19%)

Sources: U.S. Department of Education, National Center for Education Statistics, Integrated Postsecondary Education Data System, Fall Enrollment 1997–2017. Retrieved from https://nces.ed.gov/ipeds/datacenter on 07/2019. The College Board, *Trends in Student Aid 2018*. The College Board, *SAT Suite Annual Report, Total Group* (1997, 2007, 2017). U.S. Census, *Money Income in the United States* (1997, 2007, 2017).

forefront this shift with changes in the demographic makeup of the United States in the past two decades, diversity along many other characteristics is notable among today's college students, including gender identity, socioeconomic status, sexual orientation, and age, as well as in their attitudes, values, and beliefs. Emerging populations, such as international students, nontraditional students, gender-nonconforming students, and students with disabilities continue to increase among the student body at rates surpassing "traditional" populations. Montenegro and Jankowski (2017) observed that this trend is only expected to continue as the United States moves into a majority-minority nation.

Considerations Based on These Trends

The diverse and "complex mosaic" of today's student population will have a profound effect on the future of the academic enterprise. Trends in demographic shifts, along with changes in student expectations, attitudes, values, and beliefs, will push institutions to rethink past approaches to enrollment, teaching, learning, budget priorities, and the student experience. Amid this new reality, higher education leaders must reimagine the academic enterprise by strategically focusing on what the data informs. The strategic takeaways will help leaders address these new challenges and garner support for the resources necessary for a sustainable future.

Enrollment and Recruitment. Many institutions were already facing enrollment challenges, and the demographic shifts have forced enrollment management administrators to adjust their strategies to successfully recruit new students. While tried and true recruitment efforts remain effective, institutions need to intentionally develop programs to introduce students to the campus community, and promote equity and access to higher education. Additionally, this data informs that it is imperative for the academic enterprise to make diversity a priority at all levels. Diversifying faculty and staff must also be a priority if institutions wish to be successful at recruiting and retaining students from underrepresented populations. Finally, it will be important for the enterprise to re-examine its policies and practices related to entry and transfer portability. Test-optional admission practices, along with ease of transfer procedures, will enable them to attract a larger share of students.

Teaching and Learning. A diversified student body means that students coming to campus will bring with them an array of lived experiences that will place demands on teaching and learning. The adoption of inclusive teaching pedagogy will ensure that faculty are better able to meet student needs and support the learning of all students regardless of their backgrounds or identities. Additionally, to meet varied student learning styles, institutions should integrate new learning technology tools into teaching practices. Changes in student attitudes around "degree value" will also influence discussions centered around blending vocational and academic education into their overall learning. Finally, offering a variety of course delivery options is crucial for student outcomes. Implementing new technologies, along with different course modality methods, will position the campus to be more effective in improving teaching and learning.

Budget Priorities. Shifts in demographic trends and student attitudes about "degree value" will also have a profound influence on institutional budget priorities. Budget-conscience students and their families may choose a more "no-frills" approach to their education and look more closely at institutional financial aid packages and other tuition-discounting offers. Institutional policies and budgeting modeling around tuition discounting and resource allocations will have a greater significance than in previous years. The idea of academic value will become a greater priority over campus amenities, such as recreation centers and highly customized residence halls.

Student choice of majors and careers will also have an effect on the academic portfolio that an institution offers to students. Resource allocation to certain academic programs will need to adjust to meet demands. Conversely, academic program offerings that fail to meet certain metrics such as demand, retention, margin, and yield may result in program elimination or reductions in spending priorities. All of these trends will impact an institution's budget priorities and their modeling. Institutions that prove to be more agile in their approach to putting structures in place based on data-informed practices will find themselves well-suited for dealing with the demographic and attitudinal shifts.

Student Experience. The student experience will significantly be affected by changes in demographic shifts, student expectations, attitudes, values, and beliefs. Institutions will need to invest in priorities that help develop inclusive campus culture and climate. To achieve this outcome, institutions must develop programs and services that support inclusive learning excellence and promote student retention and success. Additionally, institutions must also create an educational learning environment where they have more control over their educational experience. An example might include the instruction of shorter academic calendars compared to the traditional semester or quarter terms. For-profit institutions have long offered various academic entry points and the rest of higher education must catch up. Another tactic would be to look at blended approaches to teaching and learning. As discussed earlier, hybrid methods and course modalities give students more flexibility. Finally, these data changes also will require institutions to look at alternate ways for students to blend career certifications with their academic program of study. The blending of career and program of study could be accomplished through short-term credentialing (badges), certifications, and mini-courses.

The data shared highlight and subsequent considerations based on these trends highlight how the ensuing changes will impact the future of the academic enterprise. The environment will be challenging, and yet there are some major takeaways to help institutions face these challenges. The academy has responded to other seismic shifts, yet the consequences of not adequately planning for these challenges could be more detrimental to survival.

Notes

1 Within the Hispanic population in 2017, the largest subgroup was Mexican, Mexican American, and/or Chicano (62.7%), followed by Puerto Rican (9.3%), South American2 (6.3%), Central American excluding Salvadoran3 (5.6%), other Hispanic4 (4.9%), Cuban (3.9%), Salvadoran (3.8%), and Dominican (3.6%).
2 Within the Asian population in 2017, the largest subgroup was Asian Indian (24.4%), followed by Chinese (22.3%), other Asian5 (17.1%), Filipino (14.4%), Vietnamese (9.1%), Korean (7.7%), and Japanese (5.0%).
3 Note that national data sources for gender specificity are challenging to locate since neither the NCES nor the U.S. Census track this information. However, there are a few sources as far back as 2008. See the "Enrollment by Sexual Orientation and/or Gender Identity" section for discussion on this information.
4 Like gender, there have been changes to collection of ethnicity/race over the years. In 2010, federal surveys changed, and race/ethnicity became a two-part question. This allowed NCES and other federal entities to better identify those of Hispanic origin and to track multiracial as a separate group.
5 The 2019 *CCSSE* Cohort is composed of member colleges that participated in *CCSSE* from 2017 through 2019.
6 NCES started tracking new transfers in 2006. From 2007–2017, number of new freshmen rose by 9.1% while new transfers rose 26.7%

References

American Council on Education (2005). *College students today: A national portrait*, Washington, DC: Author. Retrieved on April 15, 2022, from https://www.acenet. edu/news-room/Documents/College-Students-Today-A-National-Portrait-2005.pdf

Cataldi, E. F., Bennett, C. T., & Chen, X. (2018). First-generation students college access, persistence, and postbachelor's outcomes. (NCES 2018-421). Washington, DC: U.S. Department of Education, National Center for Education Statistics.

Center for Community College Student Engagement. (2018). *Show me the way: The power of advising in community colleges*. Austin, TX: The University of Texas at Austin, College of Education, Department of Educational Leadership and Policy, Program in Higher Education Leadership.

Community College Survey of Student Engagement (2019). *2019 benchmark frequency distributions – main survey* (Weighted, Support for Learners). Austin, TX: The University of Texas, Center for Community College Student Engagement. Retrieved on April 15, 2022 from http://www.ccsse.org/survey/reports/2019/standard_reports/CCSSE_2019_coh_freqs_support_std.pdf

Couch, V. (2018). *2017 Your first college year survey. (Research Brief)*. Los Angeles, CA: University of California, Higher Education Research Institute (HERI).

Greathouse, M., BrckaLorenz, A., Hoban, M., Huesman, R., Rankin, S., & Stolzenberg, E. B. (2018). *Queer-spectrum and trans-spectrum student experiences in American higher education: The analyses of national survey findings*. Rutgers – The State University of New Jersey, New Brunswick, NJ: Tyler Clementi Center.

Liu, A., Sharkness, J., Pryor, J. H. (2008). *Findings from the 2007 administration of your first college year (YFCY): National aggregates.* Los Angeles, CA: University of California, Higher Education Research Institute (HERI).

McFarland, J., Hussar, B., Zhang, J., Wang, X., Wang, K., Hein, S., Diliberti, M., Forrest Cataldi, E., Bullock Mann, F., & Barmer, A. (2019). *The Condition of Education 2019 (NCES 2019-144).* Washington, DC: U.S. Department of Education, National Center for Education Statistics. Retrieved on April 15, 2022, from https://nces.ed.gov/pubs2019/2019144.pdf

Montenegro, E., & Jankowski, N. A. (2017, January). *Equity and assessment: Moving towards culturally responsive assessment (Occasional Paper No. 29).* Urbana, IL: University of Illinois and Indiana University, National Institute for Learning Outcomes Assessment (NILOA).

National Survey of Student Engagement. (2007). *Experiences that matter: Enhancing student learning and success (Annual Report 2007).* Bloomington, IN: Indiana University Center for Postsecondary Research.

National Survey of Student Engagement. (2017*). Engagement insights: Survey findings on the quality of undergraduate education – Annual Results 2017.* Bloomington, IN: Indiana University Center for Postsecondary Research.

Patton, L. D., Renn, K. A., Guido, F. M., & Quaye, S. J. (2016). *Student development in college: Theory, research, and practice* (3rd ed.). Hoboken, NJ: Jossey Bass.

Pryor, J. H., Hurtado, S., Sharkness, J., & Korn, W. S. (2008). *The American freshman: National norms for fall 2007.* Los Angeles, CA: University of California, Higher Education Research Institute (HERI).

Redford, J., & Hoyer, K.M. (2017*). First-generation and continuing-generation college students: A comparison of high school and postsecondary experiences* (NCES 2018-009). Washington, DC: U.S. Department of Education, National Center for Education Statistics.

Stolzenberg, E. B., Eagan, M. K., Aragon, M. C., Cesar-Davis, N. M., Jacobo, S., Couch, V., & Rios-Aguilar, C. (2019). *The American Freshman: National Norms Fall 2017.* Los Angeles: Higher Education Research Institute, UCLA.

U.S. Census Bureau (1997). *Table 1. Educational attainment of persons 15 years old and over, by age, sex, race, and Hispanic origin: March 1997.* Retrieved on April 15, 2022, from https://www.census.gov/data/tables/1997/demo/educational-attainment/p20-505.html

U.S. Department of Education. Institute of Education Sciences, National Center for Education Statistics (1996a). *National Postsecondary Student Aid Study: 1996 Undergraduates.* Available from https://nces.ed.gov/surveys/npsas/

U.S. Department of Education. Institute of Education Sciences, National Center for Education Statistics (1996b). *National Postsecondary Student Aid Study: 1996 Graduates.* Available from https://nces.ed.gov/surveys/npsas/

U.S. Department of Education. Institute of Education Sciences, National Center for Education Statistics (2008a). *National Postsecondary Student Aid Study: 2008 Undergraduates.* Available from https://nces.ed.gov/surveys/npsas/

U.S. Department of Education. Institute of Education Sciences, National Center for Education Statistics (2008b). *National Postsecondary Student Aid Study: 2008 Graduates.* Available from https://nces.ed.gov/surveys/npsas/

U.S. Department of Education. Institute of Education Sciences, National Center for Education Statistics (2016a). *National Postsecondary Student Aid Study: 2016 Undergraduates.* Available from https://nces.ed.gov/surveys/npsas/

U.S. Department of Education. Institute of Education Sciences, National Center for Education Statistics (2016b). *National Postsecondary Student Aid Study: 2016 Graduates.* Available from https://nces.ed.gov/surveys/npsas/

3

DIVERSITY AMONG TODAY'S COLLEGE STUDENTS

Mark Anthony Torrez

Mark Anthony Torrez (he/him) currently works as an academic adminis-trator, serving as Loyola University Chicago's diversity, equity, and inclusion Program Manager (Health Sciences Division); and leading Loyola-Stritch School of Medicine's Office of Diversity, Equity, & Inclusion. As an emerging scholar-advocate, Mark's research and teaching integrate training in creative and performing arts, strategic communication, social-psychology, college student learning and development, and critical social theory, to advance how educators understand and engage today's increasingly diverse college student popula-tion. Before moving to Chicago, Mark directed community engagement and social justice education at Emory University in Atlanta, GA. He completed his doctoral coursework at Loyola University Chicago in higher education; earned a MEd from the University of Georgia in College Student Affairs Administration and a BA in strategic communication from The Ohio State University.

In an editorial in *Change Magazine* published in 1991, Arthur Levine discussed diversity and its emerging tensions within higher education discourse. It reads with eerie precision, as a clairvoyant foreboding of the now–present-*future* state of U.S. higher education. While addressing the magnitude of the challenge of diversity, he notes,

> The full contours of the issue remain uncharted; its ultimate implications and consequences are unknown; even the questions that need asking today are uncertain. [...] As a consequence, diversity is scary: to confront it is to let the genie out of the bottle. No one knows what will happen if this occurs – so the temptation has been to ignore diversity or to offer palliatives.
>
> *(p. 4)*

DOI: 10.4324/9780429319471-3

What is perhaps most helpful to bring forward and into this chapter's consideration is Levine's central declarative to a highly resistant academe at the brink of sociodemographic change: *"Diversity will not go away. Palliatives don't work"* (p. 4). Indeed, diversity is an essential aspect of the 21st century and especially integral to higher education in the United States, given the nation's increasingly diverse youth and college student populations (see Frey, 2015; Marsden, Smith, & Hout, 2020). Yet, he was wrong about one important assumption: "We [higher education] cannot continue in this manner" (Levine, 1991, p. 4). Three decades later: much has changed but much has also remained the same – and of course, there is much (perhaps, too much) which remains uncertain.

#Diversity

At the first quarter-turn of the 21st century, the United States is a geographically vast, culturally rich, and technologically advanced democratic capitalist society. As a relatively young nation, global effects continue to impact the United States in powerful ways, catalyzing a turbulent phase of sociodemographic, economic, cultural, and political change (Marsden et al., 2020). In this modern time of global, social, and technological transformation, industry and education are increasingly bound together, through neoliberal alliance, as the central propellers for U.S. prosperity. In particular, the U.S. system of higher education is called to educate and train a more diverse society, capable of meeting the evolving civic and workforce demands of an increasingly globalized world (e.g., AACU, 2012, 2015; Marope, 2017).

Today, one would be hard-pressed to find a Fortune-500 company or a top-ranked university mission statement, set of organizational values, or "About Us" web page that remotely frames *diversity* – or any similar term connoting or related to difference (e.g., *inclusion, multiculturalism, pluralism*) – in a negative fashion. In fact, most major U.S. companies and accredited colleges and universities offer newly modernized mission statements that explicitly name diversity as a core institutional value – or at least implicitly reference its educational and economic "utilities" (see Gurin et al., 2002). These commitments are commonly materialized and marketed, at the microlevel, via organizational recruitment strategies such as company brochures or college "look-books," websites, and walking tours; and, at the macrolevel, via massive postsecondary data monitoring and reporting systems – which altogether portend a growing (omni)presence and value of diversity within higher education.

Indeed, much like "leadership" and "innovation," *diversity* is a mass-popular social concept currently trending within and well beyond the educational sector. Yet, in the wake of the virulent racial politics, identity-based violence, unprecedented social inequality, which was laid bare in the year 2020, and continues to dominate national media headlines, there is strong warrant to wonder what meaning lies beneath the social veneers of such trends. For example, if diversity is such a prominent and popular discourse in our society, what exactly does it mean for a person or institution to "value diversity"? What should we expect when a colleague assures you that you'll "really get a sense that there is a presence of diversity" on a campus? When do we determine if we live in "a diverse neighborhood"? How do I learn to "contribute to diversity?" – and why is it important to recognize that we live in "an increasingly diverse society"? Ultimately, these questions compel higher education stakeholders to critically reflect and (re)consider: *What does diversity mean in modern times?*

Deconstructing "That Diversity 'Nonsense'"

Despite the growing chorus harkening diversity as the "new normal," public and political opinions often fall silent on the meaning and implications of an evolving college student population for the U.S. system of higher education. In part, this stems from the reality that the early socialization of most living adults has been primarily facilitated by national discourses (e.g., media) and schooling mechanisms (e.g., curriculum) that, at best, generally neglected thoughtful engagement with issues of culture and identity – and, at worst, actively reproduced color-blind and cultural deficit-based, dominant ideologies (Gordon, 2020). By socialization, I refer to "the systematic training into the norms of our culture" or "the process of learning the meanings and practices that enable us to make sense of and behave appropriately in" our society (Sensoy & DiAngelo, 2017, p. 36).

Through some intricate combination of formal and informal education, each of us develops a learned meaning of diversity, and at the center of our meaning(s) is a working definition or conceptualization that we apply, *inevitably* – but *with varying consciousness* – to the many thoughts, decisions, behaviors, social interactions, and relational contexts that altogether constitute our life(s). Often, our conception of diversity is learned and applied *subconsciously* or *pseudoconsciously*. That is to say, more often than not, people operate with an abstracted concept of diversity that is partially inherited from family or early childhood guardians, and further cultivated, deepened, and internalized over the life span – more or less subliminally – with little *conscious thought* and even less *premeditated thought* or *intent*.

However, it is critical to note: (1) there are, in fact, also many people who possess and enact *more-certain* meaning(s) of diversity – with greater consciousness – and which are enacted with varying *degrees* and/or/of *decrees* of intent, and (2) even if our internal concepts of diversity remain abstracted, whatever meaning(s) we hold will inevitably manifest in very concrete ways, such as in a simple statement, a casual perception, a perception with formalized value(s) (i.e., an assessment or evaluation), a specific interpersonal event or social interaction. Ultimately, our most abstract concepts will construct certain thought(s); our certain thoughts will lead us to make certain decisions and engage in particular behaviors; finally, it is our own process of collective consciousness – beginning with our most abstract considerations of our*selves* and our *society*, ending with an array of complicated concepts carried out – that transforms the material circumstances of our lives and the lives of others.

Diversity as Social Construct

At the core of this text is the fundamental assumption that *diversity is a social construct* – an idea both manufactured and maintained by human culture(s). If essentially a social construction, then we must also recognize that diversity is an inherently dynamic phenomenon, plural in definition and form. Each definitive form is necessarily unique; and, furthermore, contextually bound by particular social and historical (sociohistorical) intercepts of time, place, culture, and language (Triandis, 1995). A quick scan of the literature confirms myriad definitions and interpretations of the term, even within a single field such as higher education (see Manning, 2009). This has led Sara Ahmed (2012), derria byrd (2019), and other critical scholars to interrogate how such proliferation of diversity discourse(s) yields positively (e.g., increased presence in public consciousness, steady diversification) or negatively (e.g., devolved meaning, vacuous term with diminished effect). Yet, the ample literature that effectively normalizes the conceptual variation of diversity is undeniable, and, therefore, scholars suggest a hermeneutical examination of particular *modes of differentiation*. According to van Ewijk (2011), "[M]odes of differentiation are historical bookmarks: they only constitute difference at a certain moment in a certain place, and these differences are influenced by certain conditions under which they persist or perish" (p. 685). Given the sociopolitical history of race relations in the United States, the "multidimensionality" of human diversity is popularly reduced to "single-axis" snapshots of racial and ethnic difference (Crenshaw, 1989, p. 139) – and, more often than not, only pictured in Black and white. As Tatum (2017) explains, the Black-white American racial binary is "a function of the legacy of slavery, the African American struggle for civil rights, and the fact that in the twentieth century Blacks represented the largest minority group" (p. 2). In congress with the historical events shaping national discourse, social movements led by civil rights activists, college student activists, and college administrators have long centered racial and ethnic differences in higher education policy to attempt to dismantle and rectify an intricate system of exclusionary practices, which have operated since the field's founding to inhibit the educational opportunities and life trajectories of Black/African American and other youth of color (Espenshade & Radford, 2009).

Of course, diversity entails many other dimensions of identity. As introduced in Chapter 1, U.S. college students embody a broad array of sociodemographic characteristics, pre-college personal and educational experiences, ideologies (e.g., political and religious attitudes, beliefs), college aspirations, enrollment patterns, and many other aspects of identity – which collectively piece together the modern college milieu like a "complex mosaic." Yet, while the profile of our study body changes, our collective conceptualization of that student body does not. We persist in our thinking based on outdated information and thus perpetuate outdated ideas of dominant and nondominant persons, ideas, and identities leading to decision-making that, in turn, commonly results in a non-sensical recertification of old practices that are misaligned with the needs of the majority of *current* students (see Gulley, 2021; Kilgo et al., 2019). So, instead of our institutions being changed by these adjustments in student identities (i.e., embracing the natural effects of an evolving human ecology), U.S. higher education remains stunted by a malignant culture of reproduction (Bourdieu & Passeron, 1977; hooks, 2015; Kumashiro, 2002). That is, a culture in which imperatives for college student success and well-being are increasingly (mis) calculated by administrations that simply refuse to let go of familial "secret recipes" – institutional "common sense" carefully passed down over generations, (in)effectively centering the new minority at the cost of othering/ignoring the current majority.

Implications of Changing the U.S. Sociodemographic Landscape

By 2040, the United States will transition into a minority-majority nation (Frey, 2015). In response, the U.S. system of higher education is called to educate and train a more diverse society, capable of meeting the evolving workforce demands of the 21st-century global economy (St. John et al., 2013). As McClellan and Larimore (2009) astutely noted, "demographics are destiny," and therefore, diversity is no longer a viable option but an inevitable reality for higher education – no longer a possibility of the distant future but a past-future that is, in fact, emerging *now.*

From this present vantage point, yesterday's questions of *whether* or *if* colleges will pursue diversity are no longer relevant. Scholars and practitioners may now merely decide *how* to pursue diversity – as a modern indicator of institutional quality and relevance (see AACU; Holland & Ford, 2021) – through strategic integration or discerning "where it can serve as a powerful *facilitator* of institutional mission and societal purpose" (Smith, 2009, p. 3; original emphasis). Of course, it would be audacious to assume diversity no longer faces sizable contenders. Addressing resistance remains a preliminary, and resurgent, task for higher education and student affairs professionals seeking to advance campus diversity efforts, which are always already under threat of a pervading, oppositional system of "white supremacist capitalist patriarchy imperialism" (hooks, 2015). In response, Smith (2012) suggested the field has an ethical responsibility to engage in critical reflection and acknowledge the potential consequences of institutional (in)action(s) related to diversity – such as, in considering "[w]hat is the price of *not* creating these conditions? What can be said about *not* engaging diversity at the institutional level?" (p. 241).

For example, a recent report by the National Center for Education Statistics projected that by 2026 the number of U.S. public high school student graduates will decrease by 10% white, increase 19% Black, increase 30% Hispanic, increase 18% Asian/Pacific Islander, decrease 13% American Indian/Alaska Native, increase 42% two or more races (Hussar & Bailey, 2018). These numbers may raise important questions about the future of higher education, particularly in light of the nation's college completion goals (Pendakur, 2016) and the increasingly competitive college market (St. John et al., 2013). From an institutional planning perspective, the evolving sociodemographic landscape of the United States – and, therefore, the prospective "college student market" – raises important questions about college marketing and recruitment and enrollment strategies (Holland & Ford, 2021), student services and support infrastructure (Gulley, 2021), and campus climate assessment and evaluation practices (among many other aspects of higher education; Safir & Dugan, 2021). As Smith (2009) noted, institutions primarily dependent on enrollment/tuition-based funding models are most affected by emergent diversity dynamics, yet it is also arguable that "demographics are destiny" (McClellan and Larimore, 2009), and therefore it may be considered inevitable that the *institutional viability* (Smith, 2020) of any college or university in the 21st century United States involves "the need to attract and keep students from diverse backgrounds in order for the institution to survive" (p. 67; see also, Renn & Reason, 2013; St. John et al., 2013). Thus, while significant research and scholarship emphasizes a common focus on social identity and other forms of difference at the individual or group level, diversity must also be considered at the institutional level.

Beyond individuals and groups, diversity also influences – and is influenced by – the organization of higher education (Smith, 2020; St. John et al., 2013). From the organizational perspective, we can observe how issues of culture and identity also manifest in relation to the administration, finance, governance, law, policy, strategic leadership, and study of colleges and universities as social institutions. To that end, Smith (2012) offers helpful prompts for engaging in critical reflection on how diversity may impact higher education at the institutional level, asking,

> How should we think about diversity in an institutional context? How is the presence or absence of diversity in the study of higher education as organizations influencing how issues are framed, what is studied, and the conclusions that are drawn? What do we know about the experiences of individuals in the context of higher education as a workplace? Finally, what are the implications for the next generation of work on diversity and organizational studies in higher education at the institutional rather than the group or individual level?
>
> *(p. 226)*

Generational Context and Considerations

Although far from an exact science, the generational study of human behavior and development can contribute important insights into time-and-place-bound college student cultures. According to the Pew Research Center (2019), the millennial generation includes persons born between 1981 and 1996, which means even the cohort's youngest college students are aged beyond 24. As a point of reference, the average age of undergraduates is about 26 and approximately 32 for graduate students. However, recent postsecondary data remind us that the U.S. college student population is characterized by an increasingly broad age range, which varies across institutional types and settings (see Chapter 1 for full review). Bearing this disclaimer in mind, higher education and student affairs professionals are signaled to consider the implications of transitioning generational cohorts and particularly the matriculation of *Generation Z.*

Composed of people born between 1995 and 2010, Generation Z currently accounts for nearly one-third of the U.S. population and has emerged as the central cohort for higher education (Pew Research Center, 2019; Seemiller & Grace, 2016). Of particular note, Generation Z has also emerged as the most racially and ethnically diverse cohort in the nation's history (Pew Research Center, 2019). Students of Generation Z are also assumed "digital natives" – born into a technologically advanced world and, subsequently, raised through educational experiences (re)shaped by the possibilities of the internet, social media, "smartphones" and classrooms, and many other pedagogical technologies (Pew Research Center, 2019). For all its advantages, modern technology may also present unique challenges for higher education and student affairs professionals seeking to engage the *hyper*interconnected Generation Z college student.

Finally, it is critical to consider the troubled times into which Generation Z students were born and continue to be educated. For those born on the earlier end of the generational spectrum, the horrific tragedies of September 11, 2001, are early memories that (re)defined the social world(s) in which they would come to develop through childhood, adolescence, and emerging adulthood. Violence has seemingly increased over the last two decades, or, perhaps, it is that social awareness of violence has increased because of growth in public news broadcasting and "viral" reporting enabled by social media platforms – or, perhaps, violence is growing because of a toxic interplay between the two, which have altogether constructed the violent fashion of the 21st-century United States.

In her revised seminal text, *Why Are All the Black Kids Sitting Together in the Cafeteria,* Beverly Tatum (2017) offered urgent insight into the racial politics and social climate of the modern United States, which shape the particular developmental contexts, processes, and, therefore, outcomes of Generation Z youth and college students across the life span. At this particular junction in history, the precision of Tatum's perspective-taking is perhaps most striking and instructive given the unprecedented active presence of four generational cohorts operating and interacting across U.S. campuses. Given the markedly divergent racial/ethnic compositions between the older generations and the emergent Generation Z adult cohort, higher education faculty and staff may be especially well-served to critically reflect on the unique sociopolitical realities of Generation Z – including those that may shape the everyday experiences and perspectives of Black and other minoritized college student populations – by following Tatum into one example of a highly plausible (if not probable) frame of mind. Before reading the following excerpt, take pause to consciously consider your age and how your reality/frame of mind may relate to that which is presented here:

> If you were born in 1997, you were eleven when the economy collapsed, perhaps bringing new economic anxiety into your family life. You were still eleven when Barack Obama was elected. You heard that we were now in a postracial society and President Obama's election was the proof. Yet your neighborhoods and schools were likely still quite segregated. And in 2012, when you were fifteen, a young Black teenager named Trayvon Martin, walking home in his father's mostly White neighborhood with his big bag of iced tea and Skittles, was murdered and his killer went free. When you were seventeen, Michael Brown was shot in Ferguson, Missouri, and his body was left uncovered in the streets for hours, like a piece of roadkill, and in the same year, unarmed Eric Garner was strangled to death by police, repeatedly gasping "I can't breathe" on a viral cell phone video, to name just two examples of why it seemed Black lives did not matter, even in the age of Obama. When you were nineteen, Donald J. Trump was elected president and White supremacists were celebrating in the streets. How would a twenty-year-old answer the question posed to me, "Is it better?" The answer to that question would probably depend a great deal on the social identities of that twenty-year-old.
>
> *(Tatum, 2017, pp. 71–72)*

Arguably, the tenor of our times and ***intersectional identity politics*** have emerged at the forefront of the U.S. sociopolitical climate – most recently inflamed by an upswell in racial and ethnic tensions following the election and presidency of Barack Obama and, subsequently, Donald Trump and Joe Biden (Crenshaw, 2019; Winant, 2015). As Plummer (2018) explains, since 2016, U.S. presidential elections and broader sociopolitical landscape(s) have escalated in a distinctly polarized fashion:

> With the aftermath of an atypical 2016 U.S. presidential election season focused on gender, age, and race issues; the public struggle between advocates of religious liberties and advocates for LGBT equality; immigration reform's impact on the economy; movements like Black Lives Matter; and

pressure by millennials and Generation Z workers to align businesses with disabilities, diversity remains a central critical aspect of future workplace trends.

(p. 7)

Furthermore, and as poignantly depicted in Tatum's account, such recent events and related concerns about the national climate have amassed heavily, compelling scientists to evidence the burgeoning impact of racism, classism, sexism, and other forms of oppression, on permeating the modern American psyche (Giroux, 2018). In the 21st-century United States, *who you are matters to a critical degree* – especially within higher education, where sociopolitical forces have (re) defined modern college student, faculty, and staff experiences (see Giroux, 2018; Morgan, 2021; Tatum, 2017).

In such a volatile state, there is no such thing as a "safe space" – not even on the (once) moral grounds of higher education. Nearly 30 years ago, the Association of American Colleges and Universities (AACU; 1995) described how "[s]tudents carried these [social-political] realities with them on the campuses like books in their backpacks" (p. 11). Given the vastly transformed racial, ethnic, gender, religious, sexual, and social class diversity "landscapes" of our campuses, it is inevitable that a growing number of college students will be impacted by the current sociopolitical climate and identity politics of the 21st-century United States (given the weight of which I fear is, comparatively, over-packed for any manageable backpack on the market). Depending on the current fluctuating policy and curricular changes, these issues may become even more central to the work of higher education practitioners.

What is critical for us to further grapple with is *how* and *to what extent* higher education faculty and practitioners will maintain a sense of authority over their own social identities and affiliations, particularly within an increasingly politicized climate. As agents of the institutions, Higher Education Student Affairs (HESA) professionals have traditionally been forced to strip themselves of various aspects of social, cultural, and political affiliation, including operating under racialized frames of whiteness as "professionalism" (e.g., Jones, 2021). Yet, given the virulent sputter-politics at the first quarter-turn of the century, how does the 'sterilization' of higher education faculty and staff model what we can reasonably (or rightfully) expect of our standard-bearers – particularly given what we articulate as model behaviors and desired outcomes for student development and civic and political engagement (see Morgan, 2021)? Here, I advance Giroux's (2018) incisive charge to the institution and academy of higher education to recognize its consequential function as "a moral and political practice actively involved not only in the production of knowledge, skills, and values but also in the construction of identities, modes of identification, and forms of individual and social agency" (p. 204).

Indeed, like Giroux (2018) and other critical scholars, I am concerned by the diverse possibilities for higher education at this current historical moment – when it has never been more apparent that "education is at the heart of any understanding of politics and ideological scaffolding of those framing mechanisms that mediate our everyday lives" (p.). Accordingly, higher education and student affairs scholars, educators, and administrators alike must consider: To what extent am I aware of the backgrounds, identities, and experiences that today's college students are bringing with them to campus? How prepared am I – or my institution – to holistically support and succeed the students we admit? For example, what will we need to know – how might practice need to shift – when the surviving children of Sandy Hook Elementary and the 2018 immigration detention centers and the countless other families and communities under assault in the United States or elsewhere in our increasingly interconnected world are the new "traditional college student"? *What new faculty will we have cultivated and practiced, when our future finally comes to campus? Perhaps, most urgently, how are we prepared or actively preparing to respond to the ongoing racialized violence, economic collapse, and spatial disruptions of competing global pandemic(s) that are presently reshaping modern human society as we know it? What are the most urgent personal and institutional transformation(s) necessary to, at minimum, do no (further) harm to the most diverse cohort of emerging adults in U.S. history? – and who, if not I, is taking any of these questions into consideration for 'me', as people also intersectionally (im)positioned within the present-day academy and institution of higher education? (see Ahmed, 2021).*

Conclusion

In their compelling new book, *Street Data: A Next Generation Model for Equity, Pedagogy, and School Transformation*, Safir and Dugan (2021) effectively demonstrate the many "traps and tropes" of contemporary diversity and equity-based practices within the U.S. system of education. Their book is both convincing and constructive for educators and administrators who are genuinely committed to learning how to lead for equity. At the core of the text is an unwavering call for critical thinking and conscious action (critical praxis). Why? Because of our fundamental human propensity for implicit biases and, therefore, for error: "Our intentions may be spot on, but if we aren't aware of our discourse, understanding, and the moves we are making, we are liable to reinforce the system we seek to dismantle" (Safir & Dugan, 2021, p. 44).

In the context of this chapter (and book), *college student diversity* is positioned as a central discourse which fundamentally orients the research, theory, organization, and practice of U.S. higher education in the 21st century (Ahmed, 2012; byrd, 2019). As defined by Sensoy and DiAngelo (2017), discourses are a powerful form of language that "represent a particular cultural worldview" and include "all of the ways in which we communicate ideology, including verbal and non-verbal aspects of communication, symbols, and representations" (p. 71). Because people's worldviews and ideologies are related to their decisions and behaviors, as we learn more about how higher education stakeholders differentially perceive diversity, we may also gain critical insight(s) into their differential motivations and modalities of engaging today's college student population. Whereas Chapter 1 presents a statistical overview of today's college student population, the purpose of this chapter is to establish a theoretical foundation for understanding diversity within the context of higher education and a critical framework for analyzing how college student diversity may be understood, conceptualized, depicted, or otherwise communicated among various institutional constituencies. In the following chapter, Davis and Barnes direct more focused attention to the roles and types of higher education constituency stakeholders to cultivate reader capacity for strategic *social perspective-taking* – integrating the unique vantage points of various higher education constituencies more thoroughly into professional practice(s) – and offer a framework for considering the implications of competing stakeholder needs, interests, and other motivations.

References

Ahmed, S. (2012). *On being included: Racism and diversity in institutional life*. Durham, NC: Duke University Press.

Ahmed, S. (2021). *Complaint!*. Durham, NC: Duke University Press.

Association of American Colleges and Universities. (1995). *Diversity in higher education: A work in progress*. Washington, DC: Author.

Association of American Colleges and Universities. (2012). *A crucible moment: College learning and democracy's future*. Washington, DC: Author.

Association of American Colleges and Universities. (2015). *Committing to equity and inclusive excellence: A campus guide for self-study and planning*. Washington, DC: Author.

Bourdieu, P., & Passeron, J. (1977). *Reproduction in education, society and culture* (R. Nice Trans.). London: Sage.

byrd, D. (2019). The diversity distraction: A critical comparative analysis of discourse in higher education scholarship. *The Review of Higher Education, 42,* 135–172. doi: 10.1353/rhe.2019.0048

Crenshaw, K. (1989). Demarginalizing the intersection of race and sex: A black feminist critique of antidiscrimination doctrine, feminist theory, and antiracist politics. *University of Chicago Legal Forum, 1989*(1), 139–166.

Crenshaw, K. (2019). How colorblindness flourished in the age of Obama. In K. Crenshaw, L. C. Harris, D. HoSang, & G. Lipsitz (Eds.), *Seeing race again: Countering colorblindness across the disciplines* (pp. 126–151). Berkeley, CA: University of California Press.

Espenshade, T. J., & Radford, A. W. (2009). *No longer separate but not quite equal: Race and class in elite college admission and campus life*. Princeton, NJ: Princeton University Press.

Frey, W. H. (2015). *Diversity explosion: How new racial demographics are remaking America*. Washington, DC: Brookings Institution Press.

Giroux, H. A. (2018). What is the role of higher education in the age of fake news? In M. A. Peters, S. Rider, M. Hyvonen, & T. Besley (Eds.), *Post-truth, fake news: Viral modernity & higher education* (pp. 197–215). Singapore: Springer.

Gordon, L. N. (2020). Causality, context, and colorblindness: Equal educational opportunity and the politics of racist disavowal. In K. Crenshaw's (Ed.), *Seeing race again:*

Countering colorblindness across the disciplines (pp. 224–244). Berkeley, CA: University of California Press.

Gulley, N. Y. (2021). Challenging assumptions: 'Contemporary students,' 'nontraditional students,' adult learners,' post-traditional,' 'new tradition.' *SCHOLE: A Journal of Leisure Studies and Recreation Education, 36*(1–2), 4–10.

Gurin, P., Dey, E. L., Hurtado, S., & Gurin, G. (2002). Diversity and higher education: Theory and impact on educational outcomes. *Harvard Educational Review, 72*(3), 330–366. doi:10.17763/haer.72.3.01151786u134n051

Holland, M. M., & Ford, K. S. (2021). Legitimizing prestige through diversity: How higher education institutions represent ethno-racial diversity across levels of selectivity. *The Journal of Higher Education, 92*(1), 1–30. doi: 10.1080/00221546.2020.1740532

hooks, b. (2015). *Yearning: Race, gender, and cultural politics.* New York: Routledge.

Hussar, W. J., & Bailey, T. M. (2018, April). *Projections of education statistics to 2026* (NCES 2018-019). Washington, DC: U.S. Department of Education, National Center for Education Statistics.

Jones, A. M. (2021). Conflicted: How black women negotiate their responses to racial microaggressions at a historically white institution. *Race Ethnicity and Education,* doi:1 0.1080/13613324.2021.1924136

Kilgo, C. A., Linley, J. L., Renn, K. A., & Woodford, M. R. (2019). High-impact for whom? The influence of environment and identity on lesbian, gay, bisexual, and queer college students' participation in high-impact practices. *Journal of College Student Development, 60*(4), 421–436.

Kumashiro, K. K. (2002). *Troubling education: "Queer" activism and anti-oppressive pedagogy.* New York: Routledge.

Levine, A. (1991). The meaning of diversity. *Change, 23*(5), 4–5.

Manning, K. (2009). Philosophical underpinnings of student affairs work on difference. *About Campus, 14*(2), 11–17.

Marope, M. (2017). *Reconceptualizing and repositioning curriculum in the 21st century: A global paradigm shift.* Geneva: UNESCO International Bureau of Education.

Marsden, P. V., Smith, T. W., & Hout, M. (2020). Tracking US social change over a half-century: The General Social Survey at fifty. *Annual Review of Sociology, 46,* 109–134. doi: 10.1146/annurev-soc-121919-054838

McClellan, G. S., & Larimore, J. (2009). The changing student population. In G. S. McClellan, J. Stringer, & Associates (Eds.), *The handbook of student affairs administration* (3rd ed.), pp. 225–241), San Francisco,. CA: Jossey-Bass.

Morgan, D. (2021). Nuancing political identity formation in higher education: A phenomenological examination of precollege socialization, identity, and context. *Journal of Diversity in Higher Education, 14*(1), 12–24. doi:10.1037/dhe0000153

Pendakur, S. L. (2016). Empowerment agents: Developing staff and faculty to support students at the margins. In V. Pendakur (Ed.). *Closing the opportunity gap: Identity-conscious strategies for retention and student success* (pp. 109–125). Sterling, VA: Stylus

Pew Research Center. (2019, January). Generation Z looks a lot like millennials on key social and political issues. https://www.pewresearch.org/social-trends/2019/01/17/generation-z-looks-a-lot-like-millennials-on-key-social-and-political-issues/

Plummer, D. L. (2018). Overview of the field of diversity management. In D. L. Plummer (Ed.), *Handbook of diversity management: Inclusive strategies for driving organizational excellence* (2nd ed.), pp. 1–48). Westborough, MA: Half Dozen Publications.

Renn, K. A., & Reason, R. D. (2013). *College students in the United States: Characteristics, experiences, and outcomes.* New York: John Wiley & Sons.

Safir, S., & Dugan, J. (2021). *Street data: A next generation model for equity, pedagogy, and school transformation.* Thousand Oaks, CA: SAGE Publications.

Seemiller, C. & Grace, M. (2016). *Generation Z goes to college.* San Francisco, CA: Jossey-Bass.

Sensoy, O., & DiAngelo, R. (2017). *Is everyone really equal?: An introduction to key concepts in social justice education* (2nd ed.). New York: Teachers College Press.

Smith, D. G. (2009). *Diversity's promise for higher education: Making it work.* Baltimore, MA: Johns Hopkins University Press.

Smith, D. G. (2012). Diversity: A bridge to the future? In M. N. Bastedo (Ed.), *The organization of higher education: Managing colleges for a new era* (pp. 225–255). Baltimore, MA: The Johns Hopkins University Press.

Smith, D. G. (2020). *Diversity's promise for higher education: Making it work* (3rd ed.). Baltimore, MA: The Johns Hopkins University Press.

St. John, E. P., Daun-Barnett, N., & Moronski-Chapman, K. M. (2013). *Public policy and higher education: Reframing strategies for preparation, access and college success.* New York: Routledge.

Tatum, B. D. (2017). *Why are all the black kids sitting together in the cafeteria? And other conversations about race. Revised and updated.* New York: Basic Books.

Triandis, H. (1995). The importance of context in diversity studies. In S. Jackson & M. Ruderman (Eds), *Diversity in work teams.* Washington, DC: American Psychological Association.

van Ewijk, A. R. (2011). Diversity and diversity policy: Diving into fundamental differences. *Journal of Organizational Change Management, 24*(5), 680–694. doi: 10.1108/09534811111158921.

Winant, H. (2015). The dark matter: Race and racism in the 21st century. *Critical Sociology, 41*(2), 313–324.

4

WHO HAS A STAKE IN TODAY'S COLLEGE STUDENTS?

Tiffany J. Davis and Yolanda Barnes

Tiffany J. Davis, PhD (she/her) is a higher education leader and scholar whose classroom teaching, scholarly work, and professional service broadly addresses two major strands: socialization and professional pathways for the higher education profession and issues related to equity, justice, and inclusion. In her work, Dr. Davis draws on over 15 years of leadership experience, spanning academic and college student affairs, and currently serves as clinical assistant professor and program director for the higher education leadership and policy studies programs (MEd/PhD) at the University of Houston.

Yolanda M. Barnes, PhD, (she/her/hers) is a scholar–activist who worked for several years in higher education. There she conducted research, collaborated with senior faculty, oversaw multifaceted projects, and coached students to become leaders in their communities. Barnes's research focused on how federal and state policies support or undermine equitable pathways toward college affordability. Barnes currently leads Arnold Ventures contraception choice and access portfolio, which sources and manages investments to promote autonomy, access, and justice.

Institutions of higher education have many stakeholders who are invested in the success of their students. Some of these stakeholders include college administrators and faculty, secondary educators, government officials, consultation firms, parents, and college students themselves. The term "stakeholder"

DOI: 10.4324/9780429319471-4

was first coined in management literature within an internal memorandum at the Stanford Research Institute in 1963 (Freeman, 2010), and the motivation behind the introduction of the term was to identify those individuals and groups whom management teams within the organization needed to be sensitive toward (Jongbloed et al., 2008; Mainardes et al., 2011). The term stakeholder is defined differently among researchers, yet there is a general principle that is reflected within their definitions: institutional managers should make every effort to consider the needs, interests, and influences of persons, groups, neighborhoods, organizations, societies, and natural environments that either impact or are impacted by the institution's policies and operations (Mainardes et al., 2011; Mitchell et al., 1997). Scholars have crafted a varied pool of definitions to identify the unique role of a stakeholder within higher education. However, despite leaders' widespread usage of the term, there is no definitive explanation as to what a stakeholder is (Donaldson & Preston, 1995; Mainardes et al., 2011). For our current endeavor, we identify stakeholders as groups and individuals that have the ability to influence or be influenced by the systems (e.g., behavior, direction, processes, or outcomes) within education (Mitchell et al., 1997).

In this chapter, we will explore the question, "Who has a stake in college students?" We begin by offering a brief background of stakeholder theory for context and then identify specific stakeholders, delineating their connection to higher education broadly and interest in college students specifically. We then offer a taxonomy of higher education stakeholders that describes the different ways that stakeholder type influences the way they view college students. Finally, we conclude this chapter by articulating the changing role of stakeholders, including how colleges and universities are prioritizing stakeholder needs and interests.

Background of Stakeholder Theory

In 1984, Edward Freeman introduced the stakeholder theory concept. Before stakeholder theory was adopted, businesses and organizations relied heavily on Milton Friedman's model, shareholder theory. The stark difference between the two models centers on whether the organization's goal is to make a profit. Friedman's capitalist lens promotes the idea that an organization's principal goal is to make a profit; therefore, satisfying only its shareholders leads to success. In contrast, Freeman's (1994) stakeholder theory expanded the idea of shareholders by recognizing the relationship between an organization and its external environment – i.e., any individual or group that either influences the organization or is influenced by it (Mainardes et al., 2011), which includes not only shareholders but also any individual or organization. Throughout the years, institutions of higher education have interacted with an increased number of individuals and groups who have put demands on the education sector (Jongbloed et al., 2008), who bring a variety of lenses with them, capitalist and otherwise. The result has led educational administrators to examine relationships more explicitly between institutions and external sources, in addition to internal stakeholders (Jongbloed et al., 2008).

Stakeholder theory attempts to identify which groups of stakeholders are deserving of, or require, leadership's attention (Mitchell et al., 1997). Multiple scholars believe stakeholder theory was developed so that organizations, such as institutions of higher education, would be able to recognize, analyze, and examine the unique characteristics of stakeholders influencing or being influenced by organizational behavior (Clarkson, 1995; Donaldson & Preston, 1995; Mainardes et al., 2011; Rowley, 1997). Stakeholder theory draws from four key academic fields – sociology, economics, politics, and ethics (Mainardes et al., 2011) – and one of the central tenets of the theory is to equip institutional leaders with tools to understand stakeholders and how to best manage them (Frooman, 1999). The development of stakeholder theory has traditionally centered on two elements: defining what it means to be a stakeholder and classifying stakeholders into categories to explore their relationships with each other and to institutions of higher education (Rowley, 1998). Considering the various roles stakeholders adopt within organizations, developing the ability to properly identify and categorize stakeholders allows for institutions of higher education to appropriately respond to their needs, interests, and feedback.

Categories of Stakeholders

Stakeholders are categorized based on their ability to harness three attributes: power, urgency, and legitimacy. The unique combinations of these attributes determine the amount of attention institutional leaders may give to specific stakeholders (Frooman, 1999; Mitchell et al., 1997). Stakeholders navigate spaces with different forms of capital that can cause them risks; consequently, as an entity, they have something to win or lose depending on the behavior of the educational organization (Rowley, 1997; Clarkson, 1995). Therefore, it is important for institutional leaders to be able to identify stakeholders to learn what they are seeking before allowing them to influence the organization, as understanding the nature of the symbiotic relationship is key to determining resource allocation when engaging with particular stakeholder groups.

Higher education stakeholders fall into two categories: primary or secondary. Without the involvement and continued participation of primary stakeholders, institutions of higher education would not be able to survive (Clarkson, 1995). Students, faculty, staff, and governing boards of colleges and universities represent primary stakeholders within higher education (Clarkson, 1995). Failure to keep primary stakeholders satisfied leads to a higher chance of failure for that educational organization (Clarkson, 1995). However, stakeholder theory affirms institutions of higher education hold responsibilities toward entities beyond their governing boards and primary stakeholders. Educational leaders must balance and pay attention to the interests and well-being of those that influence and are influenced by the organization (Phillips et al., 2003), categorized as secondary stakeholders. In contrast to primary stakeholders, secondary stakeholders are not essential for organizational survival (Clarkson, 1995) – however, the shifting landscape of higher education (particularly funding models) makes this delineation increasingly difficult to state with absolute certainty. Professional associations, industry and friends of higher education, and the media are examples of secondary stakeholders. As a caveat, secondary stakeholders should not be disregarded, because stakeholders are naturally intrinsically motivated and will ultimately make decisions that benefit their goals and interests (Donaldson & Preston, 1995, p. 67). Thus, secondary stakeholders can enact damage or remedy challenges, depending on their specific needs (Clarkson, 1995). The primary and secondary categories of stakeholders are often used interchangeably with internal and external stakeholders, respectively (Lawrence, 2017).

Once stakeholders have been identified, educational leaders must work to craft an ethically driven relationship with them to serve the needs of all parties involved (Goodpaster, 1991). This is easier espoused than enacted, as there is not a single, uniform approach to working with educational stakeholders. Institutional diversity is a distinguishing feature of higher education in the United States, which contributes to the uniqueness of institutions along a variety of dimensions, including governance structure, mission, institutional size, educational profile, and research orientation, to name a few. Therefore, it is imperative for colleges and universities to effectively identify the stakeholders that influence or are influenced by their unique organization and how to best respond to them. In fact, a standardized, one-size-fits-all, approach may produce negative impacts for some institutions, as stakeholder theory tells us that each organization has a unique relationship with its stakeholders, and we are unable to predict relationships across institutions (Rowley, 1998). Yet, there are some groups of stakeholders that remain constant across institutional type, size, and mission; it is the expectations and relationship of the various stakeholders (Lawrence, 2017) that contribute to the differentiation of stakeholder relationships with individual institutions.

Who Are Higher Education's Stakeholders?

There are many stakeholders that influence the day-to-day operations, finances, strategic practices, and policies of institutions of higher education. It is important to identify stakeholders that have the power and influence to enact change, create partnerships, and support the mission, vision, and values of institutions. Some of these stakeholders, which are further examined in the following sections, include current and former students, families, administrators, and faculty, industry and friends of education, K–12 administrators and teachers, professional associations, oversight groups, the general public, foreign countries, and government officials.

College Students, Families, and Alumni

Most would agree that the most important stakeholders are the students who attend(ed) the colleges and universities and their families. College students and their families articulate return on investment, lower tuition, shorter time to degree, and greater employability (Lawrence, 2017) as important considerations when reflecting on their role as stakeholders. Moreover, quality is a central area that students and families weigh when making enrollment decisions: the quality of course curriculum (including availability of majors), quality of teaching, and quality (and accessibility) of academic and support resources that are available at the college/university (Temmerman, 2018). Alumni play a critical role in helping to craft the brand of their alma mater through word-of-mouth promotion that has the potential to recruit prospective students and other stakeholders to engage with the university (Gaier, 2005). From an alumni vantage point, the university's ability to not only maintain but also increase the value of their degree is an important consideration for alumni that in turn influences alumni involvement and giving.

College Faculty and Administrators

The institutional employees who engage in the day-to-day work of the college and university, such as presidents, vice presidents, faculty, student affairs professionals, and academic advisors, represent internal stakeholders who have a significant investment in the quality of the collegiate experience, as well as the success of students. College affordability, student learning and retention, graduation rates, and post-graduate employment are all important success metrics that drive the decision-making of executive college leadership. From a faculty and student affairs perspective, college students are the reason for our work. The implementation and delivery of degree programs, student services, and interventions are contingent upon and responsive to the academic and developmental needs of students. As a result, faculty and staff have a stake in the quality of students that are admitted, and subsequently, enroll in the college, as well as the creation of mechanisms for challenging and supporting students along their developmental journeys (Temmerman, 2018).

Industry and Friends of Education

Fostering partnerships between individual industries and institutions of higher education provides opportunities for organizations to address specific workforce needs within their region, advance economic opportunity, and cultivate research and technological innovations (King, 2015; Soares, 2010). Industry, broadly, maintains a stake in college students from two primary vantage points: (1) a pipeline of well-prepared employees and (2) resource sharing. A good example of an industry's desire for employees is the Greater Houston Partnership (n.d.), which articulates,

> [A] regional focus on developing tomorrow's workforce through educating young people on emerging industries and re-training mid-career professionals for high-demand careers. Houston has developed a strong bridge between the talent needs of various industries and the educational programs being offered through colleges, universities and technical programs.
>
> *(para. 1)*

Some employers have placed less importance on graduates' actual degree discipline in favor of the more generic skills that they have acquired.

In terms of resource sharing, higher education becomes market-oriented and must find alternative funding sources to support its research production (Kettunen, 2015) in the face of budget cuts; oftentimes, industry and philanthropic organizations fulfill this need by providing grants and donations to colleges and universities that not only fund research that can drive innovation and lead to profit-making but also assist in enhancing the overall quality of education, such as attracting top-notch faculty. Forging long-term collaborations within the academic sector becomes an advantageous endeavor for industries due to increased access to premier research and scientific talent that has the potential to contribute to advances within science, technology, and engineering (Lutchen, 2018).

Secondary Education (K–12) Administrators and Teachers

Making college accessible to everyone is one of the most pressing challenges facing U.S. higher education (Eckel & King, 2004). However, according to the College Board's *Education Pays Report 2016*, "among students with similar high school math test scores, college enrollment rates are higher for those from the highest socioeconomic status (SES) quartile than for those from the lowest and middle SES quartiles" (Ma, Pender, & Welch, 2016, p. 3). Moreover, higher education participation varies among racial/ethnic groups, with Black and Hispanic students of traditional college age being less likely to enroll in postsecondary institutions compared to their white and Asian peers (Ma et al., 2016). Thus, there is a critical need to focus on issues of college access, especially for those students from historically marginalized racial/ethnic and socioeconomic backgrounds, as well as first-generation students. This 'college access problem' begins early in the education pipeline. Thus, superintendents, principals, teachers, and guidance counselors are stakeholders to higher education, as they are responsible for educating students to ensure that they will be academically prepared to enter higher education, as well as knowledgeable about the diversity of postsecondary education and training opportunities.

Professional Associations

College and university professionals are often connected to and involved in diverse professional associations for varied reasons, from professional development and learning, the building of and dissemination of research and quality practice, to the development of cross-institutional collaborations and partnerships through networking. In addition, the two leading umbrella student affairs associations, NASPA – Student Personnel Administrators in Higher Education and ACPA – College Student Educators International, fulfill a crucial advocacy need for higher education broadly, and on behalf of student affairs staff specifically. In their advocacy roles, both NASPA and ACPA often craft responses to higher education proposals coming down the federal and state policy pipeline and work to alert and educate their membership base about looming legal and legislative conversations. Professional associations also assist in leveraging relationships with other stakeholders such as nonprofit organizations, educational technology companies, college vendors, and policy think tanks.

Oversight Groups

Oversight groups, such as members of accrediting organizations (national, regional, and programmatic) and college and university governing boards, are considered stakeholders for they influence an institution's ability to operate. Members of accrediting organizations and governing boards assure institutions are meeting standards of quality. Governing boards "occupy a middle ground; they are 'of' the university, but not 'in' the university" (Lawrence, 2017, p. 57). This distinction is important as the members of the governing boards are not easily identified as either internal or external stakeholders, as they are often successful leaders in business or government who may or may not have an institutional connection beyond their professional roles. If accrediting organizations and boards find that the institution's educational practices are not aligned with the mission of the organization or are low quality, they run the risk of receiving sanctions and potentially losing federal funding.

The General Public

Higher education provides a range of public and private benefits. Higher earnings are often associated with obtaining a college education, which ultimately leads to higher tax revenues, increased savings, and investments for postsecondary degree holders. In addition, an educated workforce is less likely to depend on government assistance (Bloom, Hartley, & Rosovsky, 2007). Institutions must continue to highlight their ability to produce graduates that will ultimately enter society with marketable skills to contribute to a growing economy. Moreover, state and federal investment in higher education, through direct funding and financial aid systems also create significant interest in ensuring a positive return on investment through innovation, practical research, and service.

Foreign Countries

Institutions of higher education experience benefits when collaborating with foreign countries, whether that is recruiting their students to campuses in the United States or working to open a global campus in another country. During the 2019/2020 academic year, 850,000+ international students were enrolled at various U.S. institutions of higher education (IIE, 2020). Several institutions rely heavily on international students to pay full tuition in order to keep their operating budget moving forward. Many institutions support the enrollment of international students, as it aligns with their campus mission statements to create a diverse learning environment. There are perceived economic benefits to help explain foreign countries' role as a stakeholder in the U.S. higher education system. The United States is viewed as a competitive producer of science, technology, engineering, and math (STEM) post-graduates. One-third of STEM graduates in the United States are foreign-born (Han et al., 2015). Many foreign countries fund their students to study abroad with an expectation that they will return to their home countries to advance innovation and excellence within the STEM fields.

Government Officials

Government officials (federal, state, and local) are stakeholders due to their ability to fund institutions of higher education. Institutions must follow regulated policies to receive both federal and state aid. In addition, government officials implement policies to help ensure institutions of higher education are creating programs, resources, and services to best meet the needs of a diverse student population, or in some cases, legislative action may narrow access. The United States has a desire to be globally competitive within the education sector. With this in mind, government officials' stake in college students is the result of needing an educated workforce who are equipped with 21st-century skills and knowledge, especially within STEM fields.

The Changing Role of Stakeholders

The accountability movement in American higher education continues to shape the administration of institutions amid shrinking federal and state support, mounting tuition prices leading to massive student debt, ensuring physical and psychological safety on campuses, and increasing calls for improving employability skills. In the previous section, we outlined nine groups of stakeholders who hold a legitimate interest in colleges and universities broadly, and college students specifically. We now turn our attention to how colleges and universities prioritize their stakeholders using Jongbloed et al.'s (2008) lens of saliency as it incorporates the factors of power, legitimacy, and urgency.

In theory, any group or individual can be a stakeholder, but their ability to garner the attention of leaders within the college or university determines their saliency. Saliency is the degree to which leaders give priority to competing stakeholder expectations and needs (Mitchell et al., 1997). Stakeholder analysis (Jongbloed et al., 2008; Lawrence, 2017) is one strategy leaders can use to support universities in their goals to classify stakeholders and determine their saliency. In order to decipher saliency, Frooman (1999) outlined three questions institutional leaders have to address about stakeholders:

1. Who are they? (This question deals with the characteristics of the stakeholder.)
2. What do they want? (This question concerns their ends.)
3. How are they going to try to get it? (This question concerns their means.)

When determining the saliency of a stakeholder, it is vital for leaders to identify the different ways (i.e., roles and reasons) stakeholders may interact with institutions of higher education. Assessing the legitimacy, urgency, and power of the individual or group assists leaders in determining how important a stakeholder is, or could be, for organizational thriving and survival. Moreover, the assumption of the strength of individual and group stakeholders within these domains may influence how institutional leaders prioritize different stakeholders, often demonstrated by decision-making and resource allocation.

Stakeholder Legitimacy

Stakeholders are seen as having legitimacy when higher education leaders identify how the relationship aligns with the mission, vision, or priorities of the college (Suchman, 1995). In addition to being viewed as desirable, having legitimacy allows stakeholders to negotiate at various levels within the organization (Mitchell et al., 1997). University-industry partnerships, such as those found at North Carolina State University, serve as an excellent example of how stakeholders gain legitimacy through strategic collaborations:

> There are 115 universities in the U.S. classified as having the highest research activity by the Carnegie Classification of Institutions of Higher Education. But only NC State has a unique combination of resources that makes it an ideal university with which to partner. The university's award-winning Centennial Campus is a national model for highly successful public-private partnerships, home to more than 75 industry partners alongside an equal number of academic departments and units.
>
> (North Carolina State University, 2019, p. 2)

Stakeholder Urgency

A stakeholder's level of urgency is established when they require the immediate attention of the institution because the nature of the relationship is time-sensitive or critical to the stakeholder (Mitchell et al., 1997). Government relations is a good example of the role of urgency in determining how to prioritize stakeholders. While the university is consistently aware and responsive to the changing legal and fiduciary requirements set forth by the federal government, there are times when the salience of government officials as stakeholders becomes even more clear. Consider the Obama-era "Dear Colleague" Letter (Morrison, 2011) issued by the Office for Civil Rights that reminded institutional leaders they have an obligation under Title IX to prevent and address sexual violence, as all schools that receive federal funding must take immediate and effective steps. While the U.S. Department of Education has since withdrawn the 2011 letter, this guidance shaped how institutions had to review and align their processes to comply with the guidance set forth in the letter in a timely fashion. The more than 7,000 colleges who received federal aid dollars at that time recognized the urgency to comply with the demands of one of their primary stakeholders.

Stakeholder Power

A stakeholder is not seen as highly salient by organization leaders if the stakeholder is unaware of the power they hold. Yet, power alone does not grant saliency. With respect to the higher education context, a stakeholder has power when it has the ability to exert its will within the relationship with institutions of higher education (Mitchell et al., 1997). Boards of trustees are examples of stakeholders who are highly salient and hold power within the organizations. Serving as the governing body of colleges and universities, boards of trustees operate as the final authority for most university business. The board of trustees at Miami Dade College wielded their power when, to the dismay of a search committee of community stakeholders, they made the decision to reopen the search for the college's next president. After a vigorous year-long search process that produced four candidates, the board decided to reject three of those candidates and operate a new search governed by the board. Campus community members were not in support of this decision and felt blindsided by the perceived lack of transparency. However, due to its high level of saliency, the board has the power to realign the search process to best fit their needs and goals as a unit. A Miami Dade spokesperson was asked to comment on the sudden change, and they stated, "This is a decision of the Board of Trustees. It is not the place for the institution or staff to comment. The board are the policy makers" (Hazelrigg, 2019).

Power, Legitimacy, and Urgency Intertwined

There must be delicate interaction between power, legitimacy, and urgency in order for a stakeholder to be labeled as highly salient by organization managers. However, a stakeholder's power must effectively interact with both their level of legitimacy and urgency in order to experience heightened saliency within the organization (Mitchell et al., 1997). The dynamic nature of the power, legitimacy, and urgency attributes suggests that stakeholder saliency is not static; stakeholders may be reclassified, or reprioritized, by institutional leaders depending on the relative absence and presence of or change to all or some of the attributes (Jongbloed et al., 2008; Mitchell et al., 1997). Stakeholders are at risk of losing saliency due to their attributes being variable, socially constructed, and lacking willful exercise (Mitchell et al., 1997). Said differently, the attributes of legitimacy, power, and urgency are not permanent stakeholder states (i.e., variable) given environmental factors that may influence its goals, behaviors, or means, and the relative presence and strength of an attribute are largely a matter of subjective perception, rather than objective measure (i.e., socially constructed). Furthermore, stakeholders themselves may not be conscious of possessing an attribute or be unwilling to exercise its full extent, which influences the dynamics of the stakeholder relationship (Mitchell et al., 1997).

Stakeholders are placed into different classes based on the possession of one, two, or three attributes (Jongbloed et al., 2008). There are seven classes of stakeholders separated by three themes: latent, expectant, and definitive. "Stakeholder salience is low for the group of latent stakeholders, moderate for expectant stakeholders, and high for definitive stakeholders" (Jongbloed et al., 2008, p. 310). Educational leaders often do not recognize latent stakeholders because they only possess one attribute, demonstrating a low level of stakeholder saliency. Examples of latent stakeholders could be local businesses within proximity to the university. Expectant stakeholders require a minimum level of attention because educational leaders view them as an entity that is expecting something from the organization currently or will in the future. An example of an expectant stakeholder could be a local organization that tracks job placement within the city and has a desire to partner with the institution to connect students with internships. Definitive stakeholders require the maximum level of attention because they carry all three attributes (power, legitimacy, and urgency) and can influence institutions of higher education at a greater level. National and state governments are examples of definitive stakeholders due to institutional dependence on funding, either through federal grants and financial aid or state allocations. It must be noted that any stakeholder at the lowest saliency levels has the ability to move into a definitive stakeholder role by acquiring more attributes (Leisyte & Westerheijden, 2014).

Conclusion

Stakeholders guide the strategic behavior of colleges and universities, and higher education's viability and sustainability are in large part dependent on how well it approaches stakeholder management. A common adage often attributed to Abraham Lincoln and others seems most appropriate as we conclude this chapter: "You can please all of the people some of the time, and some of the people all of the time, but not all of the people all of the time" (Lawrence, 2017, p. 53). It is crucial that college administrators and leaders understand the relationships they have with their stakeholders in order to understand their expectations and better engage in decision-making and actions that cultivate, steward, and strengthen the relationships (Mainardes et al., 2012). In addition, understanding stakeholder relationships is also useful in leveraging relationships between stakeholders for institutional benefit and anticipating reactions of stakeholders to various institutional decisions. Knowing the perspectives of stakeholders and understanding their lenses is vitally important in navigating the political behavior and context that operates within higher education. According to Kettunen (2015), "neglecting stakeholder relationships may lead to limited success and insufficient quality assurance in a higher education institution" (p. 56).

In this chapter, we provided a background of stakeholder theory and identified nine broad categories of stakeholders for higher education, delineating their connection to higher education broadly and interest in college students specifically. The changing role of stakeholders requires that as administrators and faculty, we are not only aware of stakeholder needs but also prioritize their needs and interests in ways that support the success of our colleges and students.

References

Bloom, D. E., Hartley, M., & Rosovsky, H. (2007). *Beyond private gain: The public benefits of higher education.* In J. F. Forest & P. G. Altbach (Eds.), *International handbook of higher education* (pp. 293–308). Springer.

Clarkson, M. E. (1995). A stakeholder framework for analyzing and evaluating corporate social performance. *Academy of Management Review, 20*(1), 92–117.

Donaldson, T., & Preston, L. E. (1995). The stakeholder theory of the corporation: Concepts, evidence, and implications. *Academy of Management Review, 20*(1), 65–91.

Eckel, P. D., & King, J. E. (2004). *An overview of higher education in the United States: Diversity, access, and the role of the marketplace.* American Council on Education.

Freeman, R. E. (1994). The politics of stakeholder theory: Some future directions. *Business Ethics Quarterly, 4*(4), 409–421.

Freeman, R. E. (2010). *Strategic management: A stakeholder approach.* Cambridge University Press.

Frooman, J. (1999). Stakeholder influence strategies. *Academy of Management Review, 24*(2), 191–205.

Gaier, S. (2005). Alumni satisfaction with their undergraduate academic experience and the impact on alumni giving and participation. *International Journal of Educational Advancement, 5*, 279–288. https://doi.org/10.1057/palgrave.ijea.2140220

Goodpaster, K. E. (1991). Business ethics and stakeholder analysis. *Business Ethics Quarterly, 1*(1), 53–73.

Greater Houston Partnership. (n.d.). *Workforce development.* Retrieved April 15, 2022, from https://www.houston.org/why-houston/workforce-development

Han, X., Stocking, G., Gebbie, M. A., & Appelbaum, R. P. (2015). Will they stay or will they go? International graduate students and their decisions to stay or leave the US upon graduation. *PloS one, 10*(3), e0118183.

Hazelrigg, N. (2019, July 29). New search, new problems. Retrieved online https://www.insidehighered.com/news/2019/07/29/miami-dade-board-reopens-search-despite-faculty-anger

Institute of International Education. (2020). International Student Enrollment Trends, 1948/49–2019/20. *Open Doors Report in International Educational Exchange.* Retrieved from http://www.opendoorsdata.org

Jongbloed, B., Enders, J., & Salerno, C. (2008). Higher education and its communities: Interconnections, interdependencies and a research agenda. *Higher Education, 56*(3), 303–324.

Kettunen, J. (2015). Stakeholder relationships in higher education. *Tertiary Education and Management, 21*(1), 56–65.

King, M.D. (2015, July 17). Why higher ed and business need to work together. Retrieved online https://hbr.org/2015/07/why-higher-ed-and-business-need-to-work-together

Lawrence, S. E. (2017). In B. D. Ruben, R. De Lisi, & R. A. Gigliotti (Eds.), *A guide of leaders in higher education: Core concepts, competencies, and tools* (pp. 53–64). Stylus Publishing.

Leisyte, L., & Westerheijden, D. F. (2014). Stakeholders and quality assurance in higher education. In H. Eggins (Ed.), *Drivers and barriers to achieving quality in higher education* (pp. 83–97). Sense Publishers.

Lutchen, K.R. (2018, January 24). Why companies and universities should forge long-term collaborations. Retrieved from https://hbr.org/2018/01/why-companies-and-universities-should-forge-long-term-collaborations

Ma, J., Pender, M., & Welch, M. (2016). *Education pays 2016: The benefits of higher education for individuals and society* [Trends in Higher Education Series]. College Board.

Mainardes, E. M., Alves, H., & Raposo, M. (2011). Stakeholder theory: issues to resolve. *Management Decision, 49*(2), 226–252.

Mainardes, E. M., Alves, H., & Raposo, M. (2012). A model for stakeholder classification and stakeholder relationships. *Management Decision, 50*(10), 1861–1879.

Mitchell, R. K., Agle, B. R., & Wood, D. J. (1997). Toward a theory of stakeholder identification and salience: Defining the principle of who and what really counts. *Academy of Management Review, 22*(4), 853–886.

Morrison, D. (2011, July). *Dear Colleague letter* [Manuscript/mixed material]. The Library of Congress. https://www.loc.gov/item/cosmos000071/

North Carolina State University. (2019). Why partner with NC State. Retrieved from https://eaped.ncsu.edu/partnerships/partnerships/why-partner/

Phillips, R., Freeman, R. E., & Wicks, A. C. (2003). What stakeholder theory is not. *Business Ethics Quarterly, 13*(4), 479–502.

Rowley, T. (1998). A normative justification for stakeholder theory. *Business and Society, 37*(1), 105.

Rowley, T. J. (1997). Moving beyond dyadic ties: A network theory of stakeholder influences. *Academy of Management Review, 22*(4), 887–910.

Soares, L. (2010, October 4). The power of the education-industry partnership. Retrieved from https://www.americanprogress.org/issues/economy/reports/2010/10/04/8518/the-power-of-the-education-industry-partnership/

Suchman, M. C. (1995). Managing legitimacy: Strategic and institutional approaches. *Academy of Management Review, 20*(3), 571–610.

Temmerman, N. (2018, April 13). The importance of listening to university stakeholders. Retrieved online https://www.universityworldnews.com/post.php?story=20180410151237739

Who Are Today's College Students?

5

WHO ARE TODAY'S COLLEGE STUDENTS?

Stakeholder Essays

Charles (Chuck) Ambrose, Chris Copes, Spencer Frye and Ellen Neufedlt

Who Are Today's College Students?

Dr. Charles (Chuck) Ambrose (he/him/his) is the President and CEO of Knowledgeworks, a national foundation helping create the future of learning through systems change with personalized competency-based learning. Dr. Ambrose bridges the world of higher Education and K–12 as a leader with over 35 years of service including two decades as a college president at Pfeiffer University and the University of Central Missouri.

Yesterday's college student was defined by the college – the identifiers such as institutional reputation, traditional versus nontraditional, programmatic quality, rankings, cost, and student loan debt – that have historically defined higher education and college students. Today's student is caught in the middle of a demanding shift to a new era, thanks to the 2008 recession and heightened economic insecurities, anti-racist practices, and a global pandemic challenging higher education. The established academic norms of what is expected of college students is becoming increasingly questioned and deconstructed as forces in the world challenge those notions.

As institutions strive to return to "normal," today's college student disrupts the system, accelerating the ways in which learning pathways, outcomes, and expectations are being redefined – broadening the number of ways in which a student will determine how they will access the learning required to meet their own personalized needs. The outcomes for students that will define success will

DOI: 10.4324/9780429319471-6

be based on community-based core competencies that prepare them to expand what's possible for both life and work. The institutions that do not follow the learner will risk experiencing an accelerated loss of reliance, purpose, and meaning for tomorrow's students, becoming irrelevant in a changing education and workforce landscape. The need to move from college-centric paradigms to student-centric paradigms is imperative – so where does that leave tomorrow's college student?

When Students Define College

The future for tomorrow's college student will be defined by the student or learner. Throughout my 34-year journey in higher education, I learned that following the learner to see what students discovered, championed, and pioneered is a strategic way to advance many of the true innovations and new paradigms across the system. The lines have been blurred among traditional sectors redefining pathways from high school to college, the school-to-work continuum, and degrees, licenses, credentials, and skills – most discovered by the learner. As these lines blur or disappear for more seamless learning pathways, barriers crumble, resulting in increased innovation.

As learning becomes more personalized, the more the student-/learner-centered paradigm for college is being turned upside down. This inversion of models is driven less by degrees, credit hours, and tuition and instead by concepts of competencies, experiences, acceleration, and affordability. KnowledgeWorks calls this systems-level paradigm personalized, competency-based learning. It centers each student's strengths, needs, and interests and provides differentiated supports and ways to demonstrate what they know and can do, ensuring each learner graduates ready for what's next.

Take Josh Adams, a learner from Blue Springs, Missouri, with a passion for graphic design. Adams's aggressive pathway was filled with dual credits, and he became a college student during high school at Summit Technology Academy. After high school, Adams enrolled at the University of Central Missouri, bringing in 28 hours of credit, eliminating at least a year of enrollment on his journey to earning a bachelor's degree. As an undergraduate student, he secured a paid internship at Hallmark Cards, Inc. Adams maintained work during the school year and the Hallmark internship during the summer, continuing to earn course credits. He graduated at the end of his third year, moving into full-time employment with one of Kansas City's top 50 global companies. It took Adams less time and significantly less cost with no skills gap and no student loan debt; his college was ultimately funded with the added support of his paid internship.

Adams took ownership of his passion to learn and his experiences help define what is known today as a P–16 accelerated pathway Innovation Campus Model, a seamless model for a regional educational ecosystem that demonstrates what is possible when we redefine college. President Barack Obama recognized the University of Central Missouri's accelerated pathway model as

> exactly the kind of innovation we need when it comes to college costs. That's what's happening right here in Warrensburg. And I want the entire country to notice it, and I want other colleges to take a look at what's being done here.[1]

Supporting Tomorrow's College Student

As the future of college evolves, so does the empowerment of students, educators, and communities to consider that all members of their communities are able to learn and are supported in the process. Learning communities need to be bolstered by data-informed strategies and innovative, future-ready, flexible, and resilient education policy changes that reflect student-centered supports, human capital and infrastructure, evidence of learning, and system accountability.

To help facilitate learning possibilities like Adams's in a personalized, competency-based learning environment, we must rethink the potential of the entire learning community. Students must adopt learner agency by making daily important decisions about their value-added learning experiences, how they create and apply knowledge, and how they demonstrate learning. Innovative pathways ensure learning is possible wherever and however a student is engaged – whether that's at school, college, work, or home. Learning outcomes define competencies, proficiencies, and mastery, and institutions are resourced, meaningfully assessed, and valued based on those outcomes. For stakeholders within the institutions, faculty and/or administrative roles must focus on removing the barriers, risks, and obstructive policies to make the learning pathways more seamless from school to life.

Student supports are driven by equity and individualized for specific student needs. Accountability is shared across systems and communities, requiring a business model restructure that is outcome-based, defined by student success, and regional core competencies that drive the economic and social well-being of the entire community. Resources are shared and in effect become a multiplier of increasingly scarce resources as win-wins are created across educational ecosystems as regionally developed skills drive localized economies.[2] Most public and private, two- and four-year institutions are seeking to build relationships to become more relevant to their local communities and produce measurable outcomes that demonstrate that their graduates are prepared to succeed.

Implications for the Future

I believe today's students are leading us in redefining college and what it means to be a college student. Student agency, activism, and engagement will demand that students are considered critical partners in redefining the value proposition for college and demonstrating those values with measurable outcomes. College degrees, graduation requirements, and learning engagement will become increasingly personalized. Scaffolding support tools such as intrusive advising, college completion initiatives, and micro-credentials will help meet individual student needs and future objectives. Learning communities will bring all aspects of their geographies into places and ways to learn. Economically competitive regions will be defined by the learning opportunities across their educational ecosystems spanning from school to work to life.[3] A student's journey will be defined by shared learning outcomes shaped by communities for future-ready skills built in partnerships – including work, school, and service. These community competencies can be identified, measured, and even credentialed, making the student's learning accelerate in its relevance, value, and meaning without having to rely on college only for credit hours or semesters to recognize learning.

Increasing affordability, access to, and acceleration of technology are empowering learners to consider new ways to define their own learning journeys. College students may begin their careers in high school – and they will continue to be students throughout their lives. When tools like hybrid instruction, experiential learning, P–16 pathways, and vertical transfers are considered the norm, then there is clear evidence that student-led and learner-centric experiences are reshaping college. Students who now are required to move around the impediments within the existing system are reshaping the purpose, delivery, and value of higher education. It's personalized. It's student-driven and student-centric. It looks to the future to ensure success not just for today's college student but for tomorrow's as well.

Transforming college begins with the mindset that every student can succeed. From that place, we realize more fully that today's college student is redefining what it will mean to be tomorrow's student. Sometimes it is as simple as getting out of their way.

Who Are Today's College Students?

Chris Copes (he/him/his) is a North Carolina native and proud graduate of North Carolina Central University, a historically Black college or university (HBCU). At the start of writing this piece, he was a rising senior on the campus of an HBCU, giving him not only the perspective of "today's student" but also that of a Black student with a unique and distinctly Black campus culture. He is grateful for the opportunity to contribute to this body of work and for the chance to reflect on his experiences and share his thoughts on a page. Chris currently works for the North Carolina Recreation & Park Association and the Town of Rolesville.

When asked who are today's college students, it was a little overwhelming for me to try and reflect on not only myself but also my friends, peers, and classmates. I am a more traditional college student in the sense that I enrolled immediately following high school, with the goal of graduating in four years. At the time of writing this essay, I am a senior and on track to meet that graduation time line. I am not a first-generation student, I had a support system to help with the application process, and I had advice on how to manage school financially. In responding to this question, it was important to me to think beyond my own experiences because I believe the word "nontraditional" best describes many of today's college students. We are nontraditional not only in the fact that not all of us are students straight out of high school who will graduate college in four years but also in the way that we buck at the idea of doing things the traditional way just because it is how things have always been done. Today's college students are about paving our own way to the future we want, even if it is not the most conventional way of doing things.

In my experience, the number of students who took nontraditional tracks through postsecondary education is larger than it appears at first glance. There are students who took gap years or worked before enrolling in undergraduate education; some of my classmates step out of the classroom and into their role as parents, and I have often been one of the youngest students in the room. Some of us are on a fast track to graduation, while others take their time to complete their degrees a la *Van Wilder*. A lot of today's college students do not attend four-year universities; when graduating high school, a large number of my classmates chose the local community college, which has grown at a consistent rate over the past few years.

I think a lot of today's students are less focused on degrees that will make the most money and instead are using college as a way to discover what it is they are truly interested in and then learning about those things. Our parent's generation often wants to push us toward the medical field or down the law track because those fields are typically connected to the concept of "success." When speaking to my classmates there are a few that want to be doctors or lawyers because of the general high salaries, but I do not think that is the norm. A lot of us change majors more than once looking for what it is that actually sparks our interest and what will lead to a career field that makes us happy. We value the fine arts as well as the humanities and social sciences, even if we choose not to pursue them as a field of study. On my campus, you can walk into any room and find musicians, producers, artists, DJs, and other creatives from a wide range of majors who pursue the arts outside of their degrees.

As a student at an HBCU, many of today's college students that I see are first generation. So many of my classmates and peers are paving the way as examples for younger brothers, sisters, and cousins as the first family members to have the college experience. A lot of them are the first to get out of rural small towns across North Carolina; they are the first filling out college applications and financial aid forms, the first ones taking on student loans, and they are figuring out how to manage these things on the fly. In doing so, they make it easier for the ones coming behind them to be successful. My Black classmates and other classmates of color are using their degrees to continue to break down barriers in the professional world. Today's Black college students challenge traditional ideas of what professionalism is through our hairstyles and textures. We push the boundaries of what is considered business casual or professional dress with our unique senses of fashion. We are trying to find the balance of following the guidelines of the workplace while not being stripped of our physical and cultural identities.

Today's college students are the pillars of pop culture, especially on the campus of an HBCU. Students at large, particularly Black students and those attending HBCUs, have the unique experience of seeing trends, dances, and styles we create grow into viral internet fads and phenomena that spread across the world. The songs we listen to and the styles we wear are often replicated by celebrities and appreciated by others after the trend has run its course through our campuses. College students across the globe relate to each other through these shared interests and jokes on our different social media platforms. Traditional news media and other outlets will certainly pick up the dances we create, the social media "challenges" we start, and the memes that are popularized after students have shared them with each other. Today's students are able to engage in pop culture in a way that encourages global thinking and sharing across regional and cultural lines.

I think today's students are motivated to create change; we are not willing to accept rules, traditions, or ideas that we do not agree with. We are determined to live in a world where people are unafraid of being their most authentic selves. Today's students challenge social norms in all areas from fashion and relationships to sexuality and gender. On my campus, fashion is a big part of our student culture and is a major outlet of expressing ourselves as individuals, and, in turn, these expressions push the boundaries of what is seen as "appropriate" to wear. A large number of students and professors have moved to putting their preferred pronouns in email communication in an effort to normalize the practice and allow room for people to own their gender identity instead of having it forced upon them. Activist groups such as BYP 100, Races, and Colors are full of today's college students who are interested in advocating for, protecting, and providing welcoming spaces to anyone who may need it. The student body at my school has participated in and organized events from marches to the polls to pulling down statues. We are concerned about being members of a global society. Some of my courses have been focused on global music, cultures, and ideas all with the intent of expanding our viewpoint on the world and how we interact with the different people around us.

I think today's students are creating, working toward, building, and centering a foundation for a society based on inclusivity and new ways of doing things. We do not all look one way or come from the same backgrounds, and we are pushing for a world where those differences are recognized, appreciated, and considered when making decisions. We are set on creating new traditions with new ideas and improving the ideas that were put in place by the college students before us, and there is room for all of us to do so. Today's college students are carrying the torch that was lit by generations of students before us and providing an example for tomorrow's students to let their ideas and traditions grow in the same way that we have.

Who Are Today's College Students?

Spencer Frye (he/him/his) was first elected to the Georgia House of Representatives in 2012, representing House District 118, which includes portions of Athens and Winterville; he still holds this office while also serving as the executive director for Athens Habitat for Humanity. He has also been a small business owner and a construction manager, has helped to export American ambulances overseas, and cofounded a company that began by recapturing recyclable motor oil and which now operates globally. As a business owner, nonprofit director, and now state representative, Spencer Frye has met and worked with folks from all over the community and successfully balanced the interests of citizens, private enterprise, and government.

In 1986, I migrated to Athens, Georgia, as an 18-year-old with no idea of what I wanted or needed to do for college. I had been accepted into the University of Georgia (UGA) after graduating from a high school that had such rigorous standards that extra weight was given to my grade point average (GPA) by the university. Student loans and Pell Grants allowed me an opportunity to not work and live in the dorms while focusing on school work. Distractions to my academic efforts came in the form of being a member of a fraternity, as well as the well-known music scene in Athens. After attending the university for seven quarters, I called my father and told him I was selling all of my possessions and moving to California. His reply was simple and direct, "You don't have anything." Yet, he heard my need for change and immediately set out to find me something to do. I ended up taking a year away from UGA and living and working in Haiti. Upon my return, I registered for classes but due to financial reasons was forced to drop out after one quarter. Needing money to continue my education, I began working and created a landscaping business. Shortly thereafter, I was able to return to classes and had people working for me while I attended college. My business was so successful that I, again, stopped attending college to focus on my responsibilities as a small business owner and a landlord. Fast-forward about 22 years later and after promising my wife I would complete my degree for the sake of being an example to our children, I reapplied to and was admitted to UGA to take the remaining two classes I had left to finally become a college graduate in 2014.

American author Washington Irving wrote a story that was published in 1819 about Rip Van Winkle, a man who fell asleep in the woods for 20 years, and when he awoke he had missed the Revolutionary war, and his friends, family, and village were all different from when he had last seen them. In 2014, when I returned to classes for the first time in 20-plus years, I immediately recalled this tale learned from my youth and felt like I was a modern-day Rip Van Winkle. When I was in college the first and second time, we had no internet, no cell phones, and the most advanced consumer communication technology was a giant box telephone that plugged into the cigarette lighter in a car ashtray. We researched projects using the library card catalogues and a green screen computer system that was slower than actually looking up a reference manually in the card system. Our reports were written by hand on lined paper, and members of group projects had the added difficulty of physically finding each other in large spaces without instant communication. Chalkboards with dusty erasers and giant overhead projectors were the only way to provide information to a large group in a single classroom.

When I returned to finalize my degree, things were dramatically different. I arrived in class the first day and was told to download an app on my phone that would allow us to take a short quiz each day, answering questions that were projected on a screen for the entire class, while the instructor immediately accessed this data to analyze course knowledge. Every student had a laptop computer in front of them, along with a phone. During the semester, I honestly do not recall seeing very many books or notepads on the desks. Each day as I was diligently writing as fast as I could in my spiral notebook doing everything I could to work out cramps in my hand from lack of writing much over the past two or so decades, I could see across the room of 200 students, the majority were typing into their laptops while watching the professor and not looking down to their screens but every once in a while. Due to a tip from some of my new peer group, I did not even have to purchase a single book for the classes because I could access PDF versions of previous editions online for free. This was a new generation of students, shaped by technological advances in both teaching and communication, but there were other differences I noticed.

More recently, in a legislative update while meeting with the university president and staff, we were informed that a recent freshman class had an average GPA of over a 4.0. While I do understand the weighting concept, as I benefited from it when I originally enrolled, for an entire class to have above a 4.0 average was astounding to me. This is achieved by taking advanced classes in high school and using the weighting system for the final grade. This statistic coupled with the HOPE Scholarship in Georgia, which requires the students to achieve and maintain a certain GPA in order to retain their financial aid for classes, which makes the college essentially free, has got to put a tremendous amount of pressure on these young students from an early age. If you want to attend the flagship university in this state, the pressure to perform above average is constant. Yet, in Georgia, this seems to be the overriding desire of most students for a variety of reasons, not the least of which is legacy, as in many cases their parents and possibly most members of their family went to UGA. You seem to have to sacrifice everything in your life to only focus on your grades and classroom performance from when you are 14 years old in the 9th grade! Couple this fact with increasing score requirements from the SAT and ACT, and you have an amazing amount of scholastic pressure on today's youth that only continues as they become college students.

As a legislator in Georgia, I have the opportunity to work with many current college students through my legislative fellowship, which is a student-run organization that researches policy, creates legislation for the statehouse, and learns how state government is run and how policy affects citizens lives and well-being. I spend a great deal of time as a mentor to these students and have gotten to see how they operate within the parameters of the modern education system. While this group of students has not grown up with the blazing-fast internet and powerful handheld communication devices like my young children have, they have adapted to these technological advances with amazing precision. Their ability to manipulate technology to achieve their goals is eye-opening and a joy to witness. These modern-day students and their grasp of the technological advances in our society have transformed our education system in a way that has never happened before. With the new communication platforms for smartphones and computers making communication instantaneous, and with advanced search functions of mobile applications providing a seemingly endless amount of information constantly available, we are seeing a new breed of students. Never before have we experienced these new knowledge pathways in the higher education system. This generation of students has permanently transformed not only how we educate but also who we educate, and they will lead us into a new transformation within our workplace as they mature and become the leaders of our society instituting these technological advances into the fabric of our future lives.

Who Are Today's College Students?

Ellen J. Neufeldt, Ed.D. (she/her/hers) has served as the president of California State University San Marcos since 2019, a university of approximately 16,000 students. Her extensive career in higher education has centered on student success and social mobility. While serving in her previous role as the Vice President of Student Engagement and Enrollment Services at Old Dominion University, she led the creation of a national center for social mobility. Dr. Neufeldt received her doctor of education from the University of Tennessee at Knoxville, her master of arts in educational psychology and counselor education from Tennessee Technological University, and her bachelor of science in business administration from Tennessee Technological University.

When I became president of California State University San Marcos (CSUSM) during the summer of 2019, I was excited to launch a listening and learning tour to get to know the campus community, which includes just over 16,000 students and nearly 50,000 alumni. As a former vice president for Student Engagement and Enrollment Services at Old Dominion University (ODU), I was drawn to CSUSM because of its diverse and multicultural community, as well as its established track record of student success. I was eager to meet our students and hear their stories – why did they choose CSUSM? What has their educational journey been like? What are their hopes and dreams for the future?

Of course, no two students provided the same answer. Some told me about the pride of being first in their families to go to college but the uncertainty that went along with that as they navigated the financial aid and admissions applications without parental support. Others told me about the challenges of going to school while juggling part-time or full-time jobs and/or parenting responsibilities. And still others shared stories from their previous military experience or their desire to make a career change/enhance their career trajectory. While almost universally our students shared their excitement to make progress toward their degrees, many also imparted complex combinations of family responsibilities, employment, and financial pressures, which required constant time and energy to navigate.

The student stories I heard from my current campus are not unlike the stories of students I left behind at ODU – or the stories my colleagues across higher education share about their students. But what often surprises me is that the stereotype of the "traditional" college student still very much exists. There are many who still believe that the common profile of a college student is what is commonly portrayed in popular culture. This traditional idea of college students are majority white, have parents who are college-educated, graduated from high school and enrolled directly in college, and are middle or upper class. But the truth is, times have changed and with it so have student demographics.

When *US News & World Report* began factoring social mobility into its overall scores in 2018 instead of focusing just on institutional wealth and admission rejection rates (Jackson & Lee, 2018), it was an important acknowledgment of the changing profile of today's college students. At CSUSM, more than 55% of our students are first generation, about 42% are Hispanic/Latinx, 40% are 23 years or older, 40% are Pell-eligible, and over 10% are veterans or military affiliated. Because of all these factors, the majority of our students are considered "nontraditional" – although I would argue that nontraditional IS the new tradition. And we must keep in mind that these were the demographics before the COVID-19 pandemic hit. Although the full effects of the virus are not yet known, there are signs nationally among college students of increased financial strain and food and housing insecurity, mental health challenges, and the difficulties of learning in less-than-ideal home environments, particularly among long income students and students of color.

Unfortunately, most universities and state and federal policies were built to serve the students of yesteryear, not the students of today who need extra assistance in balancing the many roles in their lives while breaking through various barriers. It is imperative that we make key shifts with an equity mindset. At CSUSM, we are investing in student success across every phase of our students' university experience: from pre-matriculation to graduation and everything in between. For example, through connections to the K–12 community, we invite middle schoolers on campus tours, inviting them to engage with current students and imagine themselves in college. Then, once they transition to university life, we offer success coaching, which focuses on building individualized relationships between coaches and students. Coaches act as academic concierges, providing guidance, answering questions, and ensuring students have graduation in mind from the very beginning.

The goal of student coaching is to support students at the start of their CSUSM journey and then transition them into high-impact practices, including college-level internships, faculty, and career mentoring programs, community-engaged learning opportunities, and undergraduate research. These practices have been shown to improve the success of all students but especially those students from diverse backgrounds (Kuh, 2008). Furthermore, many nontraditional students often report feelings of impostor syndrome, isolation, and marginality (Remenick, 2019). Fortunately, our faculty and staff truly embrace our mission to create an inclusive campus environment. As just one example, our Faculty Mentoring Program serves students who are first generation and/or economically disadvantaged by pairing them with faculty mentors who provide guidance, encouragement, and support.

In addition, we offer a range of specialized niche programs to support the diverse needs of our students. For example, a program called Project Rebound supports formerly incarcerated students; ACE Scholars Services provides former foster youth with both a literal and figurative home on campus; the College Assistance Migrant Program provides children of migrant farmworkers a place to build connections. Furthermore, our Tukwut Parent Program offers lactation rooms and child-friendly spaces, making it a little easier for our student parents to breathe as they try to juggle all their responsibilities. And our Veterans Center offers a place for our military-affiliated students to bond, with academic and career coaching tailored to their unique needs.

These innovative programs and high-impact practices, integrated into a network of academic advisors, success coaches, and faculty mentors, mean that our students are frequently hearing the powerful message that they can be the best they can be – and that we believe in them and will support them every step of the way. To date, these efforts are paying off. Not only have we closed achievement gaps for low-income and underrepresented minority students, but we are a top university in the country for social mobility, which measures the extent to which universities lift graduates into higher socioeconomic brackets.

Furthermore, focusing on student success by embracing inclusive excellence, removing barriers, and supporting students across the student life cycle is key not only for the individual and generational impact it has on students and their families but also because we know the future of our workforce and economy is facing unprecedented challenges. Thanks to rapid technological changes and new ways of working that are disrupting the skills employers need in their workforce, universities like CSUSM with a diverse population of students not only have a moral imperative to remove the barriers that stand in the way of students' success, but they are also key to the long-term viability of our communities and local, state, and national economies. According to the Public Policy Institute of California (2015), if current trends persist, 38% of jobs in California will require at least a bachelor's degree by 2030. In CSUSM's own region, our regional economic development council projects a need for an additional 20,000 skilled workers for top innovation occupations by the end of this decade. But we are proudly rising to the challenge with 80% of our graduates remaining in our region, contributing and leading in our local industries and communities.

While there is no still no simple way to define the college students of today – or a single silver bullet that will close equity gaps and support their success – it's clear that colleges and universities like CSUSM are redefining what it means to serve students across ethnic, gender, and socioeconomic boundaries, and be dedicated to their college and lifelong success. As we look ahead in a post-COVID-19 or COVID-19-integrated world, it will be important to embrace opportunities for further innovation and reinvention by extending business hours for key services and offering additional options for hybrid or online learning. We owe it to our students – with all of the wonderful diversity of backgrounds and experiences they bring to our campuses – and the broader communities we serve to continue to evolve, improve and innovate . . . because diversity, social mobility, and student success are truly the modern benchmarks of what makes a great university even greater.

Notes

1 President Obama's Speech at the University of Central Missouri, July 25, 2013, https://obamawhitehouse.archives.gov/the-press-office/2013/07/25/remarks-president-economy-warrensburg-missouri
2 Adapted from KnowledgeWorks' and Aurora Institute's definition of personalized, competency-based learning.
3 Adapted from KnowledgeWorks' *Navigating the Future of Learning – Forecast 5.0.*

References

Jackson, J., & Lee, C. (2018, October 5). College rankings and social mobility. Retrieved from https://www.ppic.org/blog/college-rankings-and-social-mobility/

Kuh, G. (2008). *High-impact educational practices: What they are, who has access to them, and why they matter.* Washington, DC: Association of American Colleges and Universities

Public Policy Institute of California. (2015). *Will California run out of college graduates?* Retrieved from https://www.ppic.org/publication/will-california-run-out-of-college-graduates/

Remenick, L. (2019). Services and support for nontraditional students in higher education: A historical literature review. *Journal of Adult and Continuing Education, 25*(1), 113–130. doi:10.1177/1477971419842880

6

ANALYSIS

Who Are Today's College Students?

Laura A. Dean and Jason Wallace

Dr. Laura Dean (she/her/hers) is Professor in the College Student Affairs Administration/Student Affairs Leadership program at the University of Georgia. Her research focuses primarily on assessment and the improvement of practice. A member of ACPA, NASPA, and the American College Counseling Association, she has also been active in the Council for the Advancement of Standards in Higher Education (CAS) for over 25 years, including service as Editor and as President. She is the co-author of Assessment in Student Affairs (2nd ed., 2016) and co-editor of Using the CAS Professional Standards: Diverse Examples of Practice (2017). Previously, she served as the senior student affairs officer at Pfeiffer University and at Peace College in North Carolina. She holds a BA from Westminster College (PA) and her graduate degrees from the University of North Carolina at Greensboro.

Jason K. Wallace, PhD (he/him) is an assistant professor of higher education in the School of Education at The University of Southern Mississippi (Southern Miss). Prior to joining the faculty at Southern Miss, Jason served as a student affairs practitioner for nearly a decade primarily in multicultural affairs and new student orientation. Jason's research broadly focuses on issues of equity and inclusion in higher education with emphasis on the experiences of Black and first-generation college students.

There is an old parable, generally attributed to the ancient Indian subcontinent, about a group of blind men and an elephant. The story describes them

DOI: 10.4324/9780429319471-7

encountering an elephant for the first time; each touches a different part of the animal, and each comes to a different understanding of what an elephant is like. In turn, they argue that an elephant is like a wall, a rope, a tree, a snake, a spear, and a fan. As captured near the end of a poem based on the fable, "each was partly in the right/And all were in the wrong!" (Saxe, 1873). The moral of the story, of course, is that our individual perceptions shape our understandings of all that we encounter, and when our own experiences reveal only one aspect of something, we can easily draw conclusions that, if not completely erroneous, are limited. The dominance of our individual lens frames and determines our understanding of the whole.

The question of who today's college students are reflects the lesson from the parable. We know that the demographics and enrollment patterns of today's students paint a picture of a group that is so varied, so diverse, and so complex that it defies easy description. The facts and figures bear this out. The perspectives represented by the essay authors in this chapter, however, as well as ours as chapter authors, reflect the truth that our perspectives shape our understandings and our answers to the question about today's college students.

The essay authors in this chapter reflect the varied perspectives of a current university president, a former president (serving as CEO of an education-related organization), a recent college graduate, and a state legislator. Moreover, the group also represents institutional experiences ranging from a small public HBCU (historically Black college or university) to a large state flagship institution, including a mid-size regional university and a small private one. Each of those authors has a distinct perspective about college students that has been shaped by their past and current experiences. This is equally true for us as chapter authors. Laura is a white woman nearing retirement after working more than 40 years in education at various levels. A graduate of a small liberal arts college and a mid-size public university, I worked in small colleges in administrative roles including dean of students before spending 15 years as a graduate student affairs faculty member. Despite having developed a more expansive view by now, my instinctive mental image of "college student" is still a traditional one, shaped largely by my time in small college settings. Jason is a Black, cisgender man who recently completed his first year as a higher education faculty member after a decade of working in student affairs. Though I was a first-generation college student and recognize the vast diversity of college students, often, my default mental image of college students (especially early in my career) displays students who attend college immediately following high school and graduate in four to five years, much like I did. Together, because of our role as graduate preparation program faculty members, we have a broad understanding of enrollment trends and the complex demographic profile of "today's college students," and yet we acknowledge that our intrinsic personal understandings are still influenced by our own histories and experiences.

It is also worthwhile to note that those who end up in the academy, especially in student-facing roles, are more likely to come from a single story – that of having been highly involved and having experienced validation and a sense of belonging in the academic environment – and so may end up inadvertently perpetuating it through framing, expectations, and failures of perspective. Those images of a traditional college experience are also reinforced through depictions in movies, television, and news stories that use "college student" as shorthand for "young, carefree, economically stable, full-time, residential students at a four-year university." Those students exist, of course, and they are college students, but so are many, many others who get less attention in the public imagination and, too often, at our institutions.

At the most basic level, today's college students are individuals who are enrolled in postsecondary educational institutions, generally for academic credit (although perhaps for some other forms of credentialing or specific skill attainment). We know quite a bit about the ways that they can differ from one another and how those differences can affect their experiences, but beyond the fact of their enrollment, what is the same? To return to the opening metaphor, what is the elephant?

Multiple Images, Learners at the Center

The perspectives of this chapter's essayists reflect the effect of experience on perception. Those whose experiences involve more different institutions and roles reflect a more expansive perspective on the question, and those whose experiences have been less varied have a narrower view. This is only natural. Reading across the four viewpoints, however, some themes begin to emerge.

Bimodal Images

As described earlier, there is the idea of the traditional college student, and then there is…something else. As Gulley (2016) pointed out, the often-used term "nontraditional" is highly problematic, in that it continues to center the traditional student as the norm, against which others are simply not that, even though they make up the majority of those enrolled in postsecondary education. Within the chapter essays, however, this bimodal view emerges, with the traditional image still firmly in focus, alongside acknowledgment of its limitations. Chris Copes acknowledges this in his essay; although his path was traditional, he recognizes not only that not all paths are traditional but also that many students pursue multiple paths simultaneously, in and outside of the academy. Spencer Frye's story is one that is framed around a traditional student experience, both his own initial years at UGA and his eventual return to complete his degree at an institution where the demographics were similar but technology and increased pressure have created a different environment. However, despite the fact that he was, himself, a college student when he returned to finish his degree, his perspective still positioned the traditional-age students around him as the "real" college students. In his essay, the college students around him were "they," not "we." As a university president, Ellen Neufeldt offers a perspective informed both by past experiences and current leadership of an institution whose student body reflects the complexity inherent in the question we are exploring. In fact, she contends that "nontraditional IS the new tradition." Charles (Chuck) Ambrose takes this a step further, arguing that we need to move away from defining students by their relationship to the college and instead shift to a paradigm that focuses on the student as learner. Echoing and expanding on Cope's description of students finding multiple ways to pursue multiple passions and goals, Ambrose focuses on the idea of student agency. Rather than being passive recipients of a predetermined curriculum that results in a generic degree, students are instead conceptualized as creators of a personalized path to individual goals.

While on the surface, the essays reflect somewhat divergent views, taken together they reflect the bimodal images of "today's college student" that exist. On one hand, the phrase tends to conjure images of young people walking across grassy quads bordered by old brick buildings, but even those of us who have had that experience recognize that as a limited view. The challenge remains that the traditional view is easy to picture and reinforced by images all around us, while the alternatives do not as easily coalesce into coherent shapes. We are left with the problem that the traditional image persists, and the alternatives continue to be described by their divergence from that "norm."

Multiple Meanings of "Traditional"

This leads to the second theme that emerged across the essays. Even within the notion of traditional students, differences were apparent. One perspective reflects a definition based on individual characteristics: a traditional college student is one who is young, financially secure, attends full time, lives on campus or nearby, engages in cocurricular activities, and is pursuing a baccalaureate degree. These are the kinds of variables that would be easy to ask on a survey – they make it easy to categorize individuals in terms of their relationship with the role of student.

A second perspective, however, reflects an understanding that students are better defined instead by their activities and by the salience of their identity as students. It is less a matter of categorization and more a matter of how students engage with their learning, how they exert agency over their educational experiences. Copes's description of students pursuing interests and activism alongside their academic endeavors and Ambrose's account of a student using an accelerated pathway model both reflect this complex web of activities and identities, even among those who by categorical definitions would be classified as "traditional."

Learner-Centered

The question of the salience of identity, and identity in relation to what, is at the heart of a theme we have labeled learner-centered. While for many students, identity in relation to their institution is important (hence the popularity of college sweatshirts, for example), increasingly we see that the identity of the self-directed learner is important and serves as a driver of decisions. Rather than being centered as a student on the basis of categorical characteristics, students are choosing to center themselves as the subject and object of their educational experiences. As captured in Ambrose's description, they are building an experience, choosing multiple ways to gain desired competencies, and creating a unique path to reach their goals. Further, they are increasingly creating an a la carte experience that consists of classes at multiple institutions and in different modalities, with additional certifications and credentials added on, augmented not only by cocurricular engagement but also by side hustles and work in the gig economy. This complex pattern of engagement can be seen even more in the ways that older returning students and part-time students choose targeted engagement designed to pick up credentials for advancement or for a change of direction. Whether this has been spurred by the economic uncertainty of the last 15 years, by generational differences, or by factors yet unknown, the picture that is emerging is that students are increasingly exercising their own agency and centering themselves in the process.

Influence of Technology

Few descriptions of the college experience today do not include some discussion of the role of technology in the experience. In his essay, Frye painted a vivid picture of the ways that technology has changed the experience between when he started college and when he finished, more than 20 years later. This became even more true in 2020 as the pandemic resulted in an explosion of remote instruction, hybrid/hy-flex approaches, and virtual engagement of all kinds. This illuminates one of the crucial questions related to the influence of technology on students today: Is it an interest in and of itself, or simply a vehicle for accomplishing other tasks? From our essayists' perspectives, as well as our own, it seems that for most students, technology is simply a means to an end – it is the mechanism through which they do what they do, whether that means taking care of administrative tasks, engaging in academic work through learning management systems, communicating with others in real time, keeping up through social media, or streaming entertainment in their free time. It is pervasive in their worlds, and sometimes intrusive, but inescapable, and necessary for participation as a student, regardless of how immersive or tangential their educational engagement is at any point in time.

Stakeholders' Perspectives

The four stakeholder perspectives on today's college students include a few over-lapping ideas, as evidenced by the aforementioned themes, as well as some dispa-rate viewpoints. Neufeldt and Ambrose each worked on college campuses and engaged regularly with college students, past and present. Working within a higher education context, and engaging with college student literature, equips them with rich perspectives on today's college students. Their intimate and longstanding con-nection with higher education cultivates their nuanced understanding of today's college students from a macrolevel. Though their perspectives are well informed, they lack the firsthand expertise that Copes provides as a current college student.

Copes's perspective on today's college student is deeply contextualized by what he is currently experiencing. His viewpoint is unique because the question of *who are today's college students* is one that he can answer by simply describing himself and his peers. While Copes's perspective, likely, does not include the depth and breadth of all today's college students, he does provide on-the-ground experience of his recent context as an HBCU student, as well as what he gleans from his peers at community colleges and other institutions. Copes and Frye share similar perspectives in that they both discuss college students from the standpoint of being one.

Frye's viewpoint is rather distinct since he was a college student in the mid-eighties and, more recently, in the mid-2010s. Though Frye returned to col-lege in 2014 and reflected on that experience, he framed his reflection from an "outsider" perspective, underscoring how he felt different from his classmates as an older student. Frye describes his classmates as "this generation of college students" completely divorcing himself as a member of that generation of col-lege students. This othering calls attention to the dominant narrative that 18- to 22-year-old students are the "traditional" college students. Nevertheless, Frye was, in fact, recently enrolled, and he and Copes provide invaluable perspectives of today's college students. As stakeholders who are not current or former leaders within higher education, like Neufeldt and Ambrose, Copes's and Frye's essays provide more of an unfiltered perspective.

What the stakeholders do not share in their essays are the experiences, outside of their current relationship with higher education, which inform their perspec-tive on today's college students. For example, readers are not privy to Neufeldt's and Ambrose's own undergraduate experiences and how those experiences may or may not inform how they view college students today. As authors, we discussed how our experiences (as people who went to four-year institutions directly after high school, lived on campus, and graduated in four years) sig-nificantly shaped our early views and beliefs about college students. What les-sons did Neufeldt and Ambrose have to learn and/or unlearn to gain a holistic understanding of today's college students? How are their ideas changing as they continue to engage in their roles in and near higher education? Similarly, Copes does not share what additional experiences, if any, inform his understanding of today's college students. Frye discusses his engagement through his role as a legislator, but does not go beyond that role. Might there be other experiences informing how they understand today's college students?

In addition to stakeholders' experiences, we do not know what social identities the stakeholders hold currently, or held previously, that shape their views on today's college students. Extant college student literature discusses the ways systems of oppression and dominance shape the experiences of college students who hold marginalized and/or minoritized identities. These systems continue to shape viewpoints of higher education stakeholders (i.e., faculty, administrators, legislators, alumni). From the essays, we know that Copes is a Black student at a historically Black university, and we get an idea of how his racial identity shapes his perspective. Yet, we do not know Copes's intersecting identities (e.g., religion, sexual orientation, ability) that may also shape his perceptions of college students. Similarly, we do not know the social identities of the other stakeholders with any certainty, though we can glean a few.

Lastly, we do not know the roles and relationships, external to higher education, that each stakeholder occupies and engages within. While we know that Frye is a state legislator, we do not know what other ways he and the other stakeholders engage with college students. How are the stakeholders interacting with today's college students outside of their stated roles (e.g., at places of worship, in community organizations, family members)? In what ways do those interactions shape their perceptions of college students? Though gaps exist, the perspectives of the stakeholders yield useful insights into today's college students. Contemporary scholarship on today's college students provides additional context around stakeholders' perspectives.

Relationship to Theory and Literature

Higher education scholars have long sought to understand college students. Renn and Reason (2013) tackled the question of who today's college student is in their text *College Students in the United States*. They begin the text by positing that most college students are not the "quintessential 'American college student'" (p. x) whom they describe as a white, middle-class, Christian (cisgender) man who is heterosexual and nondisabled. This student attends a selective public institution where he, no doubt, lives in a residence hall, takes a full course load, works part time on campus, and graduates with his bachelor's degree in four years. These are the characteristics of the stereotypical traditional college student as echoed by Neufeldt. Nevertheless, Renn and Reason (2013), much like many other higher education scholars, combat this narrative by revealing the diversity in the students who attend colleges and underscoring their fluid enrollment patterns, and noting the variance in institutional type in which the majority of the students situate themselves.

In a 2016 opinion piece in *Inside HigherEd*, Gulley troubled the use of the term "nontraditional college students," highlighting its inaccuracy in describing today's college students, as many of today's college students are older than 24, racially minoritized, first-generation college students, and attending school part time. Scholars continue to push against this caricature of a "typical" college student by spotlighting the diversity that exists among them. Critical scholarship challenges higher education administrators, researchers, and policymakers to recognize and serve students whom institutional leadership and scholars have traditionally relegated to the margins of praxis including, but not limited to, transgender students (Nicolazzo, 2017), fat-bodied students (Stewart, 2018), students with disabilities (Kimball et al., 2016), queer students (Abes & Kasch, 2007), and Students of Color (Tachine et al., 2017; Pyne & Means, 2013). Further, scholars continue to work to explore students whose identities lie at the intersection of multiple systems of oppression who are further relegated to the margins of institutional praxis, including Asian American women (Museus & Truong, 2013), Black deaf students (Stapleton & Croom, 2017), and queer Students of Color (Evans & Wallace, 2019), to name a few. These scholars, among many others, reach further in seeking to understand who today's college students are by acknowledging and honoring the intersecting identities these students hold, as well as exploring the contexts in which students are located. For example, Whitehead (2019) explored the experiences and cultural capital of queer and transgender Students of Color at a community college, while Mobley et al. (2021) investigated the experiences of white students at a public historically Black university. These distinct and nuanced explorations are necessary for understanding today's college students, as noted in Neufeldt's and Copes's essays.

It is clearly true that today's college students are not exclusively 18- to 24-year-old, white, full-time students attending selective public institutions, so why do U.S. media and society at large continue to portray them in this way? In what ways do higher education institutions, and legislatures, still perpetuate such a narrative? The authors of these essays vary in their understanding that the traditional college student is not so traditional. They each recognize that college students have their own patterns of enrollment, which contemporary college student literature supports (e.g., Crosta, 2014; Renn & Reason, 2013). Moreover, the authors echo current scholarship, which asserts that college students no longer, exclusively, subscribe to what higher education institutions feel is best for their success but make decisions based on what they feel is most beneficial to their learning needs and career outcomes (Seemiller & Grace, 2016). Yet several of the essay authors, much like contemporary literature, still center the idea of the "traditional" college students who engage with higher education with an end goal of obtaining a degree, license, or certificate. Ambrose challenges this notion by offering the idea that consumers of higher education are less interested in obtaining degrees in the traditional sense, but gaining competencies and skills in a more a la carte fashion. While competency-based learning is not a novel concept, particularly as it relates to leadership programming in higher educa- tion (e.g., Ashby & Mintner, 2017) and career education and development (e.g., Cruzvergara et al., 2018; Howard et al., 2017), the idea that some of today's col- lege students are disinterested in pursuing traditional degrees and licenses could cause significant concern for higher education leaders. Thus, higher education leaders and scholars must continue to grapple with how to meet the needs of today's college students while sustaining institutional resources and keeping the doors open.

The essays accentuate the need for higher education leaders to continue to be nimble in their engagement with today's college students while simultane- ously calling for continued refinement of college student theory and literature. These ideas are not unlike recent calls in higher education scholarship. While many of the thoughts offered in the essays still support the need and utility of student development theories, the ever-changing landscape of higher education, coupled with the continued decline of the "quintessential 'American college stu- dent'" (Renn & Reason, 2013, p. x), requires higher education professionals to continue to contend with the question of who today's college students really are.

Conclusion

Today's college students are many things. They range in demographic variables, salience of the student role, and pathways to their goals. Despite this complexity, stereotypical images persist, reinforced by media and by the visibility of insti- tutions that enroll a "traditional" student body. "College student" serves as a convenient shorthand, but the reality is far more complicated. While the only true common denominator across differences may be the fact of enrollment, the emerging answer to the question of who today's college students are may be one that results from a shift in perspective. Where conventional views of college students were framed by their relationship to an institution, a more current view shifts figure and ground. Rather than positioning the institution as primary, and defining students in relation to it, a newer conceptualization situates the learner as primary, with an array of institutions, modalities, credentials, and activities comprising the pathway to their goals.

What, then, is the elephant? The tempting interpretation is that the elephant is the full complement of enrolled students, made up of a range of groups and categories that look different, and so focusing on any one of them separately leads to incorrect assumptions about the nature of the whole. That interpretation is not wholly wrong or misleading. Perhaps, though, a more useful interpreta- tion is that the elephant, taken as a whole, represents each "college student" individually, and the disparate parts that can seem disconnected or at odds with each other are actually a complex set of experiences, choices, and avenues that work together to create one unified whole, moving intentionally toward desired outcomes.

Who are today's college students? They are, in fact, a group of individuals whose only factual commonality is that they are pursuing postsecondary education. More importantly, however, they are individuals who are increasingly taking charge of their own learning. Rather than being content with having their experience curated and dictated by institutions, they are identifying their own objectives and designing their own ways of reaching them, using institutions and other avenues as components from which to create the individual pathway that leads where they want to go. Their paradigm has shifted; higher education institutions and professionals need to shift ours, too, if we are to recognize, support, serve, and celebrate students who are ready to chart their own multifaceted courses.

References

Abes, E. S., & Kasch, D. (2007). Using queer theory to explore lesbian college students' multiple dimensions of identity. *Journal of College Student Development, 48*(6), 619–636.

Ashby, K. C., & Mintner, P. J. (2017). Building a competency-based leadership program with campus-wide implementation. *New Directions for Student Leadership, 156,* 101–112.

Crosta, P. M. (2014). Intensity and attachment: How the chaotic enrollment patterns of community college students relate to educational outcomes. *Community College Review, 42*(2), 118–142.

Cruzvergara, C. Y., Testani, J. A., & Smith, K. K. (2018). Leadership competency expectations of employers and the expanding mission of career centers. *New Directions for Student Leadership, 157,* 27–37.

Evans, M. E., & Wallace, J. K. (2019). No longer cast aside: A critical approach to serving queer and trans students of Color in higher education. In D. Mitchell Jr., J. Marie, & T. Steele (Eds.), *Intersectionality & higher education: Theory, research, and praxis* (2nd ed.,) pp. 181–189). BrillSense Publishing.

Gulley, N. Y. (2016, August 5). The myth of the nontraditional student. *Inside Higher Ed.* Retrieved from https://www.insidehighered.com/views/2016/08/05/defining-students-nontraditional-inaccurate-and-damaging-essay

Howard, A. R., Healy, S. L., & Boyatzis, R. E. (2017). Using leadership competencies as a framework for career readiness. *New Directions for Student Leadership, 156,* 59–71.

Kimball, E. W., Moore, A., Vaccaro, A., Troiano, P. F., & Newman, B. M. (2016). College students with disabilities redefine activism: Self-advocacy, storytelling, and collective action. *Journal of Diversity in Higher Education, 9*(3), 245–260.

Mobley Jr., S. D., Johnson, J. M., & Drezner, N. D. (2021). "Why aren't all the white kids sitting together in the cafeteria?": An exploration of white student experiences at a public HBCU. *Journal of Diversity in Higher Education.* Advance online publication. doi:10.1037/dhe0000298

Museus, S., & Truong, K. (2013). Racism and sexism in cyberspace: Engaging stereotypes of Asian American women and men to facilitate student learning and development. *About Campus, 18*(4), 14–21.

Nicolazzo, Z. (2017). *Trans* in college: Transgender students' strategies for navigating campus life and the institutional politics of inclusion*. Stylus Publishing.

Pyne, K. B., & Means, D. R. (2013). Underrepresented and in/visible: A Hispanic first-generation student's narratives of college. *Journal of Diversity in Higher Education, 6*(3), 186–198.

Renn, K. A., & Reason, R. D. (2013). *College students in the United States: Characteristics, experiences, and outcomes* (1st ed.). Jossey-Bass.

Saxe, J. G. (1873). The blind men and the elephant. https://www.commonlit.org/texts/the-blind- men-and-the-elephant

Seemiller, C., & Grace, M. (2016). *Generation Z goes to college* (1st ed.). Jossey-Bass.

Stapleton, L., & Croom, N. (2017). Narratives of black d/Deaf college alum: Reflecting on intersecting microaggressions in college. *Journal of Student Affairs Research and Practice, 54*(1), 15–27.

Stewart, T. J. (2018). About fat campus. *About Campus, 23*(4), 31–34.

Tachine, A., Cabrera, N., & Yellow Bird, E. (2017). Home away from home: Native American students' sense of belonging during their first year in college. *Journal of Higher Education, 88*(5), 785–807.

Whitehead, M. A. (2019). "Where are my people at?": A community cultural wealth analysis of how lesbian, gay, and bisexual community college students of color access community and support. *Community College Journal of Research and Practice, 43*, 730–742.

QUESTION 2

What Are the Needs of Today's College Students?

7

WHAT ARE THE NEEDS OF TODAY'S COLLEGE STUDENTS

Stakeholder Essays

Sarah Ali, Jason Cottrell, Mac Mayfield and Jawaan Wallace

What Are the Needs of Today's College Students?

Sarah Ali (she/her/hers) is a 28-year-old college student at San Francisco State University. She was raised on the West Coast, the Midwest, and Asia. She is the dean of student's student assistant and has had the opportunity to learn and understand the university's perspective of protocol, laws, academia, spirit, and student activities. Sarah manages the department's social media account, designs flyers, and creates and edits videos for on-campus marketing and considers herself to be an event and portrait photographer, an artist, and an environmentalist. Scheduled to graduate in May 2021 with a major in Broadcast Electronic Communications with a concentration in video production, Sarah's career goal is to produce media, share stories, and help protect the environment.

I believe the needs of college students are directly correlated to their surrounding environment. In order for a student to succeed in college, their basic human needs must be met. This includes housing stability, well-being, food security, and a stress-free zone to study. But, I suppose, that response is better suited if the question was about how a student could raise their chances of success in college. Though I believe that stakeholders in higher education should consider basic priorities as a student necessity because they can affect graduation retention rates for the university or college. If a college or university establishes resources to help students meet their basic needs, it would be helpful to advertise or market those related programs to their student population to ensure their students know how to access these basic health and wellness resources. If the institution does not have

DOI: 10.4324/9780429319471-9

related programs on campus, another option to consider would be to notify students of local organizations that offer free or student-discounted programs. Basic needs set the foundation for student success, and health and wellness programs greatly enhance that.

So, what can the universities and stakeholders do to directly benefit students or meet their needs?

I cannot stress enough the importance of student mental and physical health. The state of mind and body are in direct correlation to overall well-being and one's ability to produce successful outcomes. Individual lifestyle choices may not be as influential as environmental and community factors, and universities could provide a supportive understructure to encourage and promote learning, health, and personal growth through their campus communities. I believe it would be best to create and support programs that implement social and physical well-being among students, such as 5k's, intramural sports, community-building physical activities, psychological services, personal development workshops, mindfulness sessions, identity-based support groups and meetups, yoga in the quad, and meditation. Doing this in a way that centers both individual and community development is necessary to foster larger support networks. I believe building a sense of community and individuality among students holds significance to their physical and mental needs that would best equip them to meet high student demands and promote well-adjusted personal standards for personal and societal care.

It might benefit students if a university could provide long-term psychological services throughout their academic career versus a more triage-based model of mental health care. However, many universities do not have the staff numbers to match the mental health needs of their student population. I believe an increase in counseling and psychological services would positively impact participating students. A college education might typically take four years to complete, and for some, it takes longer. During academic years, students may experience some form of development or impactful experience that causes a need for help. Professional support and guidance when necessary could aid in student retention and graduation, as well as student wellness. During my time enrolled in five different institutions in different cities within California and Texas, I have come across a multitude of students who struggle in and outside of the classroom and later drop out due to hardship, impacted by and impacting mental health. I wonder what their chances of success would be like if they had long-standing support.

On another note, students would largely benefit from real work experience. Most college students I know work at least part time (if not full time). But most of these students are not working jobs that are directly related to their academic studies or career aspirations. If finances were not a concern, I believe most students would agree that they would rather gain work experience within an industry that would best complement their major. As technology continues to expand through electronic updates and accessibility on campuses, I think it would be beneficial to consider revitalizing certain curricula to include stimulating material and experience-based projects. For example, San Francisco State's Broadcast and Electronic Communications program offers an excellent opportunity for students who are interested in radio or television. Students lead their own radio programs as a host or structure a studio and set up a news program, led and run by students. Coursework like this allows students to engage in real-world work simulations while building a portfolio of experiences and products directly related to their intended field. A variety of internships related to each field that are specifically allocated for university students would be highly beneficial as well. These opportunities allow students to gain real industry experience to expand their resumes, gain confidence in their abilities and skills, and increase their affinity to the program and school – which I believe are strong student needs. They also allow students to network with future employers and colleagues. During my college years, I have held two internships; one in particular shifted my perspective of self as I was pushed to translate classroom knowledge into a real-world application. Through the internship, I gained a mentor, confidence, and the self-belief that "I can," and "I deserve to be here." Particular hands-on classes also supported my shift in mindset from doubting my abilities to gaining confidence and being able to expand my resume.

As far as my story goes, I started college as a financially, mentally, and emotionally independent 18-year-old without family support. I worked full time and held two jobs, sometimes averaging up to 60 hours a week of work. This meant school always took a backseat as I tended to personal basic needs, such as rent, groceries, and bills. As much as I wanted to focus on my studies and development, my basic needs were my priority. My progress was slow, and I experienced depression, anxiety, and feelings of failure. It felt like graduation was only a dream.

I attempted to use my university's counseling and psychological services; however, I learned that the services were only offered on a short-term basis – a total of six sessions. My needs were greater than this. I also learned that the services were prioritized for students whose lives were strictly endangered. My mental health needs were real but deemed less important than others. I am aware many other students feel the same with similar stories and situations. We all need help and support, and if more students had it, less might get to the point of crisis that endangers our lives. My overall point is that institutions need to create equity for the student population so that every student has the chance to succeed in their academic dream despite life development in terms of basic needs and wellness services. If a student decides to become a functional member of society through education, the institution of their choosing would be best to produce outstanding citizens and graduates who are well-informed and prepared for life in and outside of the classroom. I believe an equitable campus offers solutions, starts conversations, and creates space to help students fulfill their basic needs during their time at university so that the focus remains on studies, self-development, health and well-being, major-related work experience, and community and civic engagement which, in my opinion, creates well-rounded thinkers, speakers, and doers from all walks of life. This approach of collaboration and support may not be the reality, but it is ideal. I wonder how many great minds are lost to suffering, whether self-imposed or circumstantial? I believe if you help a determined person move away from survival mode, their ability to thrive is exponential. If everyone had a few years of support and met basic needs to solely focus and concentrate on educational tasks and goals that interest them, I believe there would be more great minds and creative leaders of our time. When one's basic needs are met, it leads to a person seeking something larger than themselves, and that could be beneficial for all.

What Are the Needs of Today's College Students?

Dr. Jason Cottrell (he/him/his) is from Berryville, Virginia, and Gaylord, Michigan. He is the Lead Research Analyst for Institutional Service within the Office of Postsecondary Education at the U.S. Department of Education. His work focuses on program evaluation; evidence-based decision-making; Titles III, V, and VII eligibility; grant performance reports; and data analysis. Prior to working at the Department of Education, Dr. Cottrell worked at North Carolina Central University (Durham) in New Student Services. He has also worked in financial aid, student activities, learning support, and with a variety of first-year experience programs at J. Sargeant Reynolds Community College (Richmond, Virginia) and Virginia Commonwealth University (Richmond). Dr. Cottrell holds a bachelor of science in sociology and anthropology and a master of education in administration and supervision from Virginia Commonwealth University. He completed his doctor of philosophy in higher education policy and leadership at the University of Virginia. His dissertation was titled "The Role of a University College on Student Engagement." Dr. Cottrell resides in Rockville, Maryland.

In the spring of 1999, I transferred from a small, private liberal arts college in Michigan (Alma College) to a large regional university in Virginia (Virginia Commonwealth University). The experience of being a transfer student at a different institution taught me a lot about who I am and what my needs were when I arrived in Richmond compared to the small rural campus in Alma, Michigan. I lived in an apartment one block from a diverse and welcoming campus and one block from a statute of Confederate General Robert E. Lee. This same statue became a symbol for change in our nation when protestors began demanding its removal in the summer of 2020. I remained in Richmond for 11 years as both a student (two years as an undergraduate and one as a graduate student) and a professional working in higher education. I learned through experience and social interactions who I was, who my city was, and what my future aspirations would be beyond college. I ultimately earned two degrees from Virginia Commonwealth University and commuted to the University of Virginia where I earned a PhD in higher education while working at various institutions of higher education (IHEs).

Reflecting on the years traversing my undergraduate experience as a first-generation transfer student, 17 years working on college campuses, and more recent experiences studying and analyzing IHEs, I almost started this essay with a checklist (funding, food and housing security, tuition costs, campus resources and services, family responsibilities, and the list goes on) that students attending IHEs in the United States require to succeed. This ever-evolving list of needs, that seemingly never changes, is heightened by research on college students, their experiences, and their development. Certainly, today's students require these things, and I would still argue these are critical for student success. The number of students who drop out and stop out due to lack of resources and/or campus involvement is well-documented (Astin, 1993; Berger & Lyon, 2005; Crissman Ishler & Upcraft, 2005; and Tinto, 1993).

However, as I began thinking about this essay, I turned to expected outcomes for college graduates and where we are as a society in 2020. What do college students and graduates need? I argue today's students require digital literacy skills to succeed in school and beyond. According to the American Library Association (2019, June 18), digital literacy is "the ability to use information and communication technologies to find, evaluate, create, and communicate information, requiring both cognitive and technical skills."

While sitting at home during the pandemic of 2020, many of us have fallen into various hobbies, binging television shows, baking, following the latest 2020 news, and of course checking social media via platforms like Instagram, Twitter, TikTok, and Facebook. Our human instinct is to stay connected with others, but now we must socially distance – leaving us with the need to interact through social media, even more than we did in 2019. With a deluge of constant news on all these platforms, it is often difficult differentiating legitimate sources, analyzing where you find the information, who posted it, and whether it is real or simply the latest meme.

Our human connections are now through platforms that are substantially different than they were a year ago, much less ten, 15, or 20 years ago, when none of them existed. It has become a running joke about the challenges we face in 2020 while simultaneously being extraordinarily difficult to discuss, decipher, comprehend, and solve the problems we face as a society. As such, I argue that we are at a place where the needs of today's students are still built into the foundation of postsecondary education: the college curriculum. With continuously changing social factors affecting our daily lives, IHEs are faced with a changing global structure based on digital footprints and information overload. Institutions must review their curriculum and put forth digital literacy as an expected outcome while also ramping up the focus on critical thinking skills. Students must learn these skills to succeed in college, work, and as informed citizens.

Today, our students are faced with data and information every waking minute from televisions and computers to phones and tablets with apps and podcasts to on-demand and live functionalities. Data and information are nonstop products of our connected lives. For our students, their focus and understanding of one topic evolve as quickly as their next login. It is truly a digital world that requires a clear understanding of information overload, data interpretation, and digital analytics. How institutions handle these factors with their students is not based on one-off optional lectures or even a yearlong series of activities that students can choose to attend. Instead, I argue building a curriculum founded on digital literacy and the need to interpret, analyze, and respond to information broadly meets the needs of students in college.

According to Hawthorne (1997, p. 30), "[C]urriculum is how we organize what we teach, how we teach, and to whom we teach." Mildred García and James Ratcliff (1997, p. 118) add that a curriculum is "defined as a body of courses presenting the knowledge, principles, values, and skills that are intended consequences of an undergraduate education." Today, institutions are challenged with teaching students the knowledge that is expected for a given subject or subjects, but also with developing the skills needed to interpret, analyze, and report information. These should be some of the intended consequences of an undergraduate education in 2020. Students have sources at the tip of their fingers, but trusting those sources and properly interpreting the data they view requires critical lenses that must be practiced.

Institutions review their curriculum, typically due to external forces such as accreditation. But, as García and Ratcliff (1997) argue, social factors often shape the curriculum. Today's digital world is one social force that should not be ignored. I would argue digital forces are both critically challenging and useful tools for IHEs to develop lifelong learners. Prioritizing skills for information and data synthesis into the curriculum, where students critically reflect on their topical courses is one such necessity that will prove useful for today's students and tomorrow's graduates.

Recently, I asked one of our neighbor's children (age nine) what they were learning in school. Their response, "I am taking a coding class. I am learning how to code a video game." Without missing a beat, their younger sibling (age five) responded, "You should see my Minecraft world. I learned how to build a castle by watching my favorite YouTube star." These children will arrive on campus in less than ten years with knowledge enhancing their experience while simultaneously challenging our methods and processes. They may trust more sources on the Internet (or its replacement) than they should. Thus, it is critical for our IHEs to begin reviewing and quickly accommodating these opportunities. IHEs must review their curriculum and ask, should we continue teaching our courses in the same manner we did in 2010? Or should IHEs begin working with students, subject matter experts, and faculty to improve our students' digital literacy?

References

American Library Association. (2019, June 18). *Digital literacy*. Retrieved July 3, 2020, from https://literacy.ala.org/digital-literacy/

Astin, A. W. (1993). *What matters in college: Four critical years revisited*. Jossey Bass.

Berger, J. B. & Lyon, S. C. (2005). Past to present: A historical look at retention. In A. Seidman (Ed.), *College student retention: Formula for student success* (pp. 1–29). Westport, CT: Praeger Publishers.

Crissman Ishler, J. L. & Upcraft, M. L. (2005). The keys to first-year student persistence. In M. L. Upcraft, J. N. Gardner, B. O. Barefoot, & Associates (Eds.), *Challenging & supporting the first-year student: A handbook for improving the first year of college* (pp. 27–46). Jossey Bass.

García. M. & Ratcliff, J. E. (1997). Social forces shaping the curriculum. In J. G. Gaff, J. L. Ratcliff, & Associates (Eds.), *Handbook of the undergraduate curriculum: A comprehensive guide to purposes, structures, practices, and change* (pp. 118–136). Jossey Bass.

Hawthorne, E. M. (1997). Institutional contexts. In J. G. Gaff, J. L. Ratcliff, & Associates (Eds.), *Handbook of the undergraduate curriculum: A comprehensive guide to purposes, structures, practices, and change* (pp. 30–52). Jossey Bass.

Tinto, V. (1993). *Leaving college: Rethinking the causes and cures of student attrition*. (2nd ed.). The University of Chicago Press.

What Are the Needs of Today's College Students?

Mac Mayfield (he/him/his) was 17 years old when he started writing this essay and was in his senior year of high school at Canyon High School in Anaheim, California. Since writing this essay, he is now 19 years old as of December 2020, and he just completed his first semester at Santiago Community College in Anaheim, California. During high school, he participated in many extracurriculars, such as the Safe Space Alliance club for lesbian, gay, bisexual, transgender, and queer (LGBTQ+) youth, the school jazz band, and graphic design and photoshop for three years. His out-of-class activity in high school was band (both marching and concert), in which he was involved for all four years. He even earned the laureate medal for instrumental performing arts in his senior year. He wants to earn his bachelor's and master's degrees in English.

My name is Mac Mayfield, I am 17 years old as of writing this, and as of now, I am heading into my senior year of high school at Canyon High School in Anaheim, California. The editor of this book contacted me asking for a high schooler's opinion on the subject of college students' identities, needs, opportunities, etc.; I was ecstatic to oblige. My mother has worked at a college since I was born, and from hearing about her days at work, I think I have a somewhat decent grasp on the college experience. Not to mention, my (now) girlfriend and many of my friends will soon be attending universities of their choice, so I guess pretty soon I'll have more insight into the college experience. In addition, we have had many speakers come to campus to talk about the application process, as well as their respective universities. All of this information and experience makes me feel confident about applying, as well as informed about what I am signing up for in terms of continuing my education.

"What are the needs of today's college students?" This was the prompt I was given to respond to from my perspective. College can be a confusing and albeit scary time, especially because everyone is coming from all different walks of life and from different backgrounds. Everyone comes to college having a different experience. And, what does that mean? Different needs. To go over all the individual and specific needs every kind of student brings with them to college would take way too long. Nevertheless, as I think about becoming a college student, I do consider some needs pretty universal.

To begin, there are a number of physical needs that college students have. Many college students choose to live on or near campus. So, there's already one need, a proper living environment. Students of course need a place to eat, sleep, and study. Again, this experience differs from campus to campus, you hear of campuses that keep up with their bills, whose rooms are generally tidy, and students are in a safe living environment. And then you hear about the rooms with no light, paper-thin walls, and rooms vaguely smelling of piss. Now yes, that was (mostly) a joke, but the point remains, students should have a place to properly eat, sleep, and study, with as minimal distractions as possible. A college should have the living conditions of students as a top priority, whether those students reside on or off campus.

One part of what makes the college experience so special is the almost infinite amount of extracurricular activities for students. This includes clubs, fraternities, sororities, sports, and (in some cases) marching band. In a club, you can meet people who have the same interests as you and in some cases build lifelong friendships. In a fraternity or sorority, students have the opportunity to partake in community service to help others. Another benefit of which would be to live close to campus because you are that much closer to those activities, as well as your classes. Students need chances to connect outside of the classroom. These opportunities make and help students feel involved in their campus, build relationships with fellow students, and just to generally feel more at home.

Another top priority should be food services. Most college students stay on campus for the majority of the time, especially if they actually, y'know, **live** there. So, generally, a campus should have a wide variety of food and restaurants for the variety of students they have attending. For example, the California State University of Long Beach (CSULB) has a wide variety of food items and choices to suit its huge campus staff and students. Again, this should be another one of the main priorities for a college campus in my mind.

Of obvious importance, of course, is the actual educational part of university. A student needs to have all the necessary materials and resources to succeed in the specific academic program they study. Most people who attend college are there to succeed; it is not like high school where you are forced to attend. College students attend to build on their education and to succeed. All of the materials and resources to succeed need to be at the student's disposal, so if a student does not succeed, they are held accountable for not taking advantage of the opportunities and resources given to them. Some of the resources needed are physical items, such as books and computers, others are human, such as professors.

My mother worked in the college library at CSULB for the longest time. There were a couple times where she came home telling some kind of story of something that ruined or severely damaged an entire section of books. For example, the most common accident that happens multiple times is leaking in the basement caused by draining of the local cafe or other drainage problems. So, this causes all the rows and rows of materials in the basement to get damaged in some form or another, causing the campus to lose a decent amount of materials. Inconveniences like these are another problem that students can temporarily face when one of their main sources is temporarily unavailable. Whether it is due to power outages or other unavoidable problems, these are sometimes problems students will have to face that could get in the way of their success and that is unacceptable.

Another resource to consider is the professors themselves. Much like any other teaching profession, college and university professors should be given extremely thorough background checks. Constantly on the news, stories are mentioned of a college professor having an affair with one of their students to benefit the student's grade. This is unacceptable and is one of the exact reasons why professors must be given thorough background checks during their interview process and annual reviews if they get the job they are applying for. Students need reliable, trustworthy, and caring faculty to guide and educate them.

Another great resource for college students is mentors and/or tutors. From what I've heard, these are college students (much like high school) who offer their services to other students. Peer-to-peer mentoring/tutoring can have a huge effect on one's success in a course or college studies in general. Most teachers are also available, typically after a class, to help out students and clarify any information a student may not have a good grip on. But once again, all of this depends on the student. It is up to them how to handle their problems and needs;

if the proper sources are there, a student just has to simply acknowledge and use said sources.

My final expected source of information is technology. In middle school, I had the majority of my classes taught to me on an Apple iPad. My generation and generations after me, have had modern technology interwoven with what is taught to us. So naturally, we expect to see that when we are at college. We expect to see outlets everywhere, access to computer sources and services on a 24/7 basis. It would be extremely unnatural, backward, and somewhat cruel to have a generation be raised and taught on technology to enter a university only to learn that the university is less technologically prepared than my high school and middle schools and teachers were, and from what I have seen and heard, that sounds pretty much the case in a lot of places. That seems unfair and stressful for students to have that stripped away at the same time one is learning to live on their own, as well as assessing and adapting to their new environment.

One thing to remember is I do not know the entirety of what a college or university has as their priorities, whether it be paying their professors, book upkeep and purchases, or, as mentioned, living conditions of students. From that knowledge, I can only assume that every college has a different set of priorities to where the budget goes.

I do plan on actually going to college. I think once my friends start their first semesters, I'll get more of a general consensus of what I'll actually be getting into. But from a high schooler's perspective, college is ramped up and held up as this scary thing. Not only am I scared of the actual application and scholarship process, but in reality, I think I'm more scared if I actually get in. But I can't help but think of all the new experiences at the same time, and that, that is really exciting to think of and look forward to.

What Are the Needs of Today's College Students?

Jawaan Wallace, PhD (she/her/hers), currently serves as Dean of College Counseling at Marlborough School, an all-girls independent school, located in Los Angeles, California. Dr. Wallace has worked in a variety of independent schools and began her career in college admissions at Johns Hopkins University as an Assistant Director of undergraduate admissions. Dr. Wallace holds a BA in history from Hampton University, an MA in higher education administration from the University of Akron, and a PhD from the University of Georgia in college student affairs administration.

Let me begin by saying that the high school students I have the privilege of working with on a daily basis are academically gifted, talented, passionate, and driven. I am often in awe when I consider the level of intellectual depth my students display when compared to my own high school experience (albeit, that was over 25 years ago). They are technologically savvy and have the ability to access just about any information they wish with the simple click of a button. When I first entered the independent school world about 16 years ago, Facebook was in its infancy, while Instagram and Snapchat were nonexistent. Fast-forward to the present day, and it would be challenging to find a high school student who did not spend multiple hours a day using these platforms. Like many educators, I worry that these platforms promote more harm than good. There is no doubt that the students I work with today are incredibly bright, but they are also much more anxious, depressed, and ultra-competitive. I cannot help but attribute that to the influence of social media. Compared to years past, I find my colleagues and I constantly having discussions about bullying, mental health, and students expressing the need to create clubs and organizations to combat these issues. They are definitely cognizant of the impact social media is having on their lives, but suppressing their use of it is almost an impossible feat. They are addicted. Last year, our school, like many others, implemented a mandatory digital citizenship class to combat the many issues we were having on campus that related to the use of social media – a concept that was not even in existence ten-plus years ago. Our students are dealing with many more challenges than in previous years, and it is imperative that we meet those challenges head-on and teach them how to cope with the many stress triggers they experience.

Add to this the tremendous amount of pressure parents can place on their children as it relates to the college search and selection process, and you have a recipe for disaster. The pressure these students feel is vast. From birth, their parents obsess over how they will get their children admitted to the most elite private schools. With price tags of over $40,000 per year, these parents will stop at nothing to ensure that their children have the "best" education. Unfortunately, many parents miss the mark when choosing the appropriate independent school for their children because they are too caught up in perception. Instead of focusing on the support services offered to their children, the average class size, or the curriculum, their interest lies in how many name-brand schools are on the high school's college matriculation list. And if schools like Harvard, Princeton, or Yale are not reflected on that list, you can be certain that that school has become a less desirable option, despite the fact that the school may be the best fit academically and socially for their children.

Fast-forward to when it is time for their children to begin the college search and selection process, the same rules apply. Their children can only go to a name-brand college that in their minds will be acceptable and perhaps even elevate their status in certain social circles. To be able to say that their son or daughter attends an Ivy League or highly selective institution is equivalent to having a luxury vehicle or an expensive handbag. Parents desire just as many "likes" on their social media as their children, and it gives them immense pleasure to be on the cocktail circuit and brag about how Johnny is headed to Stanford in the fall.

Parents paying for a falsified psychological evaluation to secure extra time on standardized tests, hiring expensive tutors that have access to test banks from previous years, and grade-grubbing until a teacher changes a grade, are all actions my colleagues and I have witnessed across the country and for many students have become commonplace. As soon as that A in Advanced Placement Physics drops down to a B, meltdowns ensue. Panic sets in and students are devastated because they feel they have failed and have ruined their chances of being admitted to a top institution of higher education. When did anything less than an A become a failure? Parents are infuriated and begin pressuring teachers and contacting the head of school to demand a grade change. They make the teachers feel guilty, claiming that the one B on the student's transcript will surely jeopardize their child's chance of getting into their dream school. All accountability has gone out the window, and parents are willing to do any and everything to ensure their child's record is free from any blemish. Students are walking away with the message that it is necessary and acceptable to do whatever it takes to cheat the system and gain admission into an elite institution. What we need to teach our students is that they need to trust the learning process and that attaining success should never involve compromising their values.

Having worked at three different independent schools, two of which were directly impacted by the college admission scandal of 2019, I have become disheartened by the lengths many parents will go to ensure their child will get into the "best" school. And even more disheartening is the passing down of their bad behavior to their children. Parent education is just as important as student education. By teaching parents how to model behaviors that send clear messages of honesty, respect, and resilience, we can create a culture of empathy and compassion that will allow our students to thrive and focus on being their true, authentic selves.

Colleges and universities must also take responsibility for creating this college crazed culture. Focused on improving their rankings, these schools encourage more and more students to apply each year with the knowledge that many of these students will be rejected —sometimes as many as 95%. At the Ivys and highly selective schools, admission officers encourage applications from students who they know never have a chance of being admitted. They tell students that they must fall in the top 10% of their class, they must take the most demanding courses available at their school, they must receive standardized test scores that are close to perfect, and involve themselves in a wide array of extracurricular activities. Parents and students hear these messages and think they've found the formula for getting in, but the reality is you can do all of those things and still never even have a shot. There are spaces set aside for legacy students, athletes, development cases, etc. When it's all said in done, students may be facing a less than 2% acceptance rate.

The unethical acts of parents and the loss of faith they have in their children are severely impacting the growth and development of our students. Instead of pressuring students with the importance of perfection or figuring out how to manipulate the college admission process, we need to focus on helping our students identify their talents and reconsider how they view the college search process. Instead of focusing only on the highest-ranked schools, we need to teach our students how to discover themselves and help them to identify colleges that most meet their needs. A strong characteristic of the students I work with is that they crave guidance and direction. Our students are closely monitoring our behaviors and the actions of those around them that they look up to and trust. We have to condemn those that act unethically and discourage dishonesty. We need to empower students to be responsible for themselves and find balance between what academic load is appropriate for their academic ability and ensure that they are identifying activities and hobbies that are meaningful and important to them, not just a checklist of things they "think" they need to do to gain entry to an elite institution.

As these students transition to collegiate life, ensuring their ultimate success will need to be a collaborative effort between secondary schools and higher education (student affairs?) professionals. By working together, we can begin to identify trends in both current and prospective student needs to allow us to create and implement programs and services that ensure student success. As students become acclimated to college life, the involvement of their parents does not dissipate. The same negative impact of technology and social media experienced in the high school setting has proven to be just as detrimental in the college setting. All of this technology allows parents to have instant access to their children and keeps them engaged in their day-to-day activities. Finding ways to engage overinvolved parents and providing them with resources and tools to better support their children could prove to be beneficial in teaching them how to let go and allow their children to be independent members of society. The more our students can become comfortable with being uncomfortable, the better prepared they will be to navigate academic and social challenges on their own.

8

ANALYSIS

What Are the Needs of Today's College Students?

Michelle M. Espino

Dr. Michelle M. Espino (she/her/ella) is a first-generation college student and is associate professor in the Higher Education, Student Affairs, and International Education Policy program at the University of Maryland, College Park. She earned her doctorate in Higher Education from the University of Arizona, her master's degree in College Student Personnel from Bowling Green State University, and her bachelor's degree from St. Mary's University (TX). Dr. Espino investigates the individual, organizational, and community factors that affect educational attainment for racial/ethnic minorities, particularly for Latinx/as/os. Using critical perspectives, Dr. Espino work also exposes the social inequities that undermine individual motivations to study and work in colleges and universities. She is also the creator of *Latinx Intelligentsia*, a podcast dedicated to uplifting Latinx communities in higher education.

This section focuses on the needs of today's college students from four vantage points: Mac Mayfield, who wrote the essay between his senior year in high school and his first semester in community college; Sarah Ali, a post-traditional college student who works in the dean of students' office at her four-year university; Jawaan Wallace, a college counselor for an elite all-girls college preparatory school; and Jason Cotrell, an education policy expert within the U.S. Department of Education. My role is to bring the essayists' perspectives together and offer insights that can help various stakeholders across higher education move forward in solving critical issues. Like the essayists, I will share how I arrived at the question about student needs. I am a first-generation college student. I was a master's student in a student affairs administration program, a full-time student

DOI: 10.4324/9780429319471-10

affairs professional, and a doctoral student enthralled with research. I am now a faculty member engaged in training future generations of student affairs professionals. I too carry various perspectives on the needs of today's college students.

Prior to reading the essays, I expected to find a multitude of needs, as well as deeply complex problems and challenges that reflected the 21st-century university. I expected to find urgency in addressing affordability, structural inequities, and higher education outcomes. As I will discuss in my response, these concerns are threaded throughout the essays. But what seemed unsettling as I reflected on the core themes across the essays was how the needs ranged from individual, microlevel needs to *perceptions* of needs from the macrolevel. The responses reflected stark differences – a chasm between student realities and the experiences of those who serve and advocate for them. These differences are not entirely surprising, but, as I will discuss in my essay, these differences are part of a systemic challenge in meeting the needs of today's college students.

Building Connections

The essayists for this section noted the critical issues that have been of significant concern for years but are now catalyzed in the present moment as U.S. society endures multiple pandemics of COVID-19, racism, and anti-blackness. Mayfield and Ali, the student essayists, noted the importance of addressing basic physiological needs and safety, harkening to the foundational constructs in Maslow's (1943) theory of motivation. Safety was depicted by the urgent need to address mental health concerns, and basic physiological needs were presented in the form of student housing. In contrast, Wallace's and Cotrell's full-time professional perspectives centered on the needs of specific student populations that have access to wealth and/or the latest technology. Their essays seemed to reflect an assumption that basic needs were already met and that institutions of higher education could focus more on higher-order needs regarding personal agency and independence. Cotrell stressed the importance of developing critical technological literacy skills to fully address disinformation and cyberbullying found in social media outlets. Wallace advocated for college choice processes that center students' interests rather than the familial behaviors and pressures to set personal interests aside for elitism and prestige. In the following section, I will discuss the core themes that are threaded throughout the essays: technological literacy, the teaching of morals and ethics, living and learning environments on campus, and support services for mental health and well-being.

Technology

Technology is discussed in the following ways: developing critical awareness for resisting pressures on social media platforms, developing critical skills to discern disinformation presented as truth, and enhancing the higher education learning environment through technology. Both Wallace and Cottrell explained that technological literacy is vital for student development prior to entering college and should be integrated into the higher education curriculum as a critical thinking outcome.

From a student perspective, Mayfield noted that it may be difficult for institutions of higher education to address these outcomes if faculty and administrators have limited training on educational technology – a perpetual digital divide. Amid the COVID-19 pandemic, faculty and administrators have been challenged to utilize technology through online and hybrid courses with most training coming from teaching and learning centers. Mayfield noted that his high school instructors seem to be much more informed on educational technology than college instructors, which is not surprising since college/university faculty are not required to update their pedagogical skills through required trainings and professional development opportunities.

However, the digital divide is not only a generational difference between faculty and students but can also be analyzed as a difference between wealthy and low-income students. It is difficult to ascertain the essayists' personal engagement with technology aside from observations of how K–12 students are drawn to technology or whether access to the latest technologies is connected to social class status. What seems missing from the essays and from ongoing conversations about the use of technology amid the pandemic are discussions about supporting students who had limited access to technology *prior* to the pandemic and whose needs are further exacerbated through the pandemic, especially for African American and Latinx/a/o students. According to Ong (2020), African Americans and Hispanics are 1.3 to 1.4 times as likely to experience limited accessibility to the internet as non-Hispanic whites, and at least two-in-five low-income households have limited access to a computer or the internet (p. 7). For some families, decisions must be made on whose learning is prioritized in the household, as not every sibling or child has their own computer. In addition, stories abound of students driving to internet hotspots and attempting to engage with coursework from a sidewalk or car. Access to technology, whether equipment or internet, is not equitable across the higher education landscape.

Much remains unknown about the impact of the pandemic on student learning and whether virtual space will become a permanent part of "traditional" teaching formats, especially considering limited technological access for low-income students and students with disabilities (Anderson, 2020). Education technology trainings are vital, but only if they also address the human element in virtual space. How does technology serve as a hindrance or a springboard for student engagement? How can technology educate students to value and respect one another in real life?

Teaching Morals and Ethics

In 2019, the Federal Bureau of Investigation uncovered an admissions bribery scandal, the largest of its kind, in which wealthy families with significant resources participated in bribing elite institutions and athletic coaching staff to admit their children into college (Richer & Binkley, 2019). The admissions scandal uncovered wealthy parents' disgraceful behavior to use whatever means at their disposal to ensure access to elite educational spaces. Unfortunately, this behavior is part of an ongoing process that begins in early childhood where wealthy families afford their children access and opportunity, while low-income families with limited access to college knowledge and social networks are unsure how to support their students in accessing higher education. It is particularly appalling that so much attention is given to wealthy families, while the concerns of first-generation college students, low-income students, and their families are relegated to the margins.

From an organizational lens, there is evidence that institutions of higher education perpetually strive to follow the latest trends set by elite universities and will adopt approaches used by aspirant institutions, even if those approaches do not fit with the culture and structure of the academic organization (DiMaggio & Powell, 2000). Based on Wallace's essay, it seems that wealthy families adopt similar determinants of prestige based on college admissions. In effect, the prestige of the institution raises the prestige of families within particular social groups. In turn, the competitive nature of college access to elite universities creates a feedback loop with little focus on students' needs and goals. The concern is not whether the student finds a sense of belonging and support at the institution but rather that the prestige and access to even wealthier social circles become available for certain families. Wealthy parents' constant quest for prestige distorts their students' educational goals and trajectories and could prove detrimental to their learning and engagement in college.

Wallace pressed for higher education to be the instructors of values and ethics for wealthy students because their families were demonstrating a lack of morality in the college admissions process. What should be the role of higher education in teaching morals and values? Is Wallace's call for values education a return to *in loco parentis* (i.e., in place of the parent), an artifact of the early formations of higher education where faculty took control of students' development and experiences when they moved to the university? There is increasing tension about who should be the teachers of morals and values, and whether students will be receptive to establishing values separate from families and community role models who, unfortunately, do not enact their own moral codes. Concerns about parental/familial involvement in secondary schooling have moved to higher education, as some families are critiqued for being too engaged (i.e., "helicopter parents") and some families are blamed for not being engaged enough, especially for low-income and first-generation college students (Espino, 2016). However, if the student is centered within the academic organization and encouraged to make informed decisions about their educational journeys and career goals, then they have ample opportunity to develop the moral and ethical frames that can guide them in the future.

Although institutional prestige was not a specific focus for the other essayists, there is an undercurrent about the role of higher education in developing an educated global citizenry that has achieved specific learning outcomes. Low-income students and first-generation college students contend with moral and ethical dilemmas as well, but their concerns are often focused on affordability and navigating higher education with limited guidance. Institutions of higher education are part of a larger educational system that has pressured low-income and first-generation college students to hone their critical navigation skills. Perhaps they should offer similar challenges for wealthy students by presenting multiple perspectives and numerous opportunities for students to apply critical thinking skills to their experiences within a supportive learning environment.

Living and Learning Environments

Supportive learning environments are often found within on-campus residential communities. Mayfield's essay stressed the importance of appropriate living environments where students, in relative safety, could learn and experience college life both on and off campus. Notably, his recent experience as a community college student may not include an on-campus residential component, which may suggest that the needs of community colleges are not as centered in his vision of higher education or in addressing specific college student needs.

This potential assumption of what comprises a "real" higher education experience also does not address the consequences of on- and off-campus residential living, especially when considering relationships with surrounding communities, police, or government. Town-gown issues are an inherent aspect of higher education, as colleges and universities become responsible for the well-being of students in the vicinity of campus. That also means holding students accountable for not adhering to local policies and state laws.

Returning to Mayfield's essay, I was drawn to the idea that students should live in "proper" living and learning environments either within campus residential facilities or off campus. Many campuses strive to enhance the local surroundings and collaborate on public-private partnerships that improve housing and transportation. Some institutions offer housing allowances that permit faculty to buy houses in the local area or rent apartments at below market value in large urban communities near campus.

The unfortunate result of those public-private partnerships and development is gentrification. Although seemingly tangential to the topic of student needs, the actions taken on behalf of colleges and universities to "beautify" the surrounding community prioritizes students' needs for an engaging environment over the needs of Communities of Color, families, and senior citizens who once populated these neighborhoods. Some communities can no longer afford increased property taxes and contend with the "studentification" of neighborhoods (e.g., noise, traffic, trash), blurring the boundaries between student life and the urban or township areas (Moos et al., 2019).

Inherent in development along the boundaries of the college or university, is the assumption that once the area is more student-friendly, the environment will be more inviting for student engagement and feeling "at home." This assumption does not account for commuter students, post-traditional students, students with children, or students who continue to live with their families. The physical environment is just one contributing factor to student retention, especially for first-generation college students and minoritized students who are questioned by campus police while walking to the library; tend to avoid certain faculty who are known to be racist, sexist, and/or homophobic; and guide first-year students to areas of campus known as safe(r) spaces. If a campus is culturally engaging, it will include faculty and administrators from minoritized populations, require ethnic studies courses and racial/ethnic representation in reading assignments across the curriculum, incorporate service-learning in communities that reflect minoritized student home communities, and validate students' lived experiences (Museus, 2014).

Feeling "at home" means not only living in a welcoming and supportive environment but interacting in validating ways. It also means that institutions of higher education are proactive in addressing student needs; not expecting students to know how to access available resources and, as Mayfield stated, relying on peer networks to navigate institutional bureaucracy and offer validation. Accountability is not just about ensuring that students are responsible for their own learning and success, yet it seems most pressing when reviewing the full-time professional essays. Institutions of higher education across all types must also be held accountable when they create barriers that hinder student success. How can institutions of higher education increase engagement and student retention aside from providing on-campus learning environments or public-private partnerships that shift who can live near a campus?

Mental Health and Well-Being

The final theme was threaded throughout the previous sections: mental health and well-being as a critical student need. In recent years, addressing students' mental health and well-being has become a significant priority for colleges and universities. Counseling centers are experiencing unprecedented caseloads with limited budgetary options for expansion of staff and services. Ali's essay expressed frustration with how counseling centers triage students' mental health concerns, limiting the number of sessions available. Ali's perception that their college's counseling center did not deem their needs as important is especially troubling because these perceptions can affect student retention and persistence.

Mayfield's essay reflected this model as well by weaving together mental health and well-being with community development and peer networks (i.e., social capital). Although peers do not always have the requisite helping skills to aid their friends through difficult circumstances, they are often the first to observe mental health challenges. In a study I conducted on Latina first-generation college students' experiences with stress and coping, I found that participants were managing several stressors and relying on close friends for help (Espino, 2020). As first-generation college students from low-income families, the Latina participants were accustomed to working multiple jobs to pay for college. Participants also experienced stress that arose from financially and emotionally supporting their families while also focusing on their academics. Unfortunately, counseling centers were not perceived as welcoming spaces because few staff reflected participants' lived experiences. Participants also felt uncomfortable seeking support outside of their families and close friends.

Despite the challenges, there is ample opportunity for innovation. Therapists and counselors should not be the only staff members addressing students' mental health concerns. Rather, counseling centers should be crafting relationships across campus that help students address academic anxiety, physical wellness, and racism (among other forms of oppression) that they may face. A collaborative care model draws upon the organizational structure to create connections across campus to support students (Mitchell et al., 2019). The connections among peers and family could serve as part of a collaborative care model. Across the essays, mental health and well-being were reflected in discussions of peer networks, inviting students to engage in values exploration, maintaining safe(r) spaces to test personal development and wholeness alongside family and community, and understanding the toll that technology can have on students' personhood.

Back to the Basics: Addressing the Foundation of Student Affairs Practice

The needs of today's college students are as varied and complex as student populations on college campuses, and it is difficult to prioritize one set of needs over others. Webs of bureaucracy interlace across various organizational systems, often limiting what can be addressed and how these solutions will be funded. The essays offered in this section point to both microlevel needs and institutional challenges cited by students, practitioners, and policymakers. Both sets of needs coexist on a college campus. However, the striking polarity among these essays is a critique of administrators, policymakers, and faculty alike who believe they have a keen awareness of student needs but rarely focus on ensuring that physiological needs are met. It is presumed that students will have access to housing and food, and that they will feel safe(r) on campus so that they can achieve learning outcomes established for them both in and out of the classroom. With these embedded assumptions in the fabric of higher education, whose needs become the focus of policy and practice?

Every year, in a professional orientation course, I learn alongside first-year master's students, many of whom are transitioning directly from their undergraduate experiences. One of the starting points for conversation is rooted in an assignment where students read the foundational documents that informed the student affairs profession (ACPA College Student Educators International, 1994; American Council on Education [ACE], 1937; Blimling et al., 1998; Keeling, 2004, 2006; Williamson, 1949).

As the graduate students engage in the commitments outlined in each of these documents, they usually note that the student affairs profession has always centered student needs. As stated in the *Student Personnel Point of View*, educational institutions have an "obligation to consider the student as a whole – [their] intellectual capacity and achievement...emotional make up...physical condition... social relationships...vocational aptitudes and skills...moral and religious values [and] aesthetic appreciations" (ACE, 1937, p. 3). The holistic development of students is at the forefront of each text as a direct response to the lack of care for students as faculty and researchers shifted their focus to research and development. With the first deans of women and men, the student affairs profession was created to foster all aspects of the student experience (Rhatigan, 2009).

One aspect of student development seems appropriate considering the essays presented in this section: "dissonance." Dissonance is the set of critical junctures in students' learning that create tensions between what they know and what they are now learning. By creating a space for students to explore these tensions, they can gain critical thinking skills. These skills are essential to deliberating between what was taught to them prior to attending college and what they gain from not only classroom discussions and assignments but also through interaction with peers and faculty who are different from them (Keeling, 2004). Within the profession, much of the literature frames dissonance as a positive lever for development. Without support structures in place, too much dissonance can be detrimental to student growth. In fact, it is possible that students who experience too much dissonance will build resistance to learning and engagement that moves them away from new knowledge and awareness. However, the commitment to educating the whole student remains.

As expressed by the student essayists, to serve the student as a whole person entails addressing fundamental needs such as access to safe(r) living and learning environments (Camelo & Elliott, 2019; Hallett & Freas, 2018). It should also incorporate aspects of the whole student that include family structures and connections. Rather than seeing parents and families as burdens, higher education needs to acknowledge and act upon the reality that students of today have deep connections to loved ones and (chosen) family external to the campus community.

Concluding Thoughts

What are the needs of today's college students? Had this question been posed to the essayists just a year before, perhaps responses would have been different. With the pandemic of COVID-19 and the ever-present pandemic of racism and anti-blackness, sheltering-in-place, and ensuring the safety and well-being of others have taken a rare focus. Recognition within the higher education community of disparities in access and opportunity is now presented at our doorstep: What role should higher education take in addressing technology, morals and ethics, living and learning communities, and mental health, among other concerns?

What do I believe are the needs of today's college students? What I found striking was the absence of centering social justice in research, teaching, and practice in the responses from these essayists. Perhaps social justice is not yet viewed as critically embedded in all facets of university life in and out of the classroom, and most especially in addressing student needs. Social justice should be the umbrella that covers all aspects of lived experience in higher education. If there is access to food and shelter, students can then focus on social affiliation, esteem, and self-actualization (Maslow, 1943). If they have access to current technology, they can learn digital literacies. If there is equity and justice on campus, they can feel safe(r) to engage in critical discourse. If there is equity in higher education, parents, families, and communities are not adhering to capitalistic notions of who "deserves" access to which schools.

Higher education, as with any social institution, is at a point of reckoning, where calls for accountability are growing to address the presence of settler colonialism and systemic anti-Black racism. If we leave social justice at the periphery, we cannot create an environment that cares for all students (Poon, 2017–2018). I believe that higher education is a right and as such, we must reframe how we go about the business of higher education to center equity and justice and to address the contestations that limit access and opportunity (Poon, 2017–2018). From focusing on ensuring that students have their foundational needs met, we can then attend to freedom of expression, commitment to community, equity and justice, and, finally, beloved community so that every student can live and learn to their full potential.

References

American College Personnel Association. (1994). *The student learning imperative: Implications for student affairs*. Author.

American Council on Education. (1937). The student personnel point of view. *Studies, Series 1, 1*(3).

Anderson, G. (2020, April 6). Accessibility suffers during pandemic. *Inside Higher Ed*. Retrieved on April 15, 2022, from https://www.insidehighered.com/news/2020/04/06/remote-learning-shift-leaves-students-disabilities-behind

Blimling, G., Whitt, E., & Associates. (1998). *Principles of good practice for student affairs: Statement and inventories.* American College Personnel Association & National Association for Student Personnel Administrators.

Camelo, K., & Elliott, M. (2019). Food insecurity and academic achievement among college students at a public university in the United States. *Journal of College Student Development, 60*(3), 307–318.

DiMaggio, P. J., & Powell, W. W. (2000). The iron cage revisited: Isomorphism in organizational fields. *Advances in Strategic Management, 48*(2), 147–160.

Espino, M.M. (2016). The value of education and educación: Nurturing Mexican American children's educational aspirations to the doctorate. *Journal of Latinos and Education, 15*(2), 73–90. doi: 10.1080/15348431.2015.1066250

Espino, M.M. (2020). "I'm the one who pieces back together what was broken": Uncovering mestiza consciousness in Latina-identified first-generation college student narratives of stress and coping in higher education. *Journal of Women and Gender in Higher Education, 13*(2), 138–156. doi:10.1080/26379112.2020.1784752

Hallett, R. E., & Freas, A. (2018). Community college students' experiences with homelessness and housing insecurity. *Community College Journal of Research and Practice, 42*(10), 724–739.

Keeling, R. P. (Ed.). (2004). *Learning reconsidered: A campus-wide focus on the student experience.* National Association for Student Personnel Administrators & American College Personnel Association.

Keeling, R.P. (Ed.). (2006). *Learning reconsidered 2: Implementing a campus-wide focus on the student experience.* ACPA, ACUHO-I, ACUI, NACA, NACADA, NASPA, & NIRSA.

Maslow, A. H. (1943). A theory of motivation. *Psychological Review, 50*, 370–396.

Mitchell, S. L., Oakley, D. R., & Dunkle, J. H. (2019). White paper: A multidimensional understanding of effective university and college counseling center organizational structures. *Journal of College Student Psychotherapy, 33*(2), 89–106.

Moos, M., Revington, N., Wilkin, T., & Andrey, J. (2019). The knowledge economy city: Gentrification, studentification, and youthification, and their connections to universities. *Urban Studies, 56*(6), 1075–1092.

Museus, S. D. (2014). The culturally engaging campus environments (CECE) model: A new theory of success among racially diverse college student populations. In M. B. Paulsen (Ed.), *Higher education: Handbook of theory and research* (pp. 189–227). Springer.

Ong, P. M., (2020). *COVID-19 and the digital divide in virtual learning, fall 2020.* UCLA Center for Neighborhood Knowledge.

Poon, O. A. (2017–2018). Ending white innocence in student affairs and higher education. *Journal of Student Affairs, (27)*, 13–21.

Rhatigan, J. J. (2009). From the people up: A brief history of student affairs administration. In G. S. McClellan, J. Stringer, & Associates (Eds.), *The handbook of student affairs administration* (3rd ed.,) pp. 3–18). Jossey-Bass.

Richer, A.D., & Binkley, C. (2019, March 12). TV stars and coaches charged in college bribery scheme. *AP News.* Retrieved April 15, 2022, from https://apnews.com/article/2450688f9e67435c8590e59a1b0e5b47

Williamson, E.G. (1949). The student personnel point of view. *Studies,* Series VI.

What Are the Most Significant Challenges for Today's College Students?

9

WHAT ARE THE MOST SIGNIFICANT CHALLENGES FOR TODAY'S COLLEGE STUDENTS?

Stakeholder Essays

Willie L. Banks, Shawn Curtis, Rasul Mowatt and Sebastian Sanchez

What Are the Most Significant Challenges for Today's College Students?

> **Willie L. Banks Jr., PhD** (he/him/his), serves as the Vice Chancellor for Student Affairs at the University of California, Irvine. He has held a number of administrative positions at Indiana State University, Cleveland State University, and the University of Georgia. He received his bachelor's degree from Mercer University and his master's and PhD in college student affairs administration from the University of Georgia.

This is an interesting question. My initial response would be to mention the (un)affordability of college, or the racial reckoning that continues to face college campuses on a daily basis, or maybe the fact that our students have had to go to school during a global pandemic, or the ongoing climate change issues affecting our planet at an alarming rate, or perhaps the uncertainty for a number of undocumented students about their futures and education, or the social justice issues faced by historically marginalized groups on college campuses including, but not limited to Black, Indigenous, and People of Color or the Lesbian, Gay, Bisexual, Transgender, Queer community. Maybe it is a combination of all these challenges that our students have to navigate on a daily basis. Or perhaps it is all of these issues taken together, along with others that I have not even listed. I am sure there are others who would be able to add to my growing list of "challenges."

DOI: 10.4324/9780429319471-12

These are all challenges and will require our students to be able to manage their own and others' expectations. They have to cope with a world of uncertainty, and they have to be resilient. So maybe our students are having to learn how to be more adept at coping and managing challenges, being resilient, and managing their own and others' expectations. It is not any single challenge that our students face but the central struggle of how to handle the myriad of challenges that are present as they pursue their education.

In my role as the senior student affairs officer for my campus, I hear about the challenges our students face on a daily basis. From the first-generation student having to navigate remote learning while living at home with their parents and grandparents, to balancing their education, along with the expectation that the student work and financially contribute to living expenses for the family. I also think about the students that have to utilize our FRESH Basic needs hub (a campus food pantry) to address food insecurity. I am also reminded of the increasing reliance on our Campus Social Work office to help students navigate a myriad of basic needs concerns from financial, housing, to COVID-related issues. And the students who are utilizing the Counseling Center to work through a number of mental health issues. The work is never dull and continues to change on a daily basis. The needs change, as do our responses as we work to support students and, hopefully, move from reactive to proactive in our support.

On top of all of these challenges add in social media and its prevalence in our day-to-day lives. Most of the students I interact with are tied to their phones. It is fascinating to see our students glued to their phones and sharing so much of their lives with a wider population. While some of our students have found a community online, I wonder how much damage has been done by social media to our ability to converse and interact with others. I also wonder how much of our students' abilities to cope have been hampered or helped by social media. I have been privy to numerous conversations with students who struggled with communicating with their peers in a meaningful face-to-face way. I am worried that our students have relied too heavily on social media to respond to problems and issues they may face and in turn, have not developed enough skills to manage or deal with the number of challenges that arise on a daily basis. I also wonder if the amount of content shared and consumed via social media causes an unnecessary burden for our students who feel compelled to take on the issues they see come across their timelines. Has the oversharing of information caused more unintended consequences than originally thought?

As I am writing this, I realize I have not provided a rosy picture of our current college students' lives. Maybe it is the pandemic or maybe it is just "life" as we know it. Every generation of students has faced issues, and year after year, the students continue to thrive and live their lives. For some reason, this time period feels different. I do worry about our students and how they are able to survive and cope while still going to school and learning about themselves, others, and the world. Things are different. Expectations are different, and our students are faced with a startling picture of what the world looks like. There are some glimmers of hope, but overall, I am very concerned with our students' ability to navigate and manage these challenges.

Back to the original question, "What are the most significant challenges for today's college students?" It would be easy for me to pick any of the previously mentioned challenges, but I think I would be missing the larger picture. All of the previously mentioned examples are significant challenges for our students. However, I believe one of the most significant challenges is around the skillset of coping and resiliency or the lack thereof. If our students are struggling at the bottom of Maslow's hierarchy of needs, how can they thrive in their educational pursuits?

What do we need to do as student affairs professionals to encourage our students to develop better coping skills when they are faced with challenging issues on a daily basis? Have we missed something in our programs and services that do not help our students progress? Are our students coming to campus with a limited set of coping and resiliency skills? How can we help our students learn to cope and be resilient? These are just some of the questions I think about when I am thinking about our students. It is not an easy task, but should not we as institutions encourage our students to learn to operate in spaces of uncertainty, to ask questions, to listen to opposing views, but also to learn how to cope with people and ideas that we may not agree with?

I am not saying that there is not a place to disagree with ideas or people, especially those views that do not value and uphold basic human principles like love, compassion, understanding, and basic human worth. What I am saying is that we will continue to face these obstacles on a daily basis, and we can choose to dwell in a space that is wrought with disappointment, fear, or anger. Or we can learn to cope with the realities of the world and all of the disappointments that accompany any life and figure out ways to manage those issues and still lead our lives in fulfilled ways.

My hope for the future and for our students is that we are preparing them to meet the demands of a sometimes cruel and unjust world. I hope that our students learn how to effectively cope with issues they face individually and collectively, and as human beings on this planet. Our students are our future leaders, and I hope they will set the example of what it means to be a leader in an ever-evolving world. They can be effective leaders if they choose to be and if they choose to do the hard work around coping and resiliency. As student affairs professionals, we should be challenging and supporting our students to navigate these issues. I firmly believe in our students and their potential to change the course of our country, but we have to be partners in helping them develop their whole selves while in college. I hope that we find ways to encourage our students to be critical thinkers, to engage in meaningful dialogue, and to be the agents of change, we need them to be. And ultimately to be people and leaders that can cope and be resilient as current challenges are met and new ones continue to rise.

What Are the Most Significant Challenges for Today's College Students?

Shawn Curtis (he/him/his) is a licensed secondary education Social Studies Teacher with more than 20 years of classroom experience. He has spent much of that time teaching college prep classes as well as a variety of other levels of courses. He has been lucky enough to teach in a diverse array of settings with some amazing students. Shawn taught in New Jersey, Wyoming, and Indiana and has spoken at national conferences like National Council on the Social Studies about successful social studies methods and using applicable/relevant skills to prepare students for their futures.

I have been a secondary education social studies teacher for 20 years. In that time, I have served in a variety of school settings across multiple levels of learning. I have been a teacher in Urban New Jersey, Rust Belt Indiana, Rural Indiana, and Suburban Indiana. I have been fortunate to serve students from all races and socioeconomic backgrounds, including students who had recently immigrated from Haiti as refugees, and also at an institution where more than 50% of the student population were migrants from El Salvador. Additionally, the Rust Belt county school I served in Indiana was in one of the poorest counties in the state. That poverty came with high drug use rates, high rate of heroin overdose, physical/emotional/sexual abuse, high teen pregnancy rates, and a population of adults in which only 6% pursued a degree beyond high school. Currently, I serve a population in which well over 90% of high school graduates attend college. I feel like it was important to lay out my background because it has informed the level of college preparedness in our classroom. From a high school teaching perspective, I might argue that the hardest thing facing college students today is the decision to go to college in the first place. Does the value of a college education outweigh jumping immediately into the job market?

The school and the community factor a great deal into the level of college preparedness we focus on in class. Obviously, in my current climate, college preparedness is a necessity, and the parents hold it up as one of the prime reasons they moved into the community. Our school currently sits at about 5,500 students, and the opportunities for post–high school life are abundant. The school boasts a very successful athletic program that feeds many Division I university athletic teams. There are almost a dozen nationally recognized show choirs, multiple levels of theater, orchestras, and bands if students want to pursue the arts. Things such as culinary teams, business teams, and robotics teams are part of the more than 500 specialized clubs and activities to set students up for future success. Starting in the fall semester, school representatives from Harvard to Stanford arrive at the school to interview prospective students. There is a radio station, podcasting studio, and TV studio. My point is the availability of college preparation programming is endless.

The value of earning college admissions and credentialing is also represented in our classrooms, as the students strive for the best GPAs they can achieve in order to get into college. I would also say that this classroom attitude is somewhat noneffective. Students who take classes only to get into college tend to miss the skills that are also required to be in college. I have had students say, "Why do you teach us how to take notes, or to participate in online discussions? I only want to know what will be on the test." I inform them that taking notes and being able to analyze information are two important college skills. Anybody can parrot and repeat information, but a college-level intellect will find them debating and processing multiple points of view to arrive at conclusions. In our class, we spend time reading primary sources and comparing and contrasting author bias. I show them my college notebooks and textbooks to prepare them for the level of work they can expect from one semester course. This semester, with COVID-19 changing our world, we got to practice a very important college skill: time management. The day before we left the building for the semester, I reminded them that they are about to get a crash course in college living. They would not be on a bell schedule; they would be expected to map out their day as to when they were going to study and when they would play, and they would have to practice self-discipline. I was very proud of the level of work and commitment my students put in during the quarantine. One day, we had an online discussion about whether or not the United States should have dropped the atomic bomb, and their level of critical thinking and reasoning was beyond impressive, based on similar conversations I have had with college-educated adults.

On the opposite end of the spectrum was the school I taught at in rural northern Indiana. This was the school with the large percentage of students who were children of migrant workers. In this school, we tended to focus less on college preparedness and more on life skills. Many of our nonmigrant students were either heading into trades, farming, or the military. Those students who did go directly onto college tended to go to Purdue for engineering or agriculture. Many of our migrant students worried about deportation of their parents or the limited opportunities they faced for being "DREAMers." My colleagues and I focused a great deal of time on cultural adaptation, language skills, time management, and citizenship in order to help our students have better chances at careers rather than minimum wages jobs. A popular saying within our school was "would you rather stay in the same job, or gain the skills to advance to management?" My colleague and I worked with our students to develop cultural awareness and interviewing skills by creating a "Skype" guest speaker program with cultural studies classes we developed. The students were given opportunities to hear from and ask questions from speakers as varied as Congressman John Lewis in our 1960s class, Malcolm Jamal Warner in our 1980s class, and Carl Erskine in our History of Baseball class. In Government class, we connected them with state and national representatives in order to tell their stories of immigration and feel that they had the power to advocate. We were able to meet Indiana Congressional reps, U.S. senators, and state officials. The students even worked on passing a bill through Congress. I was often told, "I don't need to do this work. I'm not going to college." We reminded them that life was about showcasing character. Are you the type of person who can complete a task even if you find it nonessential?

However, this is not to say that each school is a set "attend college vs. don't go to college environment." Within every school, there is always a certain population that is working on attending college, even in the schools where it is not the major value. In the same way, at the school I serve now, even though college preparedness is a major driving point, there are groups of students who still are developing basic skills in order to succeed on a noncollege path. At the school I served in New Jersey, which was a rural/suburban school district outside of Newark, I was fortunate to be able to teach both Advanced Placement (AP) U.S. History to college motivated students and English as a second language (ESL) basic skills history to a group of Haitian students with refugee status. In a given day, I moved from helping our AP students navigate college skill-based learning to helping my ESL students understand and translate critical vocabulary. At the Rust Belt school in Indiana, despite a culture that mistrusted college degrees and education in general, there was a group of students who were college motivated. I taught this group in Dual Credit U.S. History. Most of them had the same goal, to leave the town and find opportunities and careers that did not exist in the shuttered factories of the town. I taught a mixture of students in the required classes like Government and Economics. I held all students to the same standard of excellence in their work and always made sure to remind them about the opportunities that college could afford. I always have my bachelor's and master's on permanent display. I always have college brochures on the walls, usually from the University of Wyoming. I very often point out how I was not a successful high school student, failing both Algebra 2 and Chemistry. I remind them that I did always love history and teaching, and in college, I was allowed to find myself as a social studies education major surrounded by people who were as excited about history as I was. I tell them stories of being an resident assistant and we talk about scholarships. Many of my students who did choose college were given a 21st-century-scholar scholarship, which goes to first-generation college students in Indiana and offers full tuition.

I have also been known to take students to local universities so that we can sit in a real college setting and observe classroom behaviors. After class, we take the opportunity to interview the professor as to what they look for in students in class. I guess overall, I would say my approach to college preparedness has always been one of flexibility and depends on the values and needs of the students and the community.

What Are the Most Significant Challenges for Today's College Students?

Rasul Mowatt, PhD (he/him/his or they/them theirs), enters this dialogue with 17 plus years in academia and a strident focus on questions of related social justice/injustice, critical pedagogy, and cultural studies. Within those years of service, encounters with students have been through pre-college programs, first-year experiences, undergraduate curricula in a professional school, as well as a college of arts, humanities, and sciences, and master's and doctoral-level courses and seminars. Administrative roles over undergraduate and graduate education, departmental leadership, and extracurricular activities additionally inform a knowledge base that moves past easy answers to bigger questions.

This is not a hopeful essay. There will be no promise or solution at its conclusion. This is the challenge presented in this essay, can we truly embody the theories and ideals we espouse in order to better force the changes we desire? This is me being honest in a dialogue with you, based on a true critique of nearly 15 years as a professor and the students that I have encountered. But more importantly, this is based on an equal set of years (or more) studying the aftereffects of white supremacy, the "candy wrapper" it has left on the ground at a campsite that lets you know that it was there, that it did what it wanted to do, and is now off to do some more elsewhere. Those "candy wrappers" were "mild" subject matter things like the legacy of lynching, colonialism, and state-sanctioned violence. One of the biggest challenges for college students today is learning, growing, and surviving (maybe even thriving) in an educational system that is so steeped in these realities. So in the context of being a faculty member engaged with students, I pose a question to you, for us, from me: What if instead of dismantling white supremacy, we are in fact maintaining it?

Many of us in higher education have come to an understanding that diversity needs to be challenged, inclusion needs to be a given, and equity needs to be achievable in order for college teaching and student learning to positively move forward throughout the 21st century. But if we are to understand white supremacy not as some societal add-on that has corrupted the world around us, but instead *as* the actual world around us, how do you actually dismantle it within one small space? In the small space of higher education, colleges and universities cannot somehow be distinct from the society that they were birthed within, the cities that they are situated in, and the laws and resources that continuously make them viable institutions. Dismantling efforts seem to allude to an idea that white supremacy is not a fundamental part of society but is an insidious outside ideology that somehow taints higher education's mission and the various disciplines of study. As if through some increased nonwhite representation, redistributing the power dynamics would not result in a new set of actors of color engaging in the same life-threatening and non-life-sustaining endeavors as the previous white actors.

But what actually is white supremacy? Is it just the years of gross misconduct that allowed racial discrimination to thrive in the sum total of all employment, housing, and other such opportunities? This seems like a form of reductionism being integrated into the vast amount of scholarship on white supremacy. Is it just racism, the systemic antagonism of so-called and so-deemed inferior racialized populations? And this seems far too insufficient, for if white supremacy is merely racism, why give it a new name? In particular, through the years of studying racial violence, I have always taken white supremacy to mean the "political, economic and cultural system in which Whites overwhelmingly control power and material resources, conscious and unconscious ideas of White superiority and entitlement are widespread" (Ansley, 1997, p. 592).

A system alludes to more than a series of "evil" actors denying academic employment. A system alludes to a self-generating culture that both produces the "right" people to always do the "right" thing and ensures that even the "wrong" people will always do the "right" thing to maintain the system. We envision a racialized white group of people that controls and receives entitlements, but we would be remiss in not recognizing that racialization is simply a process and not a natural fact. Race or racialization creates a system to better manage salary differentials, promotional disparities, and occupational segregation in both academic and administrative roles because resources are finite, not because of some "skin stigma." White supremacy should push us to see that white is a thing to be done, and not a group of people that are. The division and access to resources, the seats of decision-making for that division and access, and the education to understand one's role in that process is doing *white*, which is beyond the sole workings of white people. But when we peer through the veil, we will see a host (through history, in many more cases than usual) of people from a swath of racialized identities servicing the division, sitting in those seats, and perpetuating that particular type of education of others. As Baldwin (1970) noted, "[C]olor is not a human or a personal reality; it is a political reality" (p. 70).

Further by extension looking at state-sanctioned violence, the "relations of White dominance and non-white subordination are daily reenacted across a broad array of institutions and social settings" (Ansley, 1997, p. 592). So, it is not enough to exist as a racially designated white "being"; white or whiteness is fundamentally about domination and subordination. White supremacy is a cultural value that places these two realities as paramount for society. Someone must dominate and someone must be dominated. Without the apparatus of racialization, racism would not be as successful as a system within white supremacy (the basis for *racecraft* according to Fields & Fields, 2012). This is why seeing racial discrimination as synonymous with white supremacy is an act of reductionism, and seeing racism as white supremacy is insufficient. Either captures only one contributing process in an array of processes.

And so more importantly, such reductionism of white supremacy within higher education results in a discourse of "dismantling" that could falsely create lines of thinking among students that the acts they engage in, the words that they craft, and the ideas that they formulate can somehow scare away the "monster" in the bell tower, or topple the very tower, itself. White supremacy is not a separate tower among the other towers on a campus. Anti-racism is not really attacking racism. It is instead "fighting" the faint of race that only results in my racialized self being more comfortable on a college campus that pays low wages to its unseen workers in the kitchens, among the pipes, and near the massive machines that wash the endless yards of linens and sheets for banquets, soirees. Decolonizing is absent of colonized countries and peoples. It is an empty cause that actually creates a net of "racially diverse" neo-colonial social media influencers who personally benefit from the self-branding exercises of syllabi construction bereft of actual care and action of off-campus residential displacement, the construction of substandard student housing, and general student and staff homelessness.

What if instead of preparing a new set of social agents to change reality for the better, we are preparing new monsters to fill those towers with new skills and tools that only succeed in fortifying that tower with better bricks and mortar? "The" white supremacy of higher education is not special, nor are we in its towers. In our academic vocations, we cannot be so pompous to think what exists on campus does not also exist in warehouses of shipping companies, factory floors, steel mills, public school classrooms, hospital beds, dock ports, and prison cells. A basic aim in academia should be becoming "good" teachers, "good" administrators who attend to students' responsibilities responsibly. In this day and age, just answering emails and responding to students has become almost "revolutionary." To teach a class on time, all the time, with a syllabus before the first class has become "liberating." Students are not either, but they illustrate things that are missing in what teach, convey, and model. On our watch, students are the absence of a negative, they are a good moment that can be had in a classroom. But a broader struggle has to go on beyond the limited scope of academia. This is the most fundamentally and terrifyingly significant challenge that students face, making sense of their own responsibility to do something about the realities that we all live in.

References

Ansley, F. L. (1997). White supremacy (and what we should do about it). In R. Delgado & J. Stefancic (Eds.), *Critical white studies: Looking behind the mirror* (pp. 592–595). Temple University Press.

Baldwin J. (1970). *The fire next time*. Dell Books.

Fields, K. & Fields, B. J. (2012). *Racecraft: The soul of inequality in American life*. Verso.

What Are the Most Significant Challenges of Today's College Students?

> **Sebastian Sanchez** (he/him/his) is a student at Delaware State University where he is on a full-ride scholarship. Before enrolling there, he attended a two-year college in Georgia and has been a part of the Deferred Action for Childhood Arrivals (DACA) program during his educational endeavors. He is studying accounting.

The DREAMers categorization and movement emerged during the time that the DREAM Act was being pushed in Congress on June 15, 2012. The individuals that make up the group are primarily undocumented students/youth. The DREAMers movement has been tackling issues regarding immigration, education, and citizenship for decades. Many DREAMers' life stories are challenging.

Hello! My name is Sebastian Sanchez, and I am a Deferred Action for Childhood Arrivals (DACA). I am extremely grateful to The Dream.US for granting me the opportunity for a full-ride scholarship to attend Delaware State University. My goal is to obtain a bachelor's of science in accounting and Management Information Systems. One of the biggest challenges I had to overcome in 2019 was leaving my parents. Although I was a dual enrollment student at Elbert County High School and Athens Technical College in Northeast Georgia, I was working a part-time job to help my parents financially. Unfortunately, once I committed to Del State, I was limited in the help I could grant them. I grew close with them after my sister had the privilege to be granted the same scholarship in 2018. I know she struggled with leaving my parents and going off to school. While I saw her pain at that time, I did not see a future in college for me. I remember my mother always telling me, "Sebas I don't see you tied down to a table and books." At first, I was growing up with that mentally; however, things can really change for the best. I had my mind set to finish at Athens Technical College with an associate's in accounting; however, after deliberating with my mentor, JoBeth, I realized what an opportunity was being granted to me. Then came the summer of 2019, and I was preparing to move to Delaware. One of the biggest fears I had was being so far away from my parents because my mother is not in a great place in her life. She has had seven surgeries, which makes it kind of hard for her to maintain a proper lifestyle. On the other hand, my father has multiple health problems like cholesterol and diabetes. I honestly felt hopeless leaving them 682 miles away to chase my dreams. Unfortunately, my mother could not go with my father and me when I was dropped off at Del State. August 19, 2019, was my orientation day, as well as the day my grandmother, who I never had an opportunity to meet, died, and with that anxiety, my father was driving 682 miles by himself without a driver's license. The fear that something could happen to him on his way home to my mother with her grief over her mother's death was super scary.

DACA allowed 800,000 DREAMers to live and work in the United States free from fear of deportation. The DREAM Act is bipartisan legislation that allows two million DREAMers to better contribute to their families and their community and boost the economy. Being a DREAMER is incredibly challenging. As a recipient, you are not eligible to receive federal financial aid. However, you are able to apply to any college you desire, but you'll be considered an out-of-state student regardless of if you graduated in the state. Many DREAMers face a tough challenge to find a solution that most U.S. citizens do not seem to mind at all. On the other hand, one way to be eligible to attend college is by receiving a scholarship. Many times, the scholarship does not cover all the expenses. As much as our parents want to be part of our academic lives, they cannot afford to pay any out of pocket. Many undocumented parents are working "under the table" (when an employer pays an employee without reporting it to the government), leading them to get paid minimum wage. As sad as it is, many DREAMers must end their dreams of achieving a college degree. I can say from my experience that once middle school hit, and my advisor started to ask about my career plan, things got intense. I honestly had no idea what to say or just made something up. I was really scared that if I told them my legal situation, things would get awkward. I ended up not telling, only then high school came around, and I regretted not saying anything. Living in a household where your parents are immigrants is frightening. I was scared that my classmates or professors would state a racist comment. Then during my high school years, I was stressed about what to do after graduation. I did not know if I should just go into the workforce or actually fight for my education. Luckily, my school offered a program called MOVE ON WHEN READY (Georgia's dual enrollment program allowing high school students to earn college credit while working on their high school diplomas). I had the opportunity my junior and senior years to complete classes at Athens Technical College. Those two years were very tough. I was taking college classes while being trained as a head bookkeeper for my job at the time. Time management and multitasking were critical components for balancing school, work, and personal life. A huge blessing for DREAMers is The Dream.US because they have granted scholarships for multiple DACA scholars for four years. Donald E. Graham, the cofounder of The Dream.US, has made the dreams of many DREAMers come to a reality and all the sacrifices parents made. The first of four cohorts at Delaware State University has officially graduated. Unfortunately, due to COVID-19, the graduates could not walk the stage; however, they were able to represent their heritage with pride.

Along the way, DREAMers overcome many more challenges. A huge problem many DACA recipients have is battling with mental health issues. Mental health issues run across the board with any college student. Nevertheless, like I previously mentioned, other DREAMers like me have the responsibility to look out for their parents. Most of the time, I can say we forget to make sure we are okay. Working, focusing on our academic lifestyles, and studying triggers us to make other things a priority instead of ourselves. I can say from my experience I've received a phone call when my parents needed me to translate for them. Everyone goes through different challenges in their academic careers; however, I am not trying to be selfish, but DACA recipients have much more challenges to overcome. Besides having other mental health issues, DREAMers also face the challenge of being accepted into grad school.

Unfortunately, many undergrad students graduating from a four-year college run into the same situation trying to get into grad school. Many grad schools do not accept DACA recipients for the same reason as undergraduate schools: federal financial aid. Luckily, there are 19 states that have granted in-state tuition for DACA students (NCLS, 2021). Having these states open another door for DREAMers is a dream come true. However, there are three states with laws explicitly barring DEARMers from receiving in-state tuition and another two that do not allow DREAMers to enroll in postsecondary education at all (NCLS, 2021).

In conclusion, DACA recipients must take an extra step to fight for their rights. I know we all have a purpose in life, and DREAMers will have their moments of success. It may happen years from now, but I know we will be so happy to know all the sacrifices our families made were well worth it. Once challenged, students face feelings of freedom. There is no adult supervising them, so they feel like they have the free range to do as they please. Another challenge college students face is time management, making their academic lives harder on them.

Some specific challenges DREAMers face:

First-generation attending college
Knowing the government knows all of your information
Knowing our parents have no protection

10

ANALYSIS

What Are the Most Significant Challenges for Today's College Students?

Shannon Dean-Scott

Dr. Shannon R. Dean-Scott (she/her/hers) is an associate professor in Student Affairs in Higher Education (SAHE) at Texas State University. Dr. Dean-Scott teaches courses in student development theory, assessment, evaluation, and strategic planning, research methods, and internship experiences in higher education. Her research focuses on multicultural consciousness of undergraduate students, teaching pedagogies, assessment, and faculty-student interactions. Dr. Dean received her PhD in Counseling and Student Personnel Services from the University of Georgia, a master's degree in College Student Affairs Administration and a bachelor's degree in Liberal Arts from Azusa Pacific University in southern California. Prior to joining the faculty, Dr. Dean-Scott worked for over 10 years in a number of student affairs functional areas including housing, leadership education, international student affairs, advising, and service learning.

When reflecting on the many challenges of today's college students, I would echo several of the challenges presented by the authors in the four essays. Today's students struggle with a variety of stressors, some of which are newly present in our current climate of higher education, even excluding the current COVID-19 pandemic troubles. I have worked in higher education for over 15 years, initially as an administrator and now as a faculty member in a preparation program for master's students who want to be college administrators. This provides me a unique lens by which to view the changes within college students' identities, development, and challenges over time. College students today face a plethora of challenges from political divisiveness, racial injustice, tuition expenses, and more.

DOI: 10.4324/9780429319471-13

Depending on the identities of the college students in question, there may be countless other struggles from financial insecurity to balancing familial responsibilities. However, there are many similarities among students that we can draw upon to better understand the experiences and challenges of today's students. In this response and analysis, I will outline some of the similarities and differences I see presented in each of these essays. Further, I will provide some context and relationship to theories on college students and literature related to our students' current struggles. Finally, I will provide additional thoughts and commentary on the topic to conclude the chapter.

Summary of Essays

The first essay is written by Dr. Willie L. Banks Jr. He is vice chancellor for student affairs at a large public institution in California. His essay focuses on the many challenges that college students might face while attending a university. He discusses a variety of topics but highlights a few poignant areas that he feels most of today's college students must negotiate, which are social media as well as learning coping and resiliency strategies for navigating the complexities of college and the United States. Dr. Banks comes from many years of working in public higher education and his perspectives offer great insight into the struggles today's college students face both from an individual and systemic level. His views make sense given his many years working directly with students and his intentionality even in his role as a vice chancellor to be connected to students directly. He responds to the question regarding student challenges by thinking of students as individual people before a collective category.

The next essay is written by Shawn Curtis, a licensed secondary education social studies teacher who has been teaching for over 20 years. His essay highlights the very real and difficult choices that students must face when considering college or a career. In this essay, Curtis discusses the ways in which he and his colleagues prepare students to enter a university or workforce. He identifies the skills needed not only to get into college but also required to succeed during their postsecondary academic experience. Curtis's perspective is valuable as we consider who today's college students are in light of their previous experiences in high school as well as how those students are being prepared prior to their matriculation into college. His insights help us evaluate how students' prior educational experiences shape the challenges these students face as they enter and pursue collegiate degrees.

The third essay is written by Dr. Rasul Mowatt, a college professor and department head with 15 plus years in academia. In his essay, Dr. Mowatt focuses on social justice and white supremacy that evades our country and academia. He discusses the struggles of white supremacy facing college students through racial inequities and state-sanctioned violence toward people of color. His essay concludes by challenging faculty, administrators, and students to face the realities of the world and create positive change within our spheres of influence. Dr. Mowatt's experiences as a college professor and as a social justice advocate enable us to view some of the challenges today's college students face in light of the systemic racial injustices he studies, argues, and discusses. His perspectives are helpful in shaping the context of the world in which today's students are pursuing their degrees and the struggles they face inside and outside of academia.

The final essay is written by Sebastian Sanchez, a Deferred Action of Childhood Arrival (DACA) recipient and (at the time of writing his essay) a community college student. He provides his personal insights on what today's college students face, particularly those who are DREAMers. The Development, Relief, and Education for Alien Minors Act (DREAM) allows temporary conditional residency and the right to work to DACA individuals. In his essay he outlines the struggles of DREAMers and many other first-generation students, including challenges with the systems and familial ties, as well as challenges such as mental health issues and balancing multiple responsibilities. Sanchez's essay is particularly insightful in helping us understand an experience from a students' perspective about the challenges he faces. Further, his lived experiences being a DREAMer and at a community college really help define his views and give us firsthand knowledge of some of the challenges today's college students face.

Each of these authors reflects a unique perspective about the challenges of today's college students that is shaped by their various identities and lived experiences both in and out of the collegiate environment. The same is true for my viewpoint as I analyze their essays and attempt to convey similarities and differences throughout their perspectives. I am a White woman who serves as an associate professor in higher education with over 15 years in administration and faculty roles and a focus on preparation programs for college administrators. In my role, I strive to create equitable spaces for diverse groups of students, focusing my research on multicultural consciousness, teaching pedagogy, and learning environments. Prior to joining the faculty, I held administrative roles in housing, living-learning communities, and international student life. These administrative roles inform my current position as a faculty member, as do the identities that I hold. I am a first-generation college student who received degrees from a mid-sized private university, as well as a large public university. These lived experiences shape my worldview and are the lens I bring to analyzing these essays and inform my perspectives on academia and today's college student.

Themes across the Essays

In analyzing these essays, there are a few themes that spread across all four responses and also some unique attributes that each author presents. The commonalities among these four essays include the discussion of the diversity of the student body within higher education and the cultural and racial inequities

present within the United States and across our institutions of higher education. Additionally, each author presented various ways in which today's college
students struggle to balance their lives, whether it be with their academic and
social lives or their collegiate and familial responsibilities. These two themes
were present in each of the four essays. In regard to the uniqueness of the essays,
much of what they uniquely determined as challenges for today's college students stem from their identities, perspectives, and roles in relation to higher education. Much of the discussion about their differences will take place in the next
section regarding the distinct positionality that each author brings to this topic.

Diversity on College Campuses

The demographics of today's college students are more diverse than ever before.
Students come from more diversified backgrounds, including race, gender, sexual orientation, socioeconomic status, and student status, to name a few. Banks
and Mowatt both discuss this at some length, with Banks explicitly noting
the increase of "historically marginalized groups on college campuses and the
social injustices faced by Black, Indigenous, People of Color and others from
the Lesbian, Gay, Bisexual, Transgender, and Queer communities" (p. 115). A
number of challenges come from this more diverse student body. Students with
nondominant identities might arrive on campuses that are unprepared to support these students or where policies do not provide appropriate support. It can
also be challenging for students to learn how to productively engage with others
from different backgrounds.

Additionally, college students have a myriad of choices in terms of college
degrees from two-year versus four-year institutions to public versus private to a
variety of schools created to increase access for marginalized populations such
as Hispanic serving institutions, Tribal colleges, and historically Black colleges
and universities. Each of these types of colleges provides students with a unique
experience. Further, the demographics of the population in the United States
are also becoming increasingly diverse. Not only is higher education a beautiful representation of the shifting demographics of the United States, but it also
becomes a testing ground for students as they grow developmentally and come
to a greater understanding of their identities.

In the last five years, higher education and the United States have also seen
increased racial tensions on college campuses. There has been an emboldening
of hate and overt forms of racism, sexism, homophobia, and xenophobia. Higher
education is not immune from these tensions either; it finds its way into cities,
communities, and onto our campus environments. For today's college students,
they are confronted with these realities amid their own development while also
navigating their development in direct relation to others who represent (intentionally or not) the very-isms that are challenging their development. Each of
the essayists discuss this at some level. Mowatt describes in great detail the social

injustices that many of today's students face both on and off campus and the impact of their identities in those spaces.

College is a time for immense personal growth and change. Many college students find new understandings of their various identities through their academic and cocurricular pursuits. Couple these contentious environments (both in the United States and on college campuses) with identity exploration, and students may struggle with reconciling their newfound ideological views about themselves, their peers, and their world. Each of the authors addressed this conflict and challenge in some way. Some were explicit in discussing privileged identities (Mowatt and Curtis) that many students struggle to understand, while other authors talked about students understanding their own identities in the midst of potentially combative spaces (particularly Sanchez and Banks).

Unique Stressors for College Students

Another theme I saw present across each of the essays were the stressors and additional struggles today's college students face in balancing their lives. Today, more than 81% of college students (full time and part time) work at least part time, and 43% work full time while also attending school (National Center for Educational Statistics, 2019). Today's students are also highly involved in academics and cocurricular activities. Balancing these obligations can be difficult for any individual, but the additional factor of many of these students being on their own for the first time creates tension. Although Banks addresses this from an upper-level administrator point of view, his sentiment is also echoed in Sanchez's personal experiences in his essay.

As a diversity of students flood our college campuses, so too do the needs of these students. Some of today's college students are also parents and/or are working full time, many also have familial obligations while also attending to their studies. Curtis and Sanchez both discuss the challenges of balancing these responsibilities while managing their curricular obligations. These challenges create a balancing act for students, and many times they do not feel they can give as much as they would like to their academic pursuits because of these commitments. The essay authors also discussed the challenges that students face in balancing responsibilities while also finding time and energy for recreational or leisure pursuits, which in and of themselves are necessary for human growth and development. The struggle to have social lives and the pressures to engage in the world through social media add further stress to today's college students.

Although these essays shared many things in common, it is often the uniqueness of their pieces that brings out the beauty and diverse nature of higher education. Since these four essays were written from various stakeholder perspectives, you can see their distinguished contribution to helping better understand the challenges for today's college students. The perspective of a chancellor is going to look different than that of a current student, for example. Each voice speaks to the nuances and challenges for students. In the next section, I will break down some of the unique perspectives each of these essays contributes not only from an author's perspective but also as each of these individuals is a stakeholder in the realm of higher education.

Stakeholder Perspectives

One of the wonderful things about reading these essays from the various perspectives is that you can see the authors' viewpoints on today's college students from their positionalities. The authors' backgrounds and lived experiences have shaped how they view and approach this topic, as does my positionality in responding to their essays. As noted in the opening chapters of this book, positionality is an important consideration in understanding and approaching this topic. Some people perceive positionality as bias, but the social and political context for how identities are shaped are incredibly valuable in considering the authors' unique contributions – in this case to understanding today's college students.

Both Banks and Mowatt currently work on a college campus, albeit in very different positions. Banks offers the perspective of an upper-level administrator who has worked in various capacities within higher education – and particularly student affairs for a number of years. Whereas Mowatt, although previously an administrator, now brings the lens of a faculty member to the discussion. Each of them helps us better understand the landscape of the challenges of today's college students but is further removed from the lived experiences than Sanchez, for example. As a current student, Sanchez offers his experiences firsthand with the challenges he and others in similar situations face. Likewise, although removed from the collegiate environment and being a student, Curtis works very directly with high school students as they consider their educational journeys or career trajectories. His perspectives on what students are struggling with as they make life decisions regarding potential college career choices is invaluable to understanding some of the challenges students bring with them as they enter institutions of higher education.

Each perspective, including my own, provides a differentiated view of the struggles that college students face. Different people are going to see these challenges from their own lenses, greatly informed by their own lived experiences. For example, a college student is going to see their peers' challenges differently than a college professor; a family member is going to also recognize different experiences than a college professor. In order to better understand their experiences and the perspectives they bring, it would also be helpful to have more information on the essayists' social identities and prior experiences. Although some of the authors provide pieces of this throughout their essays, a better understanding of the authors' racial identities, where they grew up, generational status, and their own backgrounds while in college and beyond would help frame their unique perspectives on today's college student.

These four essays are approached from the perspective of a vice chancellor for student affairs, a secondary education social studies teacher, a college professor, and a student. These individuals bring with them a myriad of lived experiences, and from what we know, they also have different experiences with the types of higher education available (private, public, two-year, and four-year). This lends these individuals to offer greater insights from their perspectives from their various positionalities. Although I have attended and worked at two-year, four-year, public, and private universities, my experience is limited to my own identities and time spent at these places. I believe each of these essays enlightens us on the various struggles facing college students today, and their various identities, perspectives, and lived experiences enhance our understanding of the factors that impact and challenge our students while attending college.

Relationship to Literature

Much of the literature on today's college students and on the unique challenges for students echoes what is written by the authors in these essays. In this section, I want to draw your attention to some of the challenges we know based on research and literature that impact a college student's experience. The first challenge is the response by higher education and administrators to the increase in historically marginalized and underrepresented populations on college campuses. The second challenge I want to address is the balancing of commitments – particularly work and family obligations. The last challenge prominently represented in the literature is the financial challenge for college students. Although this last challenge is also seen in the second challenge, and the need to work while attending college, research also shows the increase in the cost of education. There are many other challenges for students individually and collectively; however, these three are prominent throughout the literature, expressed in the authors' essays, and articulated in the lived experiences of today's college students.

Increasing Historically Marginalized Populations

Throughout most of the history of higher education in the United States, White men have been the primary recipients of a college education. These demographics have shifted in the last 30 years with women now outnumbering men and students of color almost equaling the number of White students on college campuses (Biddix et al., 2021). Additionally, we know there has also been an increase in multiracial students – or those who identify with two or more races. This is not only seen throughout the population of the United States but also among those attending college. Further, there is an increase in first-generation college students – those who are first in their families to pursue or complete a bachelor's degree (RTI International, 2019). Banks noted that the increase of first-generation college students having to navigate college, particularly remote learning in the time of a pandemic, has proved challenging. The increase in demographic diversity of the student population is wonderful in terms of increased access and continuing advancement for historically marginalized populations. However, these increases in diversity can also create a challenge for higher education institutions in meeting the diverse needs of these students, thus presenting challenges for students in acquiring the support they need to be successful.

While there are numerous benefits to diverse student bodies, there are some challenges for students as well. College campuses can increase the racial diversity on their campus but fail to provide adequate support structures for students, resulting in lower persistence and retention rates for historically underrepresented students (Chen, 2017). If administrators are not intentional about the support systems for these students, historically underrepresented students may feel isolated and unwelcome on campus. Mowatt discussed the challenges students of color face regarding their safety and feelings of inclusion both on campus and within society. Many racially marginalized students and many first-generation college students feel like they are waiting for someone to find out they do not belong on their college campuses. First-generation college students often struggle to find and access the various resources on campus to help them be successful. Students of color, or more specifically Black, Indigenous, People of Color, may struggle to get connected to other students and faculty who look like them. A sense of belonging is really important in not only helping students feel connected to each other and the campus but also in students being successful academically and socially. Thus, college administrators need to be really thoughtful in providing resources for these diverse students who are attending our campuses at higher rates than in the past.

Managing Commitments

Another important consideration and challenge for students today is the balancing of multiple commitments, such as work, school, and family. Although this is not necessarily new for today's college students, there are additional factors that play a role in the difficulty that balancing and managing commitments has for students. Both Banks and Sanchez echoed this difficulty in their essays. They each discussed the many competing priorities vying for today's college students' time and attention. Today's college student is more connected than ever – these students have been raised with the internet and cell phones in a way that previous generations were not. Thus, the connectivity to each other, family, and work looks different for this generation. Work also looks different for today's college student. It is estimated that roughly 70% of full-time college students work during college (St. Amour, 2019). Working in and of itself is not necessarily the challenge. Research shows that if you work 15 hours or less per week, this can have a positive impact on your life and education, whereas working more than 15 hours a week has a negative impact, particularly on your GPA (Georgetown

Report, 2018). Sanchez noted in his essay that many of his peers, especially those who were DREAMers, needed to work for financial purposes, yet struggled to manage this commitment with their educational pursuits. Balancing this commitment with school can be particularly challenging for students when there is a financial need that forces them to work – whether because college is costly or because they are covering additional expenses for themselves or family.

College students today are also very involved on campus and in the community, and they are continually pushed to be involved by faculty and staff. Although involvement is overall positively linked to many academic and social benefits for students, overinvolvement can again lead to difficulty in balancing their academics, commitments, and social lives. It is not just the campus involvement that can become overly burdensome to students either. Approximately, three in ten college students today are caregivers to either a minor or a parent or family member (Rothwell, 2021). These statistics vary by race and socioeconomic status and not only impact a students' ability to be academically and socially involved on campus but also their ability to balance and navigate the many commitments to family and other responsibilities they hold. This can play a large role in student persistence and graduation if students do not receive the support they need in order to balance these many pressures and responsibilities.

Finally, although seemingly tangential to managing commitments is the challenge that many students have today in managing their online engagement and presence. Banks mentioned this challenge in his essay, noting not only are students today tied more to their phones and social media, but they also feel the burden of coping with and responding to various issues they face online. As mentioned earlier, students today are extremely connected to their peers, families, and community through online platforms and social media. Students today have to navigate and manage their online presence while learning, growing, and developing. Not only does it take a lot of time for students to manage an online persona, but they may not be at a place developmentally in order to navigate this well. Many classes and programs also require students to create virtual platforms online, whether it be through LinkedIn, blogs, or portfolios. This can create a challenge for students as these activities are not only time-consuming but can also add to stress for students to be congruent across these platforms and in real life. These additional online requirements have become particularly true in a pandemic, but even outside of the traditional classroom, students are having to navigate more complexities within their online personas. This creates a challenge for students and added pressure as they seek to manage their identities, families, and various responsibilities all in a varied digital and mediacentric time.

Struggling with Finances

The cost of a college education is on the rise. Since 1980, tuition and cost of enrollment have increased 1,200% (Bhutada, 2021). More students are faced with financial difficulties in affording college tuition. With the increase in access for low-income students, many of today's college students have to decide how to fund their college experience. Thus, many college students turn to student loans in order to afford the financial constraints of college or work while enrolled, or both. In the United States, there are approximately 45 million borrowers who owe over $1.5 trillion in student loan debt (Friedman, 2020). These financial decisions can be difficult for today's college students to make because without loan options, college is unattainable for many. Yet some college students lack the financial literacy to truly understand what taking out loans for their education means. Further, some students cannot dip into a savings account or ask for parental assistance to pay for tuition, books, and other educational expenses, adding additional strain to an already stressful season of life.

Financial concerns spread even further than just the matter of student loans; finances impact the day-to-day life and choices of college students. While there are those who struggle with debt or lack of financial knowledge, many also struggle with financial anxiety and lack of satisfaction with their college experience (Archulta et al., 2013). College students have to make many choices regarding majors, involvement opportunities, work, and internship experiences, and by adding financial anxiety to the mix, college students are left grappling with choices and making decisions that may financially benefit or hurt them in the future. Further, discussions of finances are often seen as taboo in the United States, and thus many college administrators do not often engage with college students on topics of financial literacy, debt, credit cards, or investment information. Discussions related to finances are extra challenging for students from low-income backgrounds or first-generation college students who may struggle to seek out these resources of know of their availability on a college campus. Regardless of the identities of today's college students, this needs to be a continuing topic and point of discussion to better provide services and resources to address this challenge for students.

Concluding Thoughts

Today's college students face a variety of challenges, many of which are not new to higher education or college students but are exacerbated by the world in which we live today. The four authors' essays helped enlighten different aspects and challenges of students from various perspectives. Hearing from the viewpoint of a student, a vice chancellor, a high school teacher, and a faculty member allowed different voices to demonstrate the challenges from their individual positionalities. My perspective is no different in that I bring my own worldview and ideological beliefs to this topic. By grounding their perspectives and my own in research and literature, I hoped to illuminate some of the most pressing challenges that today's college students face. From there, it is the responsibility of all of us as educators to help eliminate and minimize some of these challenges by creating resources and sharing knowledge so that these challenges can be met with solutions.

References

Archulta, K. L., Dale, A., & Spann, S. M. (2013). College students and financial distress: Exploring debt, financial satisfaction, and financial anxiety. *Journal of Financial Counseling and Planning, 24*(2), 50–62.

Bhutada, G. (2021, February 3). *The rising cost of college in the U.S.* Visual Capitalist. Retrieved on April 15, 2022, from https://www.visualcapitalist.com/rising-cost-of-college-in-u-s/

Biddix, J. P., Gabourel, K. G., & Cuevas, F. (2021). *Today's U.S. college students by the numbers.* In N. Y. Gulley. *Multiple perspectives on today's college students: Needs, challenges, and opportunities* (p. X). Routledge.

Chen, A. (2017). Addressing diversity on college campuses: Changing expectations and practices in instructional leadership. *Higher Education Studies, 7*(2), 17–22.

Friedman, Z. (2020, February 3). Student loan debt statistics in 2020: A record 1.6 trillion. *Frobes.* Retrieved on April 15, 2022, from https://www.forbes.com/sites/zackfriedman/2020/02/03/student-loan-debt-statistics/?sh=14d02f6c281f

Georgetown Report. (2018). *Balancing work and learning.* Retrieved on April 15, 2022, from https://cew.georgetown.edu/cew-reports/learnandearn/

National Center for Educational Statistics. (2019). *College student employment.* Retrieved on April 15, 2022, from https://nces.ed.gov/programs/coe/pdf/coe_ssa.pdf

Rothwell, J. (2021, January 29). *College student caregivers more likely to stop classes.* Gallup Blog. Retrieved on April 15, 2022, from https://news.gallup.com/opinion/gallup/328970/college-student-caregivers-likely-stop-classes.aspx

RTI International. (2019). *First-generation college students: Demographic characteristics and postsecondary enrollment.* Washington, DC: NASPA. Retrieved on April 15, 2022, from https://firstgen.naspa.org/files/dmfile/FactSheet-01.pdf

St. Amour, M. (2019, November 18). Working college students. *Inside Higher Education.* Retrieved on April 15, 2022, from https://www.insidehighered.com/news/2019/11/18/most-college-students-work-and-thats-both-good-and-bad

QUESTION 4

What Are the Most Significant Opportunities for Today's College Students?

11

WHAT ARE THE MOST SIGNIFICANT OPPORTUNITIES FOR TODAY'S COLLEGE STUDENTS?

Stakeholder Essays

Caroline Angelo, Jemelleh Coes, Roslyn Gowens and Ximena Silva-Avila

What Are the Most Significant Opportunities for Today's College Students?

> **Caroline Angelo** (she/her/hers) serves as the Executive Vice President for Academic and Student Affairs at Atlanta Technical College. She has been in this role since August of 2017. Prior to this professional experience, she was the Vice President of Academic Affairs at Athens Technical College. She has been in many professional roles from adjunct instructor to faculty in English to Executive Director of Registration and Records. Her career in higher education and the technical college system began in 1991.

The overriding goal of technical community colleges is to make student development and success possible in a competitive global economy and build a well-educated, globally competitive workforce. Technical colleges, in particular, develop programs based on the current needs and forecasted growth of business and industry in their immediate service areas. Most track our graduates for months or years after graduation to ensure that they are gaining employment in their fields of study. If data indicate that graduates are not employed in their fields, these colleges can quickly reevaluate offering the program of study, consult with industry professionals to determine if the current curriculum is competitive, and, in some cases, terminate the offering in favor of other fields of study with a higher job placement rate. If *opportunity* can be defined as a pathway to employment, then opportunities in this era of grant funding for high-demand careers, employer reimbursement for higher credentials, a return

DOI: 10.4324/9780429319471-15

to more applied training opportunities, and a growing need for an educated workforce are significant.

Available Funds

Many states have instituted programs to promote college attendance. Tennessee, for example, has the Tennessee Promise program, a last-dollar program that fills in the gaps for two-year college students after any financial aid has been applied, essentially making community college attendance free. In the state of Georgia, lottery-funded grant programs managed by the Georgia Student Finance Commission (GSFC) provide tuition assistance for eligible residents (https://gsfc. georgia.gov/). The Hope Scholarship and the Zell Miller Scholarship provide tuition assistance to Georgia high school graduates pursuing associate's degrees or higher. The Hope Grant and the Hope Career Grant are awarded to any Georgia resident who is pursuing a postsecondary technical certificate of credit or occupational diploma. GSFC programs also provide a $500 tuition voucher to any graduate of a Georgia GED program. These grants pay a significant portion of the tuition each semester in high-demand fields.

All of these opportunities for state grants that do not have to be repaid, unlike a loan, represent a significant opportunity for residents of Georgia. Those who may have thought that college was beyond their reach financially have some incentive to pursue these grants and maintain the grades necessary to continue the funding. In the state's 22 technical colleges, credentials are built in such a way that the shorter credentials are embedded in the longer associate's degree. This method of stacking credentials at community and technical colleges enables students who may not have had the GPA to earn a scholarship to complete a certificate using the Hope Grant, build their GPA, and apply for an associate's degree–level scholarship at a later date. These stackable credentials allow a student to gain employment early on and return for the associate's degree better positioned financially to pay for the remaining semesters. For a student with a good counselor or financial aid advisor, grant and scholarship opportunities can pave the way to an affordable education that leads to a career.

Dual-enrollment programs offer another pathway to a career. In Georgia, for example, dual-enrollment tuition, fees, and textbooks are fully covered for any eligible high school student. As early as tenth grade, students can attend a Georgia technical college and earn transferable general education college credits, technical certificates, and even associate's degrees. Students who take advantage of this offer get a head start on college, often graduating from high school one week and walking across the stage at their local college the next week with an associate's degree. These students can then go straight into the workforce or go on to pursue a bachelor's degree with as much as two years of college credits behind them. Again, for those whose families or counselors understand the benefits and can encourage high school students to pursue this option, the opportunity is there.

Learning on the Job

Another significant opportunity for today's technical college students is the renewed interest in the apprenticeship model of learning. Since the Middle Ages, apprenticeships have been a way of training workers in a hands-on way so that they develop specific technical skills and an understanding of a workplace. In his 2014 State of the Union address, President Barack Obama pointed to apprenticeships as the pathway that could "set a young worker on an upward trajectory for life" (Zients, 2015). The Obama administration led the way in moving apprenticeships into the forefront of discussions about educating skilled workers in the United States with apprenticeship options growing by 75,000 workers from 2014 to 2016 and millions of dollars being put toward the effort (Hanks, 2016; Carlson, 2017; Roepe, 2017; Welton & Owens, 2017). The U.S. Department of Labor provided $90 million to go toward the expansion of apprenticeships, and another $175 million in grants was made available for public-private partnerships to expand apprenticeship opportunities (Roepe, 2017; Welton & Owens, 2017). This focus on apprenticeships at high levels of government and education represent a significant opportunity for the unemployed, underemployed, and undecided to earn a college credential and find rewarding employment.

At community and technical colleges, apprenticeships have taken center stage as one of the initiatives to meet employer demand. For example, as a part of a grant awarded by the U.S. Department of Labor's Employment and Training Administration, the state of Georgia created Georgia WorkSmart, a work-based learning initiative. The goal of Georgia WorkSmart is to promote apprenticeships, co-ops, internships, and other work-based learning models to develop Georgia's workforce (Georgia Department of Economic Development, 2018). Georgia WorkSmart is a strong promoter of the federal Registered Apprenticeship Program. Together with the technical college system, Georgia's Office of Workforce Development helps businesses in the health-care industry, IT industry, and advanced manufacturing create apprenticeship programs that combine on-site curriculum and specialized classroom instruction. Each technical college in the state has an apprenticeship coordinator who works through the various steps and paperwork to arrange for apprenticeships in the college's service area.

Atlanta Technical College, in Atlanta, Georgia, started its own apprenticeship program in the fall of 2017 with the Hyatt Regency in Atlanta. Through this program, students in the college's Hospitality, Restaurant, and Tourism Program work at the Hyatt and receive valuable on-the-job training that is complemented by classroom training at the college's main campus a few miles away. As a part of the Apprenticeship-USA program, this apprenticeship opportunity is being funded by the U.S. Department of Labor.

The COVID-19 national health crisis has only accelerated the need for apprenticeship-style programs. With a critical need for health-care workers, Atlanta Technical College has developed registered apprenticeships with Atlanta's Grady Health System and partnerships with local fire and rescue departments. Students will be employed full time and will attend college part-time for two to four years to complete technical certificates of credit, earn industry-recognized credentials, and gain valuable workplace experience. These are significant opportunities that either did not exist as recently as ten years ago or were not seen by employers as a workable model for developing the workforce.

Concluding Thoughts

From state-funded grant opportunities to a more workforce development focus as a measurement of success, opportunities for college students are strong and are set to become even stronger as the baby boomers continue to retire and more and more middle- to high-skilled positions open up. These opportunities for employment drive the mission of technical colleges nationwide. The role of the college is to make sure that these are not dead-end opportunities. Articulation agreements, two-plus-two programs, apprenticeships, and continued dual-enrollment initiatives will guarantee that two-year college students taking advantage of the current opportunities continue to have a pathway to higher education and personal and professional success.

References

Carlson, S. (2017). Why colleges need to embrace the apprenticeship. *Chronicle of Higher Education* 63 (38): A16–A19.

Georgia Department of Economic Development. (2018). *Georgia Worksmart.* Retrieved on April 15, 2022, from https://www.georgia.org/georgia-worksmart

Hanks, A., (2016). *Now is the time to invest in apprenticeships.* Center for American Progress. Retrieved on April 15, 2022, from https://www.americanprogress.org/issues/economy/reports/2016/11/18/292558/now-is-the-time-to-invest-in-apprenticeships/

Roepe, L. (2017). *Why apprenticeships are taking off.* CityLab. Retrieved on April 15, 2022, from https://www.citylab.com/life/2017/02/why-apprenticeships-are-taking-off/514977/

Welton, A., & Owens, D., (2017). *Scaling up registered apprenticeships at Illinois community colleges.* Champaign, IL: Office of Community College Research and Leadership, University of Illinois at Urbana-Champaign.

Zients, J. (2015). Expanding apprenticeships to invest in American workers. [Blog post]. Retrieved on April 15, 2022, from https://obamawhitehouse.archives.gov/blog/2015/09/10/expanding-apprenticeships-invest-american-workers

What Are the Most Significant Opportunities for Today's College Students?

Jemelleh Coes, PhD (she/her/hers), is Georgia's 2014 Teacher of the Year. She is a Clinical Assistant Professor at the University of Georgia and a Professor of Practice at Mount Holyoke College. She supports K–12 educators in creating environments that prioritize justice-oriented content and practices.

The most significant opportunities for students are to begin to understand the interconnectedness of their roles as future leaders and their responsibility to build a more just society. Next, I expand on the four major opportunities college students have today: to be in community, to critically critique the world, to be a voice, and to figure out what is important.

Be in Community

For the last five years, I have helped to prepare preservice educators for the teaching workforce. By their own admission, many of them have had very limited interactions with people who were different than them. This limited interaction fostered two things: fear and nonchalance. When discussing people different from those in my classroom, one student commented that she feared riding the public bus because the people who were on the bus were poor, and she was concerned about getting robbed or harassed. Another student commented that her parents told her to stay away from the "ghettos" because the people there might rape white women. Her use of the term "ghettos" was in reference to a part of town with a high residential population of people of color, as that is where she was scheduled to do her practicum work, and she was very concerned about having to potentially visit students' homes. One of my students commented that he shouldn't have to worry about all of the problems students of color would bring to school. Their problems were their own, and his responsibility should just be to teach his content.

Dear College Student,

Be in community with people who have different life experiences. People who have different identity markers than you can teach you a great deal about our society. Their experiences, while not monolithic, can shed light on places that have previously been dark for you. Gaining a better understanding of experiences of challenges people have faced, successes they have encountered, and treatment they have received can help you become more thoughtful, compassionate, and sensitive to the society around you. It may help you to better understand why #Blacklivesmatter, #loveislove, #metoo, and other movements are so important.

Critically Critique

I have found that oftentimes when my students get to me from high school, they have not been engaged in the art of critical critique. They have often been taught in ways that encourage them to consume and regurgitate the information they are being given rather than to consume the information, critically assess that information, and then construct new or nuanced ideas. Students are used to taking tests that mundanely ask them to fill in the correct bubble that corresponds with the correct answer as though all of the information on the assessments they are given only have one "best" answer. There is rarely room for further explanation or rationale to help the students demonstrate their ability to think and more importantly critically think. The efforts to train students to think in particular ways are evident even in the categorizations in which many of their tests fall within: "standardized." However, this is not limited to tests. The social curriculum that students are learning is informing the ways in which they interact with others as well as what they believe about themselves. All of these efforts to require regurgitation over thought feel very intentional. They preserve the status quo.

Dear College Student,

Be critical about your learning, past, present, and future. There is information that you have learned in the past that is just wrong. There is also information from your past learning that has been intentionally left out. As you embark on your college journey, fill in those gaps. Be willing to engage with ideas and information that you have never been exposed to before. Be willing to consider multiple perspectives in order to construct new ideas. Be willing to learn beyond the walls and the assignments of your college classroom. Then, be willing to interrogate and critically critique that information as well. The goal of college is to help you become a lifelong thinker, as well as a lifelong learner.

Be a Voice

When students get to college there are literally hundreds of opportunities presented to them at once, and most of these opportunities are presented at the start of the school year during the overwhelming orientation activities. The sheer volume of options can be daunting. This information overload causes some students to withdraw completely while helping others to dive in head first, for good or for bad. Some students end up joining the right groups that help them throughout their lives, others join too many so they never really find a passion, some join groups because they seem like they are the popular ones but have no meaning to the individual joining, still others join none at all as they are faced with too many options and are unsure how to prioritize. None of that is productive.

Dear College Student,

The goal should be to join something of interest that is meaningful to you. Join something that will help make you a better person and potentially have a positive impact on the world. Do not join everything. Be strategic. Take your time. Lend your voice to important causes. Attend a rally or a march related to an issue that is important to your community even if it seems that you will not be impacted by the outcome. (Helpful reminder: You are always impacted by what is going on in our society. Our lives are all inextricably connected.) Remember to preserve your physical and mental well-being, but also remember that there are people you will never know who are counting on you to use your privilege. Remain connected to the causes you lend your voice to.

Figure Out What Is Important

College students today have the unique opportunity to engage with the world better than any generation that came before them. They have instant access to a plethora of information including the whereabouts of thousands of their friends and what those friends are having for dinner, at any given moment. They have the opportunity to build relationships with communities of people who are hundreds and even thousands of miles away from their physical space. They have the opportunity to dialogue with people whose life experiences might have only been encountered through books, television, or other methods of one-way media. To this end, college students today can bridge generations of divide through reflection, understanding, and communication. Beyond an intrinsic, unwavering dedication to humanity, what may drive a desire to do this work is a clear understanding of how each of our lives is connected and tied to the lives of the people with whom we share the world.

Dear College Student,

The generations that have come before you have many talents and resources that you can learn from. You have the technological savvy, situational awareness, and an orientation to community and the collective good that should have long been a model for us in the United States. No. I'm not talking about socialism. I'm talking about humanity. You have the opportunity to learn the truths that the history books "missed," to think beyond your immediate spheres of influence, to make better decisions for our society than the ones that have been made for you. You have the opportunity to help the world see disability as difference, not deficit by demanding a more accessible society. You have the opportunity to destroy gender roles and discrimination by shifting your language and making pronoun distinction as part of any introduction. You have the opportunity to remind us that Black and Brown people deserve to be treated with dignity and respect by using your voice at the ballot box to elect people who support social, environmental, and economic progression for people of color.

It is my belief that college students already know many of the points outlined here. It is my hope that they will lean into their humanity to engage.

What Are the Most Significant Opportunities for Today's College Students?

Roslyn Gowens (she/her/hers) was born and raised in Greenville, South Carolina. She is currently residing in Washington, DC, where she serves as the Fraternity and Sorority Advisor at George Washington University (GW) – overseeing the Interfraternity, National Pan-Hellenic, and Multicultural Greek Councils. She also serves as the advisor to the GW Panhellenic Diversity and Inclusion Leadership Board. Prior to working at GW, Roslyn served as the Fraternity and Sorority Advisor at Western Carolina University (WCU) where she worked with Panhellenic and National Pan-Hellenic Councils. Roslyn completed her undergraduate work at WCU where she earned her bachelor's in criminal justice and political science. She returned to WCU to receive a master's of education with a focus on higher education and student affairs, graduating in 2019.

The opportunity to serve as a small touchpoint during a student's college career has been an opportunity that I will cherish for my lifetime. As a junior student affairs professional, I have worked at a midsize rural public institution and a large private institution positioned in a politically driven urban area. In many ways, the student experiences at these two institutions might seem drastically different, yet when considered holistically, they are more similar than not. Students pursue a college degree (whether associate's, bachelor's, or other) to prepare for the workforce with the skills necessary for success. While this career-driven motivation is foundational, I believe the most significant opportunity for today's college students is the ability to understand themselves and how they fit into society – including an understanding of their own social responsibility. I also believe students have the opportunity to gain the art of networking and how that will impact their future. The tangible thing that students gain is academic knowledge; however, I believe that they should develop in other areas that create a more holistic developmental experience that will help them in life after school. I am a believer that without learning social skills and what it means to become your own person in our complex world, students will not have the necessary skills to survive in the world after college.

During my time as a student affairs professional, I have witnessed students join organizations based on the fact that their values align, the urge to gain a sense of community, and to get involved in extracurricular activities outside of the classroom. After they join organizations, some students decide to run for executive positions. While running and serving in those positions, students gain a better sense of themselves by experiencing what it means to be a leader, the ability to make tough decisions based on what is going on within the organization or the greater community, and the development of collaboration skills as they work with various partners and stakeholders. By taking the opportunity to serve in organizations, students are able to manage conflict and experience what it means to motivate others to accomplish common goals. As an example, I currently advise the Diversity and Inclusion Board of the Greek-lettered council, the Panhellenic Association. The association is made up of 26 sororities that have memberships that spread nationwide. They focus on academic success, leadership, philanthropy, and other common goals. While working through current events of overt racism, national policy changes, the Black Lives Matter movement, and the COVID-19 pandemic – the student leaders have experienced what it means to be a majority white organization charged to take a stance on whether to openly support Black individuals in their council and in their college community. The board of student leaders worked with historical and majority Black organizations on campus to determine what programmatic items they could focus on for the upcoming year that would educate their members internally on diversity, equity, and inclusion; push for policy and bylaw changes that were suitable to current times; and develop a platform to encourage cultivating sisterhood and friendship across cultural and racial backgrounds. During a time when our country is experiencing high racial tensions, a board made up of a majority of white women had to unpack, some for the first time, what it means to be a part of a council that was founded on exclusionary practices and whiteness, one whose history supports racist and oppressed systems and institutions. As they unpacked their thoughts, history, and values, they acknowledged the council's past and ultimately made the decision to join their individual Greek-lettered organizations to bring their diverse perspectives to encourage change. They had to have honest discussions on how to create anti-racist and inclusive spaces to break down traditions that continue to have a negative impact on their members and those who interact with their council. Ultimately, the student leaders are gaining hands-on experience facilitating diversity, equity, and inclusion efforts before joining the workforce.

I believe that as a junior professional it is my responsibility to create a space for diverse perspectives to be expressed and challenged in order for students to gain eye-opening experiences before working full time. During the tumultuous time that our country is facing, students have gained a deeper understanding of themselves through developing programs to break down the different nuances that contribute to some historical yet discriminatory practices. While students experience what it means to be inclusive of ideals and determine what level of social responsibility they want to contribute to society, they are able to start making their own choices without the influence of their parents, guardians, or families. Through the support of peers, campus partners, and faculty and staff, these students learn life lessons that will contribute to their future success.

The opportunity to assist students with determining what major or route they would like to take is a cathartic, yet fulfilling experience and gives me a sense of purpose in the field. Meeting people and forging friendships and mentorships have helped me get to where I am today. As a Black, first-generation college student, I learned that it is important to network and build meaningful relationships with individuals who believe in me and my future success. During college I had professors, staff members, and advisors contribute to my success by teaching me how to engage with potential colleagues and supervisors. They took the time to guide me through what it means to have a strong resume and why it is important to gain experience through interning and creating lasting impressions on potential employers or those who can serve as a reference. Through these experiences, I learned that networking and relationship building are tools that you can take with you wherever you go. Developing the networking skill has informed my practice and served as a guide to encouraging students in the art of human and professional connection that can contribute to future success. Currently, I work in a metro area where students are able to intern on Capitol Hill, at the White House, and at higher-level politically driven entities requiring some levels of security clearance. Previously, at a midsize university serving a majority of lower socioeconomic status students, they did not have the same access to opportunity to intern in places that can enhance their careers in the same way. The unequal access to resources impacted their achievement unless they had connections or other avenues to assist with their success. Access for students who were outside of the majority demographic of the region struggled more with building professional relationships. For college students, opportunities to intern and network are significant, but some students have to be more strategic than others in the way that they gain access to those resources. I view my job as a student affairs professional to be breaking down some of those barriers and creating pathways to success.

Throughout my time as a professional, one characteristic of students has been solidified in my mind – they need to build confidence through their experiences and have someone to help guide them through their journeys. The opportunities that students are presented with during their college experience ultimately position them to be successful in their goals and aspirations if they are able to take advantage of them. From assisting students to unpack privilege, create systems that are equitable through organizational and social change, or creating the road map of success for that student – opportunities in college are needed and impactful. During 2020, while students are navigating high racial tensions, and the impacts of COVID-19, it is important that students are galvanized into action but also make considerations for what their future holds. As a student affairs professional, my philosophy is to use my natural strengths to help students identify their why and then, how. My hope is that students will take with them a few lessons that they have been afforded and use them to gain experience and exposure.

What Are the Most Significant Opportunities for Today's College Students?

Ximena Silva-Avila (she/her/hers or they/them/theirs) is a first-generation college student studying Latinx applied mathematics and statistics, and a political science student at Macalester College in Saint Paul, Minnesota. For the past three years, she has worked with the admissions office to recruit students from marginalized backgrounds to Macalester and serves as a mentor for various students on campus. Through their work, Ximena hopes to empower students on campus to help them achieve personal and professional goals throughout and beyond their college experience.

When choosing a university, I heavily considered the opportunities that my institution could provide to me that matched my needs. As a young person coming from a low-income, immigrant family, I was ready to make sacrifices, such as being separated from the only people I knew in this country. Knowing I would benefit from the small class sizes, generous financial aid packages, and access to significant alumni networks, I was ready to make the sacrifice to get ahead. I do not have the connections that some of my peers, whose families have been in this country for generations, take for granted. I do not have family members spread out around the country who have a network of friends who can help me find an internship, fellowship, or job. All I have is the work ethic my parents instilled in me and the relentless drive that helped me get through one of the most rigorous high schools in the country. Despite the need to move many miles to attend Macalester College, I was set on utilizing college as a way to build networks and gain career momentum. As I drove up to college on the first day of orientation, I heard my brother's voice in the back of my head, "At the end of the day, the only person you have is yourself. Not your friends, not your family. You." I did what a lot of other people I know did; I put on the mask I thought would help me blend in, took a deep breath, and dove in head first. I told myself that if I wanted to make something of my life, I would have to do it all by myself.

During my first year of college, I was only looking at the opportunities that were explicitly career-advancing. I looked for opportunities to dress in my best business casual, shake hands, and schmooze. I joined clubs that would make me look good. I thought building a network and building a community were synonymous. Just like a square can be a rectangle, your community can be your network, but your network cannot always be your community. Your network is focused on advancing you the professional in a professional capacity, but the people who make up your network probably won't know about the skeletons you hide in your closet or even know the face behind the mask we tend to wear. I cannot deny that I do, in fact, schmooze plenty. My network has gotten me far, but my community has gotten me further. I really don't know what my life would look like without the support of other Latinx students, other strong women, other low-income individuals, other survivors, and other people who understand how anxiety and depression feel. It was not the institution but my peers who told me about internships that have turned out to be the most useful. It was my peers who held me as I sobbed when I felt lonely, validated my place at my institution, and told me which professors I should go speak to in order to get more support and encouragement. It was my peers who celebrated me when I won a prestigious national fellowship, not the university. It was my peers who challenged my way of thinking, albeit it was often in the context of a course we were taking. More importantly, it was my peers who showed me I did not have to think I was alone because I was not alone. It has been my peers who have taught me to be a better person and see the world in such a positive and supportive light that has been invaluable in my career thus far.

I wish I could go back and tell freshman Ximena to spend more time with her peers and less time crying alone in the shower. Despite what I was telling myself, I was not alone in feeling inadequate. I wish I could tell myself to forgo the networking event that will "eventually help me with my career" and go hang out with my friends across the hall who are helping me now. I wish I spent less worrying about others judging me for being too nerdy and had just invited people to join me at all those free talks sponsored by the university. I wish I could tell myself to close the laptop and take a nap or eat or shower because there is nothing more important than my own health. I am so grateful I worked over 90 hours a week between two jobs, heading two campus organizations, and taking four classes during the same semester because I learned a lot through all those opportunities, but I now realize it was not worth it. Doing all of this meant that I did not have enough energy to actually enjoy the process. I tell as many first-year students as I can the things I wish I could have told myself because I know some people need to hear them.

I cannot quite pinpoint when I accepted that I needed people in my life not only to support me but also whom I can support. Needing and wanting people around and being in community does not make you weak and can be a source of incredible strength. More than anything, helping others is a way that I can pay it forward. By sharing my experiences, I feel like I can prevent others from going through the same things I did by helping provide some coping skills, validation, and context to the whole college experience. Taking the opportunities to learn about what inspires others, what makes them happy, what makes them sad, what makes them laugh and smile, to really get to know them, allows me to better understand myself. That is community building. This is how we increase access to opportunities for our people.

As I reflect on what I have written, I would be a bit upset if I were reading this. I did not name how taking advantage of internships or engaging in student organizations can lead to meaningful college experiences. Instead, I have said that making friends is the most important opportunity for college students. Therein lies the beauty of going to college. Once students have a degree, society has deemed them employable and able to get a job somewhere. Through classes, students meet people who have similar interests and might be able to open professional doors for each other. Having the right people around during college for deep relationships is more important than acquaintances we meet once and connect with on social media platforms and think are our network. Why? Friends are the ones offering up their couches when we need a place to stay, while our network probably will only give a recommendation for a great hotel. Friends go with us to find a new outfit for an important event; networks might like a social media post about it. Friends are there when we get the job and when we do not; where will our network be when we stumble? As students today we have a significant opportunity to create relationships that are deep, meaningful, and can sustain us through the highs and lows of not only college but life. Making these deep and lasting connections requires intentionality and vulnerability. Building communities requires energy, but students are not pushed to develop them as much as we are pushed to build our network. Yet, we need our friends, and college provides us a chance to create lasting and deep relationships that end in community. Although there are so many impressive national and local fellowships to take advantage of in a multitude of disciplines, I still believe that taking the time to know, understand, and learn from our peers in order to cultivate community is the best opportunity students have in college. There is no predicting the power and positive influence this community will have on their lives, but the truth is that this community can prove that just because you can do it alone, does not mean you have to.

12

ANALYSIS

What Are the Most Significant Opportunities for Today's College Students?

Karen Kurotsuchi Inkelas and Terrence Hanlon

Karen Kurotsuchi Inkelas, PhD (she/her) is a Professor in the Higher Education Program in the School of Education & Human Development at the University of Virginia. Dr. Inkelas is the founding Principal Investigator of the National Study of Living-Learning Programs, and lead author of the book, *Living-Learning Communities that Work: A Research-Based Model for Design, Delivery, and Assessment.* She currently serves as the Research Director for UVA's Crafting Success for Underrepresented Scientists and Engineers Project, which examines ways to reduce inequities in STEM education. She is also the Research Director of Undergraduate Initiatives for the UVA Contemplative Sciences Center, and focuses on how mindfulness and contemplative practices can facilitate students' overall well-being. In Fall 2018, she became the sixth Principal of the University of Virginia Hereford Residential College. Dr. Inkelas obtained her B.A. and MSEd. from Northwestern University and her PhD from the University of Michigan.

Terrence Hanlon (he/him/his) received his PhD from the Higher Education Program in the School of Education and Human Development at the University of Virginia. Mr. Hanlon has served in various roles across higher education, including positions in residential life, campus activities, health promotion, intercollegiate athletics, university strategic planning, and internal and external consulting. Mr. Hanlon earned his Master of Arts degree in Higher Education Administration from the Lynch School of Education at Boston College and a Bachelor of Science in Economics degree from the Wharton School at the University of Pennsylvania, concentrating in Management, Marketing, and Legal Studies.

DOI: 10.4324/9780429319471-16

While preparing this chapter, we were still in the midst of the COVID-19 pandemic, which resulted in most residentially based colleges and universities being forced to move their courses online and significantly curtailing – if offering them at all – their social events and informal gatherings. Thus, the question of what constitutes an "opportunity" took on a glass-half-full versus half-empty connotation: for many, simply the end of the pandemic and the ability to resume normal operations would be an "opportunity" after living our lives in isolation. For others, the lessons from the pandemic may have given us the "opportunity" to rethink residentially based education going forward. Either way, the chance to think about future opportunities in higher education is a profoundly optimistic endeavor, and the four authors tasked with this responsibility were both inspirational and aspirational, even as some of the essays were written prior to the COVID-19 pandemic.

Summary of Themes From Four Essays

The four authors chose to focus on a broad array of opportunities in the higher education landscape. Caroline B. Angelo, executive vice president for academic and student affairs at Atlanta Technical College, identified two primarily pragmatic opportunities for college students: the ability to garner more funds to attend college and more apprenticeship experiences for hands-on learning. She identified several grant programs (as opposed to loans) in the state of Georgia, where she is located, for eligible residents. She also described nontraditional ways to earn college credits while fulfilling other obligations. For example, the state of Georgia's dual-enrollment program allows high school students to attend technical colleges and earn transferable college credit, technical certificates or diplomas, or associate's degrees. In addition, students in Georgia can participate in paid apprenticeships and receive on-the-job training while earning credits toward a degree. The challenge, as Angelo asserted, was to ensure that all students learn about and take advantage of these funds and apprenticeships, especially historically marginalized groups for whom these opportunities may be of greatest benefit.

The other three authors wrote about opportunities that were more personal than vocational. Jemelleh Coes, 2014 Georgia Teacher of the Year and clinical assistant professor at the University of Georgia, outlined two intertwined opportunities for today's college students: the ability to gain an understanding of different life experiences and to learn how to think critically. The former, she wrote, helps students to appreciate diversity in all of its forms, including social and cultural backgrounds, as well as personal and political ideologies. The latter, she argued, helps students become more well-rounded, intellectually aware, and better positioned for a life of continual learning. The combination of appreciating diversity and thinking critically, she concluded, would position college students to use their degrees and places in society to better their communities and futures.

Roslyn Gowens, fraternity and sorority advisor at George Washington University, focused on students' development in the opportunities she identified for college students. She saw college as a time in which students can learn about their own identities or the ability to "understand one's self and how one fits into society" (p. 148). The role of a student affairs professional, like herself, is to facilitate this development within each student. This facilitation may turn into an opportunity, such as when a student learns about diverse perspectives when taking on a leadership role in their cocurricular or extracurricular pursuits. Similarly, helping students to extend themselves into new and uncharted experiences can become an opportunity to network and build relationships. She concluded with the challenge (not unlike Angelo's caution) that student affairs professionals face: to ensure that all students are able to access these experiences during college so that they can equally capitalize on the opportunities that arise from them.

Finally, Ximena Silva-Avila, a first-generation, Latinx, applied mathematics/ statistics and political science major at Macalester College, described an evolution in her own thinking about the opportunities that arise for college students like herself. At first, she reflected, she might have answered this prompt by underscoring the importance of networking and establishing relationships that would help her with her future vocational pursuits. In fact, she focused on those networking opportunities in the early portion of her time in college. However, as her college experience progressed, she began to feel that personal, and not professional, support from her peers was what was important. She began to see that making deep friendships and knowing that "people have your back" were more important to her than surface connections she made at networking events. Accordingly, she encouraged future college students to seek out those meaningful personal bonds.

Comparison and Contrast of Themes

The four essays differed substantially in form and tone, but they did share some themes in common. For example, they all included opportunities that were meant to be of use to students long after their time in college had ended. Angelo emphasized the utility of apprenticeships, not only as a way to earn credit while working but also because they were beneficial in learning new skills that were directly applicable to students' intended vocations. Coes stressed that appreciating diversity and thinking critically were transferrable skills in a wide variety of circumstances, most particularly in contributing to the betterment of society. Gowens mentioned that the development of leadership skills in college could be used to build relationships for the future and help students better understand what they valued. Finally, despite being the most recent to graduate from college herself, Silva-Avila came to understand the vital importance of close friendships and support – not just during college but while one is making her way in the world.

Indeed, human connection was an important aspect in all four essays. Angelo focused on human connection through an experiential form of education she found was gaining functionality in college curricula: the apprenticeship. Unlike formal learning that might take place through solitary activities like reading or laboratory science, apprenticeships are inherently social in that students experience vocational work in its social setting and are typically mentored by a more seasoned professional. Coes argued that being among people from diverse backgrounds helps students better appreciate different life experiences; thus, this type of learning can only take place when in the company of others. Gowens, while focusing on how individual students might gain increased insights into their own identities, believed that identity development was attained interpersonally – through the building of relationships and the servant leadership of others. Finally, in what was the most explicit reference to human connection, Silva-Avila drew strength and purpose through her kinship and support from her friends in college.

A final common thread among the four essays was the concept of social justice. All four essays stressed the importance of students taking advantage of the plethora of opportunities afforded to them while they are in college. However, they all also warned about two necessary steps in order for such opportunities to be capitalized upon: students' own agency and the equity with which students can access the resources. Coes and Silva-Avila strongly encouraged future students to see college as more than a series of courses to take and pass; instead, they admonished future students to exploit the riches of the college experience and support others in the process – Coes in terms of co- and extracurricular activities and Silva-Avila in terms of supportive friends. Even more importantly, Angelo and Gowens warned that institutions must work with intentionality to ensure that all students can benefit from the great opportunities they can experience while in college. Such opportunities cannot be offered haphazardly or on a first-come, first-serve basis, nor can they be provided only to those whose high social capital backgrounds predisposed them to knowing about the opportunities in the first place. Instead, colleges and universities must reorient themselves to ensure that all students stand to benefit – especially among those students who are the least likely to participate in them due to their exclusion in the past.

The ways in which the essays differed depended largely upon the viewpoints of the authors. The senior administrators, particularly Angelo, tended to emphasize broad policy opportunities, such as increased access and outcomes through increased funding and employment prospects. Moreover, the two administrators, Angelo and Gowens, described the roles that states and institutions play in providing opportunities for students, whether it be funding programs, apprenticeship experiences, co- and extracurricular programming, or leadership possibilities. On the other hand, the student perspective provided by Silva-Avila focused more heavily on interpersonal relationships as opportunities. This makes intuitive sense: When characterizing the college experience, students typically think of their own experiences and extrapolate from their own recollections.

Conversely, those who have worked at universities may tend to conceive of opportunities more often in the form of institutional responsibilities. And the more senior the level of administrator, the more likely they are to discuss general and wide-ranging opportunities, like statewide grant and apprenticeship programs. Indeed, the opportunities depicted by the four authors align very well with the backgrounds and experiences they bring to higher education.

Stakeholder Perspectives

In discussing the opportunities available to college and university students, each of the essayists presents their assessments from their unique positions as student (Silva-Avila), student affairs administrator (Gowens), educator (Coes), and executive officer (Angelo). As previously discussed, common themes bridge the four essays; however, each author's role in institutions of higher education shapes their assessments.

Silva-Avila, as a student, elaborates on the differences between the opportunities encouraged and provided by the institution and the opportunities created by being a member of a community of peers. More specifically, Silva-Avila questions the efficacy of institutional emphases on networking, leadership in student organizations, and overall resume building. Instead, Silva-Avila advocates for students, especially fellow first-generation students, to allocate greater time and energy toward building concrete and personal friendships with peers, which can lead to vocational opportunities.

Another first-generation student, Gowens similarly advocates for relationship building, but, as an administrator, reinforces the importance of networking and taking advantage of institutionally provided opportunities and resources rather than building friendships. Although recently finishing coursework as a master's student, Gowens does not discuss any in-class aspects of the higher education experience, whereas Silva-Avila briefly touches on the demands of coursework. Gowens focuses the essay on extracurricular activities expected of a student affairs administrator.

Coes, as both an educational consultant and faculty member, provides a more abstract viewpoint on the opportunities afforded to today's college students. Focusing on values of interconnectedness and critical thinking, Coes calls for students to engage in their local communities and work toward the common good. The only concrete opportunity mentioned by Coes is through a critique of activity fairs during orientations and how students may not join the most meaningful extracurricular organizations.

At the most senior level, in contrast to Coes's more theoretical perspective as a faculty member, Angelo only discusses concrete opportunities for students in Georgia's technical colleges. Given the position of serving as an executive vice president for a two-year public institution, Angelo elaborates on what public grant funding opportunities are available for students, what credit-earning opportunities are available for prospective students, and what cocurricular vocational learning opportunities exist for current students. Furthermore, rather than solely focusing on the positive impacts for individual students, such as increased access, reduced cost, and improved job placement, Angelo provides the perspective of a senior administrator of a state institution on how these opportunities can also positively impact the state of Georgia.

Across the four essays, each author provides an assessment of the opportunities available for students, and while the perspectives ranged from abstract to concrete, and institutionally provided to peer-based, none of the authors provided an overarching summary of all of the available opportunities for students. Each author's essay depends heavily on the role each author serves in the higher education landscape. With the faculty member advocating for opportunities to embolden critical thinking, the student impressing upon peers to find their own friendships, the student affairs administrator calling for student leaders to take ownership over racial inequity, and the upper-level administrator describing how students can attend, afford, and succeed in college, each essay highlights the author's perspective and responsibilities.

While these authors' roles intersect and collaborate in higher education, their essays rarely feature discussion regarding opportunities presented by other specific stakeholders. Rather, across the essays, the opportunities discussed focus more on opportunities that exist extramurally or that are provided by the faceless concept of "the institution." Although the essayists do not discuss opportunities provided by other higher education stakeholders, such as their fellow authors, the similarity in themes highlights overlapping objectives and aspirations. Even without a student, a student affairs administrator, a faculty member, or a senior administrator discussing the exact same opportunities, the shared themes of engagement, community building, and social justice reflect common purposes and even encourage further opportunities for collaboration and communication.

Relationship to Literature and Theory

From a theoretical perspective, certain well-known theories of student development and engagement mirror the narratives presented across the four essays. Across the four assessments of opportunities for students, the essayists' commentary centered around engagement, community building, and social justice. Regarding engagement, the narratives presented by the four authors reflect the literature surrounding Astin's (1984) theory of student involvement and Kuh's (2008) identification of high-impact educational activities. For community building, the essayists' emphasis on students taking individual ownership toward understanding deeper interpersonal connections shares sentiments with Chickering and Reisser's (1993) vectors of identity development. Lastly, the essayists' use of the language of positive social change through collective action parallels the social change model of leadership development (Komives & Wagner, 2009), specifically the values of citizenship and change.

Astin's (1984) theory of student involvement lays a foundation for understanding how a student's level of engagement in taking the opportunities presented during college helps determine the impact those opportunities have upon the student. The postulates of Astin's (1984) theory highlight the diversity of college student involvement, whether general or specialized, quantitatively measured or qualitatively, or with a high or low degree of involvement. Furthermore, the postulates stipulate that the amount of learning and development gained by the student is proportional to the amount of involvement and that institutions should work toward policies and programs that increase student involvement. Silva-Avila, providing the perspective of a student, specifies the finite time that college students must allocate. Specifically, in enumerating the multiple jobs, extracurricular activities, and time demands of coursework, Silva-Avila believes that the effort expended in those jobs, clubs, and classes was not as fruitful as time spent with peers. Silva-Avila provides a perspective similar to Astin (1997) in that a student's peer group is the single greatest influence on growth and development during a student's undergraduate years. Additionally, Silva-Avila argues that institutional efforts for vocational development were not as engaging and did not increase student involvement.

Across the literature about opportunities for college students, Kuh's (2008) exploration of high-impact activities serves as a gold standard to measure what opportunities institutions should provide for students in which to engage. Given the positive impacts realized from high-impact educational practices, one could argue that the opportunities described across the four essays should mirror or at least heavily draw from the list of practices endorsed by the Association of American Colleges and Universities (AAC&U, 2014).

However, the four essay authors only highlighted the opportunities for internships and career-oriented learning opportunities and the need for students to engage in their communities to better understand the diversity of the local and global communities. Regarding internships and preprofessional education, Angelo presents detailed information on the apprenticeship programs available to Georgia students and the intended outcomes for both students and the state's economy. Gowens and Silva-Avila discuss the importance of internships and building meaningful connections that can assist with the procurement of internship placements, but also highlight the inequality of opportunities that exist due to individual student circumstances and institutional resourcing. While Coes does not mention the importance of internship or preprofessional opportunities, Coes emphasizes the importance for students to take the opportunities to engage with their community and critically examine the communities around them and take active participation roles in positive social change. Gowens explains how students in Greek-letter organizations seized the opportunity of recent events to reexamine and challenge racist power structures present in their organizations.

While these four essays discuss the two high-impact practices of internships and engaging with the diverse local and global communities, the essayists did not mention first-year seminars, common intellectual experiences, learning communities, writing-intensive coursework, collaborative projects, undergraduate research, cocurricular service learning, or capstone courses and projects (Kuh, 2008). Outside of preprofessional educational opportunities, no classroom opportunities are discussed, including by Coes, a faculty member. Instead, Coes discusses how extracurricular activity in engaging with the diverse communities surrounding institutions of higher education could positively impact classroom learning, such as increasing students' awareness of and compassion toward different people's challenges.

Aside from Angelo's essay detailing the opportunities for access, affordability, and preprofessional learning, the other three essayists provide rich descriptions of how students can take ownership over opportunities for community building and can better understand the interconnected nature of the world around them. Gowen highlights the importance of college as a time for students, specifically traditional-aged students, to make their own choices of how to engage with the community around them, rather than relying on family or guardians. Coes implores students to use individual talents and privileges to work toward a shared common good, underpinned by an interconnection between the lives of community members. Silva-Avila recommends that students take the opportunities to build deep connections with others by which support can be given and received.

The calls to action for students to take these opportunities to develop their purpose, discover their identity, and grow their understanding of the interconnected world around them as they develop mature relationships mirror the developmental vectors presented by Chickering and Reisser (1993). As Gowen and Coes encourage students to find ways to personally engage with their community and find avenues for change, the authors mirror the developmental vectors of "establishing identity" and "developing purpose" as students seek to find their role in the community and how they will contribute (Chickering & Reisser, 1993). With a focus toward community, as students take the opportunities to engage with their community and build strong personal relationships with peers, as suggested in the essay of Silva-Avila, students seem to be "moving through autonomy toward interdependence" and "developing mature interpersonal relationships" (Chickering & Reisser, 1993). Chickering and Reisser's (1993) emphasis on the notion of interdependence and interpersonal relationships underscores the understanding that students' lives are interconnected and highlights the importance of the role of community in a student's development.

Lastly, the essayists' descriptions of opportunities for students to promote positive social change call to mind the social change model of leadership development (Komives & Wagner, 2009). The social change model, featuring the individual values of consciousness of self, congruence, and commitment, the group values of collaboration, common purpose, and controversy with civility, as well as the society/community value of citizenship, centers on positive social change (Komives & Wagner, 2009). For these essays, the values of citizenship and change ring through many of the authors' depictions of student opportunities. While Angelo's essay includes themes of social mobility through increased access and affordability and reflects an overall goal of positive social change, the other essays focus more on how students accepting opportunities can work toward improving society. Silva-Avila, for example, describes how students taking opportunities to learn about and from others leads to greater community building and increased opportunities, especially for first-generation or underserved populations. Gowens identifies the opportunity for college students to understand themselves and their social responsibility as the "most significant opportunity for today's college students" (p. 148). Furthermore, Gowens explains how student leaders can and should work toward combating systemic racism and injustice by promoting inclusivity and equity. Coes, as previously mentioned, provides the most direct call to action, encouraging students to "understand the interconnectedness of their roles as future leaders and their responsibility to build a more just society" (p. 145). Through taking greater action as engaged citizens, Coes calls on students to improve the world for others through understanding the interconnected nature of society.

Across the essays, given the nature of the student opportunities mentioned, student development theories provide the most foundational connections to higher education literature. From the basis of Astin's (1984) theory of student involvement and Kuh's (2008) identification of high-impact educational activities, these four essays provide an insight into how stakeholders view the importance of student engagement and the activities toward which students should direct their finite time and energy. Through the lens of Chickering and Reisser's (1993) vector model and the social change model of leadership development (Komives & Wagner, 2009), the essayists' calls for students to take ownership of the opportunities presented and work toward greater interconnectedness and positive social change are better understood.

Concluding Thoughts

Overall, from these four essays, stakeholders of higher education hold diversified views over what could be considered an opportunity for today's college students. For a first-generation student in Minnesota, the opportunities presented by the institution pale in comparison to the opportunities presented by the community at the institution. For a senior administrator in Georgia, the opportunities for today's college students begin during high school, as students have opportunities to increase the affordability of a degree while also building their capacity for specialized knowledge. For a student affairs administrator in the District of

Columbia, opportunities that build a student's capacity for socially just leadership, as well as vocational networks, are paramount. Finally, for an education faculty member in Georgia, the opportunities are almost entirely extracurricular and must be sought out by students wishing to make a positive difference in their communities.

While there may be disparate perceptions about the opportunities available for students, questions posed about equitable availability of opportunities and resources underpin all of the essays. How can student affairs administrators, faculty, senior administrators, student leaders, and other stakeholders of higher education work to ensure students of all institutions of higher education have equitable access to opportunities, especially those high-impact practices described by Kuh (2008)? Given all of the resources currently available to students at their fingertips (given access to the requisite technology and high-speed connections), how are opportunities offered to students? Does increasing and improving technology allow for opportunities to be more equitable and irrespective of institutional type and resources?

Also, as illustrated by Silva-Avila and Coes, many opportunities for today's college students exist extramurally from the institution. As shifts in technology and networking continue to materialize, will the moniker of "college student" be necessary for individuals to take advantage of these resources? Does enrollment in an institution of higher learning serve as the prerequisite for an individual to be eligible for certain learning or developmental opportunities if they are entirely housed online? In what ways will the roles of faculty, administrators, and staff shift to better serve these individuals accessing these opportunities?

For all of these questions, more engagement with the stakeholders of higher education will allow for greater insight into the future. As the higher education landscape continues to shift, including in response to COVID-19, stakeholders will continue to evaluate what opportunities are available to college students and what needs should be met. As these four essay responses illustrate, college students have a plethora of opportunities available to them currently, whether provided by the institution or not. Across all of the essays, the most important aspect of any of these opportunities is how students take advantage of the opportunities presented to them.

References

Association of American Colleges & Universities. (2014, June 24). *High-Impact educational practices* [Text]. Association of American Colleges & Universities. Retrieved on April 15, 2022 from https://www.aacu.org/node/4084

Astin, A. (1984). Student involvement: A development theory for higher education. *Journal of College Student Development, 40*, 518–529.

Astin, A. W. (1997). *What matters in college?: Four critical years revisited* (1st edition). Jossey-Bass.

Chickering, A. W., & Reisser, L. (1993). *Education and identity* (2nd edition). Jossey-Bass.

Komives, S. R., & Wagner, W. (2009). *Leadership for a better world: Understanding the social change model of leadership development* (1st edition). Jossey-Bass.

Kuh, G. D. (2008). *High-impact educational practices: What they are, who has access to them, and why they matter.* Association of American Colleges.

QUESTION 5

What Can You Do to Support Today's College Students?

13

WHAT CAN YOU DO TO SUPPORT TODAY'S COLLEGE STUDENTS?

Stakeholder Essays

Anonymous Parents, Talia Bailey, Pressley Rankin and Vernon Wall

What Can You Do to Support Today's College Students?

> **Anonymous Parents*** (she/her/hers and he/him/his). The parent and step-parent are both North Carolina natives. The parent (father) got his start as a serial entrepreneur in the software industry. He left that field for a bit to become an organic farmer and restaurateur and still serves as an angel investor and consultant for tech companies and venture funds. The stepparent has worked in government, fundraising, and politics. She co-manages the organic farm and restaurant while also being a successful cookbook author. Their children grew up in affluent households, splitting time between the farm and the home of their biological mother.
>
> *In order to protect the privacy of their children, the authors have opted for anonymity in their response. This allowed them to speak the most freely about their experiences and insights.

We are writing as parent and stepparent of four children who have all been educated, to varying degrees, at public universities in the South. We also have regular and in-depth contact with college students on a daily basis in our business lives. We have owned two restaurants in college towns and employed hundreds of college students in both. We also own an online farmers market and delivery business, and the changing nature of delivery schedules means that our delivery staff tends to be a mix of retirees and college students – always an interesting balance of personalities. And, finally, we live on and own an organic farm that

DOI: 10.4324/9780429319471-18

supplies our farmers market and restaurants. Many of the people who work at the farm are college interns. So, whether we like it or not (and it is a mix of both), we seem to constantly be surrounded by students.

How to support the college students in our lives is a giant question – one that we struggle with as parents and as employers. The simple answer is, be there – be physically available to the student and provide a judgment-free space for them to learn. It gets tricky there, though. Every student and set of needs are different, and resisting judgment is often quite difficult.

As parents, we have raised four very different children, who all experienced college in incredibly different ways. The lesson we learned again and again with all four is that we needed to be present and do our best to support their ideas, even when they seemed far-fetched. We also learned that there are times when you need to step in and help get things back on track and other moments when you just need to offer encouragement or a little incentive to do better.

Our oldest is the quintessential oldest child. He is organized, in charge, possessive, and the best at everything he does. We never had to do much to motivate him, we just needed to acknowledge and celebrate the awards and pay for the many opportunities that came his way. He needed us, and his professors, to be open and listen to his many ideas and questions. Further, he needed the space to learn any and everything he wanted, whether it was permission to take an extra class at another university in upper-level stats or permission and support to travel abroad for a semester. His hard work and our support paid off. He's still a student – in his last year of a fully funded PhD program. And he plans to stay in academia. It worked for him.

Our second born looked at school and learning from a very different point of view. He's always the friendliest person in the room. He's the life of a party and a pretty decent athlete. He also suffers from a mild case of dyslexia that he mostly conquered as a child in intensive one-on-one therapy, but it occasionally rears its head, and he was worried about it going into college. This child wanted to attend a major state institution, where many of his friends were going, but he didn't have the grades in high school and honestly was not academically prepared. He ended up at a smaller regional (and rural) comprehensive institution with plans to transfer later. The things he needed from us and the folks at his institution varied as he settled into college. Before he even started classes, we took him to campus to meet with advisors who could help him navigate classes and were there if he had issues in class because of his dyslexia. Just knowing that he had a special advisor to talk to made him feel more comfortable. He continued to visit the same advisor all four (well, 4.5) years he was there. She always made him feel better, even if it was only having someone to talk to. Unfortunately, this child ran into some trouble with the law at the end of his freshman year, so his plans to transfer derailed. That was an especially tough moment for him. In that instance, and for the next couple of years, what he needed from us was encouragement and incentives. He needed us reminding him that he was smart enough and could make it through four years in the mountains, and he also needed the incentive to force himself to do better. We made him a deal that if he kept his grades up and stayed out of trouble, we would pay for him to study abroad in London, and when his semester was done, we would come tour around Europe with him. He never made anything under a B after that and started finding ways to enjoy the rural environment and even some of what he was learning.

Birth order theories are sometimes very on point. Our third child, on good days, is everyone's best buddy and on bad days is the lost child. Growing up, he wanted to tag along and do everything his older brothers did. If that didn't work, he would do what I was doing or what his dad was doing. He always wanted to be with someone and directly intensely engaged with that person. He was not a self-starter and was not the kid to go off and play alone or read in a corner. As a child, "being there" for him was obvious – you just needed to let him be with you. As a young adult, and especially as a college student, being there for him was much harder. He no longer wanted to just hang out with us; we weren't very fun (by his definition), and he did not enjoy anything about his academic life at college. Unfortunately, he never found a faculty or staff member that he connected to and never felt connected to a class. Even more unfortunately, he did feel very connected to his fraternity and their party lifestyle. His partying landed him in jail, in the hospital, in fights, but never on the honor roll. He never had what most would call a successful academic semester, no matter how many times we tried to intervene, discipline, or incentivize. After multiple starts and stops and dropouts, the best way we could be there for him was to acknowledge that it was ok for him to not be a student. It took a bumpy adjustment period, but he has a good steady job now that didn't require the degree he never really wanted, but we did.

Our youngest is our only girl and fits right in that birth order mold, as well. She always gets what she wants, but she's not loud about it and is quite happy in her own corners. The thing she has always needed and wanted most from us is space. She wants to know we are around if she needs us, but she doesn't want us, or anyone else, that close. We made her the same deal we made her two older brothers – keep the grades up, and you can study abroad and travel. That was all she needed. She did what she had to do with as little input from us or her teachers as possible and headed out. She is just two months out of college, so the verdict is still out on what she will do with her four years of learning Italian at a flagship state university in the South. She may be in Italy next month. And we will still just need to remind her that we are around if she needs us.

In a strange twist, the physical needs of the college students who work for us are generally much greater than our own children. Farm interns need us to be physically beside them teaching them how to use the tractor, feed the pigs, and pick the tomatoes. They need explanations of how to do something, and then they need to see it done. It's why things like farm internships exist. You can read about driving a tractor all semester long, but you don't know how the shifting works or the scary sound the plow makes when it drops unless you physically do it. More accredited programs should probably offer options for students to go out and get their hands dirty, whatever their field might be.

Another thing our intern students need is the room to learn from experience and have room to make mistakes without terrible consequences. If they leave the gate open and the cows get out, they need to get the cows all back in, but they don't need to be screamed at for making the mistake. Once you've left that fence unlatched once, you never forget again.

The hardest thing, and the thing our student interns seem to need the most, is access to us personally. We have tried many times over the years to create boundaries between our public and private lives, but they never stick. We live in the middle of the farm, and our lives always end up somewhat entwined. So, we cook dinners; we tell stories; we take them fishing and to ball games; we let them talk. In many cases, coming to live on our farm is the first unstructured space they have ever lived in. They somehow feel freer here, maybe it's the wide-open spaces. We have often ended up as practice stand-ins for parents as they try out a coming-out speech or an "I'm dropping out of school to be a farmer" idea. And all we can do is listen and accept. In the end, it's probably all we should be doing for college students anyway.

What Can You Do to Support Today's College Students?

Talia Bailey (she/her/hers) was raised in Washington state and is a second-year student at Cincinnati State Technical and Community College majoring in cybersecurity. She is actively involved in student organizations such as the Gamer's Club and the Leadership Club. She volunteers to help the institution any chance she can by helping with recruitment events, representing the student voice, and encouraging students to get involved on campus. She does her best to help other students and listen to their concerns so she can bring attention to those concerns in order to facilitate change where it is needed.

My name is Talia Bailey, and I am a first-year student at Cincinnati State Technical and Community College. I've been asked to write this piece due to my active involvement on campus (prior to the coronavirus pandemic). I am earning credit toward an associate's of applied science, specifically in computer networking engineering technology with a concentration in cybersecurity. I am also earning credit toward a leadership certificate. This is my third time attending college, and I have made an extra effort to get out of my comfort zone and network in ways I previously have not, including engaging in student organizations. Some of my leadership roles throughout campus include being president of the Cincinnati State Gamer's Club and communications coordinator for Leadership

Club. Additionally, I have been energetically involved with student activities in general. I took on these roles not only to help my confidence but also to help other students. My experiences have shaped how I feel about the cruciality of campus resources and student opportunities in order for students to succeed and go above and beyond expectations.

Something that needs more exposure when discussing this is the importance of counseling services. Mentally, I would not be where I am at today had it not been for free counseling services provided by my current school. I have battled with depression and anxiety since childhood and in the last six years post-traumatic stress disorder. When I first moved to Cincinnati, I was upset because I had moved four times previously in the year, left some of my family and friends behind, and had a stress fracture in my foot from a previous job. My confidence was shot, and the counseling services helped me get a hold of my anxiety and cope healthily. Having counseling included in student tuition is extremely important because many students struggle with paying for books, supplies, lab fees, etc., and worrying about whether they can afford to take care of their mental health should not be added to that list.

Certainly, there is simply not enough exposure when it comes to the importance of counseling resources. Many students feel uncomfortable discussing counseling and like they will be judged if they use them. Many college students do not seek help because of this fear of judgment, and some resources come with more of a stigma than others. For example, I feel at times the counseling center is brought up and briefly discussed because instructors *have* to speak about which campus resources are available. Most know what syllabus day is like: tedious and boring. Everyone wants it over with, but discussing the importance of mental health continuously throughout a student's time on campus is so important. When I have held conversations with peers, many did not even know that the service is offered for free as part of our tuition. In fact, a peer of mine during my first semester is who guided me and told me that the counseling center was included in our tuition. The key to normalizing this is to keep talking about resources, whether a student or instructor, and letting students and our peers know that they will not be judged, most are confidential in nature, and resources are always available.

While it may be difficult for instructors to connect, it can make a huge difference to a student to see a professor trying to relate to them. Most likely, a student has, at some point, had an instructor who did not take the time to understand their students. During my first attempt at college, I had a math instructor come into the room, set her things on her desk, and tell the class, "It's my last semester teaching here, so don't expect much help." What a wonderful first impression, right? It was one of the first classes I had ever failed. One, because that abrupt introduction immediately turned me off from seeking any type of support from her, and two, it was extremely difficult to go to the math lab. The lab only had specific and short times they were open, and appointments booked up quickly.

I compare this to a positive instructor I had last semester who continues to push me to achieve my goals, not to give up, and provides leads on new opportunities. Just because a class ends does not mean the student interaction has to end as well.

To students reading this, the more you put an effort into forming a relationship and networking on campus, the more others will be willing to reciprocate the effort. In my experience, students typically learn a great deal from other students, and this should be encouraged regardless of being at a community college or a university. I have come to realize students are typically more receptive to help when it comes from friends. An instructor could talk all day about a specific resource on campus; however, once a student can speak to the validity of it among friends, it begins to hold a different weight. Having other students share their experiences with others makes a big impact because it not only makes them seem more relatable and less intimidating but can also encourage strength and courage, and let them know that they are not alone in their thoughts and feelings while attending college. Had it not been for instructor and peer encouragement, I most likely would not have taken on leadership opportunities while in college because I was incredibly shy and did not believe in myself at the time.

Finally, not only do activities and opportunities increase student involvement, but they also help student retention because they are activities that appeal to students' needs outside of studying, which helps sustain their motivation and interest. Having opportunities for student leadership (such as officer positions for clubs and volunteering opportunities) encourages students to achieve higher-level thinking, assess their critical problem-solving skills, and be creative with outside-the-box thinking. These opportunities are rewarding because club and organizational events normally offer stress relief for many students, not just those who worked on the event. Employer opportunities, such as co-ops, internships, and career fairs, that benefit the future of students can encourage students to keep striving in their studies because they can visualize themselves in the workplace. Resources on campus that further help with future employment such as resume building, interview attire, and what to expect after graduation also help a student feel less lonely in the process while also being supportive of furthering one's education. Offering hours and adequate help in all tutoring centers and writing labs can also make or break a student's success. As with my story about a previous math lab I have been to, not having the appropriate amount of help can make a student's willingness to seek help fade. Instructors and students should all do their part in reassuring that it does not matter how well one does in school, tutoring centers are for any and all levels.

Altogether, awareness of resources and encouraging peer-to-peer involvement is a great start when discussing how to support college students because it lets them know there is nothing wrong with receiving help. Do not let pride get in the way of success. It is not a sign of weakness to ask for help but shows determination, readiness, and strength to better oneself. College can be intimidating, tiresome, stressful, and it can be difficult to find the motivation to keep going, but it is also a fun and diverse experience that helps us grow in ways we never thought possible. We must unite as students to support one another, celebrate our strengths, and encourage each other to learn and improve upon our weaknesses. Get out of comfort zones, make friends, be kind to one another, push each other to keep going above and beyond expectations.

What Can You Do to Support Today's College Students?

Dr. Pressley Rankin (he/ him/his) has been involved in online higher education for over ten years. He is currently a Program Director and Associate Professor in the School of Education and Leadership at City University of Seattle. He has designed classes and programs at the bachelor's, master's, and doctoral levels. His course topics include organizational leadership, strategic thinking, research methods, instructional strategies for adult learners, and program design, assessment, and evaluation. Pressley is passionate about creating classes that make learning easier and create a solid sense of community in the online space.

During my years working with adult students at primarily online universities, I have attended conferences and workshops where I often a part of discussions focused on what we can do to support today's college students. In these conversations, there are several more focused questions, the answers to which I believe all come together to explore the more significant question how to support college students. In this essay, I explore those and make some overarching points about student support.

For context, I work at City University of Seattle (CityU), which is a nonprofit private university with mostly adult students, predominantly online. In teaching adult students here over the past five years, I have used multiple learning management systems (LMS) and modalities (in person, online, and hybrid). I have found that while there are multiple ways to support today's college students, there are some support options that resonate across modalities and ages.

Know and Share Information

It has been my experience as a program director that we must know who our students are and where they are in their program of study. Studies have shown that persistence is linked to students understanding their long-term schedules and being able to see when they will finish. Spaulding and Rockinson-Szapkiw (2012) found that managing students' expectations about a program plays a significant role in student persistence. Golde and Dore (2001) assert that a lack of adequate information increases the likelihood that a student will withdraw from a program. Students who are unsure of what to take, when to take it, and how their progressing along their educational plan find themselves frequently experiencing anxiety and loss of focus. This can lead to attrition. I believe it is crucial for institutions to track their student's progress both at the program and institutional levels and share progress and path information frequently.

Tracking students also allows program directors, advisors, and others to adequately plan for staffing, recruitment, and course offerings. I assert that students are happier when they understand their schedule and know someone is watching out for them and their progress. Further, connecting with students about their path creates a relationship with a real person that can ease their anxiety.

Show Students They Are Seen

When thinking about what students care about most, my first inclination is to say their grades. Much of the student-initiated interaction I have with students is around grading, both on assignments and in courses overall. That being said, I also have students worrying about deadlines, their family commitments, the number of readings or assignments, or the level of rigor in a course. Adult students focus on their education from different points of view depending on the reason they are enrolled. However, while students have many reasons to reach out, I believe the most important thing they care about is to be seen – to know the instructor/institution sees them as an individual, seeks to understand who they are, and acknowledges what they have accomplished before ever coming into the classroom. When we see our students, they can see themselves in our institutions, which leads to a sense of belonging that can lead to student success.

Encourage Intentional Faculty Engagement

Similar to helping the students feel seen, I have found that faculty presence in the course is valuable to assure student success and satisfaction. This is particularly challenging, yet important, in the online environment. In my programs, I encourage faculty to use their phones to record weekly video announcements. These are meant to be off the cuff and to supplement what is also written in the announcement for the week. I have found that faculty who post videos have higher end-of-course scores in the area of presence in the course.

Videos are helpful but not the only way to help students feel the presence of the faculty. Another way is for faculty to participate in the class discussions online through discussion boards. We must expect the faculty to interact with the students, not just score the students' engagement with each other. The interaction does not have to be a response to every student's post but must include a substantial synthesis of student ideas and questions.

While in online education it is typical to create discussion boards where the student creates a post and then peers respond to that post, the nature of these posts creates a conversation between the student, peers, and professor. Yet, if the professor provides the initial post and not just a prompt, it creates a more social form of student response similar to engagement on social media. To accomplish this at CityU, we have each faculty start a discussion thread that gives context to what will be learned that week in class. The faculty then will pose a question to consider for the week. As students complete their weekly readings, they consider the question and then respond to the instructor's thread. The instructor can also comment back to them. This conversational method closely resembles the way we interact on social media and has proven to be more popular than having the students complete individual posts in response to a prompt and having peers respond to those individual student posts.

Offer Variety in Learning Opportunities

Particularly for online students, I have found that students need variety in the types of assignments they are expected to complete. Horton (2012) describes three types of assignments for online learning: *Absorb, Do,* and *Connect.* "Absorb" activities are described as having students view a presentation, read from articles or a textbook, listen to a class lecture, or go on a field trip. The students' main goal is to absorb the information they are presented, and then they may be asked to recite that knowledge back in some way (typically on a discussion board or paper).

Horton (2012) describes "Do" activities as those where knowledge is applied through activities like case studies, role-playing, games, or simulations. During and after these activities, learners are provided feedback in a safe environment. I have created other meaningful activities in lieu of discussion boards. For example, in research class, I ask students to complete a table identifying various aspects of a research article. This find-and-fill-in exercise feels like active engagement, and I get, "Thank you for not giving us all boring discussion boards."

The final type of activity is a "Connect" activity. Horton (2012) states, "If Absorb activities are the nouns and Do activities are the verbs, then Connect activities are the conjunctions of learning" (p. 163). Connect activities join what the students have learned in class to their actual lived experiences. These activities are ones of application, such as the creation of original research. For adult learners, the need to know what they are doing matters in the real world is important. Offering variety in assignments allows students to vary their engagement and keeps their interest. This helps them answer the ever-present question, "Why is what I'm learning important."

How Do Your Classes Support Today's College Students?

As a college faculty and administrator, I believe that we can best support students by showing students they are seen, have faculty intentionally engage students, and allow students to engage with course materials in a variety of ways. Additionally, we (particularly those of us working in predominantly online environments) can support students by doing the following:

- Putting ourselves in our student's shoes; understanding our students are diverse and have many life circumstances that weigh on them beyond their educational endeavors
- Creating class structures that are easy to follow
- Synthesizing weekly topics, readings, and tasks into one succinct location in the LMS. Links should open up new windows, so the base is always there waiting for them to return
- Providing context and rationale for learning. Anticipate and answer the questions: Why am I reading this? Why should I watch this video? How deeply should I engage with this material?
- Finally, when teaching online, we must be in constant communication. Communication, no matter how short will help students feel that we are there and that will make their experience less lonely

References

Golde, C. M. & Dore, T. M. (2001). *A cross purposes. What the experiences of doctoral students reveal about doctoral education.* The Pew Charitable Trust.

Horton, W. (2012). *E-learning by design* (2nd ed.). Pfeiffer.

Spaulding, L. & Rockinson-Szapkiw, A. (2012). Hearing their voices. Factors doctoral candidates attribute to their persistence. *International Journal of Doctoral Studies, 7,* 199–219.

What Can You Do to Support Today's College Students?

Vernon Wall (he/him/his) is the 2020–2021 President of ACPA College Student Educators International. Vernon has over 30 years of professional experience in Student Affairs at a variety of institutions around the country. He is the Director of Business Development for LeaderShape, Inc. and is President and Founder of One Better World, LLC – a consulting firm specializing in engaging others in courageous social justice and equity conversations. Additionally, he is one of the founders and facilitators of the Social Justice Training Institute.

When we think of the "average college student," several common characteristics seem to arise. Most believe that the typical college student attends a four-year institution (full time), right out of high school, has no children, lives on or near campus, and has extra money for food, travel, clothing, and alcohol. That, my friends, is simply not true today. In reality, most students live off campus, are older, have children, and are struggling financially.

In October of 2018, Higher Education Learning (a nonprofit advocacy organization working to shift federal policy from higher education to higher learning) released a report that sheds light on the actual demographics of today's college students. The survey asked simple true and false questions of two different demographics: A representative sample of one thousand Americans and a group of "education insiders" (higher education policymakers, politicians, government staff; leaders of higher education associations, institutions, and organizations; and think tanks).

Here's what today's college students really look like:

- 58% of students work while in college
- 55% of today's students are financially independent
- 42% of independent college students live at or below the federal poverty line
- 41% of college students are older than age 25
- 39% of students in 2016 attended an institution part time
- 36% of undergraduate students attend two-year colleges
- 34% of undergraduates are first-generation college students
- 26% of today's college students are parents
- 13% of first-year students live on campus

As someone who travels to campuses throughout the year giving presentations and trainings for students, faculty, and staff on issues of equity and inclusion, I would like to add that our campuses are more diverse than ever, and students are very concerned about social justice issues. I have also found that students from historically marginalized groups do not trust university staff, faculty, and administrators. The focus here is on power. Who has the influence to make change? Who can make their college and university experience better? In their minds – university staff, faculty, and administrators. They experience bias-related incidents at alarming rates and do not believe that the university has their best interests in mind as policies to counteract these incidents are developed and employed. University mission statements are seen as hollow promises. All of this begs the question: "Are the systems that are in place to assist students in being successful on campus not meeting their needs?"

In order to better assess your capacity to support all students, I suggest reflecting on these ten questions:

1. Are your services, programs, and academic programs flexible enough to support students with varying schedules and priorities?
2. Do your campus administrators engage in conversations on food insecurity and provide services for students who might not have the resources to feed themselves adequately?

3. Are students that are not of the traditional age (18 to 21) involved on campus? What are you doing to engage them?
4. Do part-time students on your campus feel that they are part of the university community?
5. Has your campus developed partnerships with two-year colleges? The goal of higher education should be to increase access.
6. Are your policies on reporting and responding to bias-related incidents on campus transparent and responsive?
7. What conversations are you having with the university community on the importance of providing a welcoming environment for all?
8. Is your campus adequately equipped to attend to the increase in mental health–related issues that today's college students possess?
9. What does community mean to you? How can you encourage students to be supportive of each other?
10. How can we continue to be current and effective in our work as we support the multifaceted and personalized goals of student success?

So what can be done to begin to answer these questions?

− Dust off that climate survey that you did a few years back and revisit the themes. No need to institute another one (that's honestly just a stall tactic). That data has not changed. You might want to do follow-up focused questions to get more details from specific student populations.
− Research your peer institutions. How are they engaging these issues on their campuses?
− Develop workgroups to tackle specific issues in more depth. These groups could discuss possibilities in more detail and offer potential initiatives.
− Involve community leaders in the process.
− Update students along the way. Be transparent about your progress and struggles.
− Develop a professional development curriculum for faculty and staff that focuses on enhancing the college and university experience of today's college students.

Now, more than ever, we are called to be more nimble and responsive to our changing student demographics. There is no archetype for today's college students. Our students represent every person from every walk of life. We must continue to challenge ourselves to be advocates for all students. It is our responsibility. It is our duty.

References

Association of American Colleges and Universities. 2018, November. Facts & figures: Misconceptions about today's college students. *AAC&U News*. Retrieved April 15, 2022, from https://www.aacu.org

Higher Learning Advocates. (2018). *How well do we really know today's students?* Retrieved on April 15, 2022, from https://ejm0i2fmf973k8c9d2n34685-wpengine.netdna-ssl.com/wp-content/uploads/2018/10/10-18-HLA-TodaysStudents-Survey-Deck-FINAL.pdf

14

ANALYSIS

What Can You Do to Support Today's College Students?

Julie E. Owen

Julie E. Owen, PhD (she/her) is Associate Professor of Leadership Studies at the School of Integrative Studies, George Mason University, where she coordinates the leadership studies major and minor. She is affiliate faculty with the Higher Education Program, and with Women and Gender Studies. Owen is the author of numerous scholarly publications, including: *We are the Leaders We've Been Waiting For: Women and Leadership Development in College* (Stylus, 2020) and *Women and Leadership Development in College: A Facilitation Guide* (with Dr. Jennifer Pigza, Stylus, 2021). Her research explores the intersections of leadership identity and women's adult development, as well as the scholarship of liberatory leadership teaching and learning.

Even before the COVID-19 pandemic revealed stark discrepancies about college students' access to health care, education, and employment opportunities, there were persistent unaddressed social forces that profoundly shaped students' experiences in college. This chapter examines themes from essays written by people inhabiting four different social locations vis-à-vis the academy: a second-year college student pursuing a technical degree at a regional community college, parents who put four children through college and who regularly employ college students at their restaurants and businesses, a program director and associate professor who predominantly teaches in online modalities, and an experienced higher education consultant who is also the president of an international association focused on college student educators. These narratives reveal important points of congruence and areas of vast discrepancies in their views on how to support today's college students. This chapter explores these areas of agreement

DOI: 10.4324/9780429319471-19

and difference, connects resulting themes to extant theory of student learning and development, and concludes with a call to action for readers to activate on behalf of college students, no matter their positionality.

Stakeholder Perspectives

Students Supporting Students

In Talia Bailey's thoughtful essay about her involvement and experience as a second-year student majoring in cybersecurity at Cincinnati State Technical and Community College, readers can witness the difference peer support and advocacy can make in the lives of other students. Talia describes her involvement in student organizations, as well as her service to the university at recruitment events and involvement fairs. For Talia, prior college experiences "shaped how I feel about the cruciality of campus resources and student opportunities in order for students to succeed and go above and beyond expectations" (p. 171). She is dedicated to helping her peers navigate and avoid some of the struggles she has faced in college. Her motivation is personal and profound.

Counseling Services. Talia describes the importance of counseling services being included as part of a student's tuition and fees "because many students struggle paying for books, supplies, lab fees, etc. and worrying about whether they can afford to take care of their mental health should not be added to that list" (p. 171). Additionally, she advocates for "discussing the importance of mental health continuously throughout a student's time on campus" (p. 171) and destigmatizing counseling. Despite the recent rise in anxiety disorders on college campuses, support for counseling resources on most campuses has not kept pace. Psychologist Albert Bandura suggested that positive psychological and affective states are essential for building the efficacy needed for successful learning and development (1997). Talia's experiences underscore this point in a dramatic fashion.

Faculty Support. Talia sheds light on distracted and distant faculty when she describes her own experience of being discouraged from asking for help in a math class. She warns that many students have been in classes where they felt no connection with faculty. In contrast, some faculty work hard to relate to students and support them in discerning and attaining their goals. The rapport developed between a faculty member and students may be the vital thread that keeps them connected to campus (Gallup and Purdue University, 2014). Talia wisely concludes that "just because a class ends does not mean the student interaction has to end as well" (p. 172). Faculty mentorship can continue far beyond the bounds of the academic term or campus.

Advice to Peers. Talia describes the differential effect of peer-to-peer mentoring and support. She notes frank conversations among classmates "can encourage strength and courage, and let them know that they are not alone in their thoughts and feelings while attending college" (p. 172). She suggests that involvement in campus activities and programming opportunities are vehicles for learning leadership as well as can help students "achieve higher-level thinking, assess their critical problem-solving skills, and be creative" (p. 172). They are also a source of motivation, socialization, and even stress relief for students. She offers a beautiful rallying cry for how students can support other students, and indeed campuses would be more welcoming spaces should her vision become a reality.

Parents as Presence

What can parents do to support today's college students? In the anonymous essay, a parent and stepparent of a family of four children discuss their various approaches to higher learning. Their biggest insight from their years of experience supporting their children is that "every student and set of needs are different, and resisting judgment is often quite difficult" (p. 168). They wisely echo Nevitt Sanford's (1967) theory of challenge and support when they state, "[T]here are times when you need to step in and help get things back on track and other moments when you just need to offer encouragement or a little incentive to do better" (p. 168). They describe the differing needs of a self-motivated, first-born child; a gregarious child with a learning disability who needed support navigating institutional systems and structures; a third child who found community with peers who did not have his best interests in mind and who later realized college was not the path for him; and a youngest child who craved independence. They also stress the importance for students to "learn from experience and have room to make mistakes without terrible consequences" (p. 170).

Faculty Matters

In Dr. Pressley Rankin's cogent essay on how faculty can support students, especially adult learners in online learning environments, he speaks to the importance of managing expectations, mattering, intentionality, and variety in learning. First, Dr. Rankin asserts "that managing students' expectations about a program plays a significant role in student persistence" such that when students are unclear or unsure, the result is anxiety and even withdrawal from college. He suggests "connecting with students about their path creates a relationship with a real person that can ease their anxiety" (p. 174). Communication is an essential driver for making students feel they matter.

Above all else, Dr. Rankin believes that students care most about being seen and knowing that "the instructor/institution sees them as an individual, seeks to understand who they are, and acknowledges what they have accomplished before ever coming into the classroom" (p. 174). The role of belonging as essential to student success cannot be understated. A third way to help students feel they matter is to ensure faculty presence in courses, especially in online learning environments. Presence can be communicated by posting weekly impromptu videos related to class themes and ideas or by faculty-led prompts on discussion boards where faculty are active participants in student engagement. Faculty can provide a context and rationale for learning that promotes motivation and growth mindsets (Dweck, 2006).

Dr. Rankin's fourth suggestion for how faculty can support students is perhaps the most compelling: offer variety in learning opportunities. The scholarship of teaching and learning underscores the role of novelty in promoting deep learning. Horton's (2012) "absorb, do, connect" approach to learning is one suggested route such that assignments vary from traditional learning to action and relation learning. Rankin emphasizes that these pedagogies help students "answer the ever-present question, *why is what I am learning important?*" (p. 175).

The Role of Association Leadership in Student Support

After a 30-year career in higher education, Vernon Wall assumed the presidency of ACPA College Student Educators International. Wall brings his expertise from numerous campuses and higher ed organizations to his role in shaping an agenda for college students to thrive. Wall rightly troubles the dominant narrative of the typical college student who "attends a four-year institution (full time), right out of high school, has no children, lives on or near campus, and has extra money for food, travel, clothing, and alcohol" (p. 176). He cites recent reports showing today's college students as older, more culturally and ethnically diverse, more likely to work full time, more likely to be poor, working-class, or first-generation students, to live off-campus, and to be parents or have additional family responsibilities.

Wall issues this clarion call: "Now, more than ever, we are called to be more nimble and responsive to our changing student demographics. There is no archetype for today's college students. Our students represent every person from every walk of life. We must continue to challenge ourselves to be advocates for all students. It is our responsibility. It is our duty" (p. 178). He describes how far we must go to reach this goal as students from marginalized groups experience bias incidents at alarming rates and feel university mission statements offer "hollow promises." Wall suggests a systems-level shift is needed to meet the needs of today's students. In his essay, he offers ten powerful questions that directly and indirectly address power, inclusion, and inequality on today's campuses.

Exploring Themes and Connecting Literature

Whether the stakeholders who contributed essays to this section were aware of it or not, each of their responses to the prompt of what can they do to support today's college students echoed aspects of the scholarly literature on college student development. The association president and college professor likely made use of formal theories of development, while the parents and student essays likely drew from implicit or informal theories each stakeholder had formed about the college-going experience. This section integrates insights from the contributed essays to foundational student development theories about mattering and marginality, developmental readiness, and challenge and support. Next, the essays are examined considering diverse notions of social, academic, and community capital. Finally, involvement theory and theories of well-being, including resilience, flourishing, and purpose, are addressed.

Mattering, Readiness, Challenge, and Support

Talia Bailey's essay is a primer for why mattering indeed matters. Schlossberg (1989) describes the importance of marginality and mattering to healthy student development. She describes how feelings of marginality can emerge when students are in transition, such as when they take on new roles, or when they feel as if they do not fit in with a group. For some members of underrepresented communities, marginality can be a permanent condition, while for others it is more episodic. Schlossberg defines mattering as "our belief, whether right or wrong, that we matter to someone else" (1989, p. 9) and suggests it consists of four components: (1) *attention*, or feeling noticed; (2) *importance*, or feeling cared about; (3) *ego-extension*, or the feeling that someone else cares about one's failures and successes; and (4) *dependence*, feeling needed. Bailey notes how both instructors and peers can be essential sources of mattering. She describes, "[H]ad it not been for instructor and peer encouragement, I most likely would not have taken on leadership opportunities while in college because I was incredibly shy and did not believe in myself at the time" (p. 172). Fostering feelings of mattering in students is essential to a host of college student success outcomes. As the *Gallup-Purdue Index Report* (2014) reveals, if college students "had a professor who cared about them as a person, made them excited about learning, and encouraged them to pursue their dreams, their odds of being engaged at work more than doubled, as did their odds of thriving in their well-being" (p. 6).

Vernon Wall, the higher education association leader, issues an important caveat: "I have also found that students from historically marginalized groups do not trust university staff, faculty, and administrators" (p. 177). Consider these words in relation to concepts of mattering and marginality. If trust is a prerequisite for establishing caring, mutual relationships, it follows that underrepresented students may not feel connected to their peers, faculty, or campuses. Wall suggests the blame for this erosion of trust stands squarely with the institutions. It is no wonder, as students "experience bias-related incidents at alarming rates" and "do not believe that the university has their best interests in mind" (p. 177). When schools and administrators fail to take appropriate action, students can experience a phenomenon called institutional betrayal (Linder & Myers, 2018).

Though originally referring to how institutions delegitimize instances of sexual violence, it may be expanded to include how students from any marginalized group may be more vulnerable to their stories being ignored, minimized, or delegitimized by the institution (Linder & Myers, 2018).

Dr. Rankin offers specific suggestions for how to ensure that students feel seen. He offers a road map to mattering such that "[w]hen we [faculty] see our students, they can see themselves in our institutions, which leads to a sense of belonging that can lead to student success" (p. 174). One of the antidotes to marginality, according to Rankin, is faculty presence. Whether in face-to-face or distance learning environments, faculty can establish presence in a course through personalizing course content, engaging in dialogue along with students, and modeling authenticity. Online learning experts developed the Community of Inquiry Model (Garrison, Anderson, & Archer, 2000), which proposes three dimensions of presence: social, teaching, and cognitive. Social presence occurs when faculty and students "project their personal characteristics into the discussion so they become 'real people'" (Garrison, Anderson, & Archer, 2000, p. 89). Teaching presence is communicated via course expectations, materials, and delivery. Cognitive presence refers to the "extent to which the professor and the students are able to construct and confirm meaning through sustained discourse (discussion) in a community of inquiry" (p. 89).

In the essay by parents and employers of college-aged students, the parents summarize the conundrum:

> The simple answer is, be there – be physically available to the student and provide a judgment-free space for them to learn. It gets tricky there, though. Every student and set of needs are different, and resisting judgment is often quite difficult.
>
> *(p. 168)*

Though likely unknown to them, these parents are paraphrasing the scholarship of psychologist Nevitt Sanford, a pioneer of college student development. Sanford (1967) describes the essential processes of *challenge*, which occur in situations where a student may not have the skills, knowledge, or ability to cope, and *support* where intentional actions, programs, and environments can be created to help students meet challenges and to be successful. The idea is to find the optimal dissonance between challenge and support, where a student is motivated to learn and develop, but not so challenged that they shutdown, regress to earlier stages of development, or even drop out. An often overlooked component of Sanford's model is *readiness*, or the contention that students will not exhibit certain behaviors until they are developmentally ready to do so.

The parents go on to describe how they supported and challenged each of their four children in uniquely different ways based on their unique personalities and readiness. For their oldest self-motivated son, they recall that "we never had to do much to motivate him; we just needed to acknowledge and celebrate the awards and pay for the many opportunities that came his way" (p. 168). When an individual seeks out challenges on their own, then parents being sources of emotional and financial support offers an important balance. For their next oldest child, who also suffers from a mild case of dyslexia, the parents had to balance challenge and support. They describe this process as "he needed us reminding him that he was smart enough and could make it through four years in the mountains, and he also needed the incentive to force himself to do better" (p. 169). For educators, incentives usually refer to the benefits of good grades and credentialing to career attainment, civic contribution, and lifelong learning. These parents adopted a more transactional approach where they rewarded good grades with travel and study abroad opportunities, a form of incentivizing rarely available to lower-income families. Research shows that extrinsic forms of reward are less durable and lasting than internal forms of reward, which build self-motivation and resilient habits of mind (Ryan & Deci, 2020). Though perhaps these parents' insight into their son's developmental readiness caused them to use more transactional approaches, which worked well to spur success.

With their third child, the parents describe what happens when students do not access institutional supports. They note their son's feelings of marginality in that "unfortunately, he never found a faculty or staff member that he connected to and never felt connected to a class" (p. 169). And no amount of challenge or support by the parents could counteract those feelings. Finally, the parents expanded their notion of support to mean that college might not be for all of their children. Their youngest child was an independent self-starter, so the parents' main role was "to remind her that we are around if she needs us." Each of these presented cases underscores the importance of foundational student development theory to student success. While the importance of mattering, readiness, challenge, and support cannot be overstated, they are also dependent on a student's access to social, academic, and cultural capital.

Community Cultural Wealth

Though there are many contested definitions of social capital, the concept broadly refers to how people access power through social connections and how these networks can produce or reproduce inequality (Bourdieu, 1997; Putnam, 2000). Vernon Wall's narrative reminds us that "there is no archetype for today's college students" and that many of today's college students do not have access to the forms of social capital that prior generations had – including generational wealth, housing and food security, access to mental health resources, and freedom from bias, discrimination, and violence to name but a few areas of difference. Talia Bailey describes her lifelong battle with depression and anxiety and her recent diagnosis with post-traumatic stress disorder and how these affect her college-going experience. She reminds us that students are managing many things, and mental health should not be among them. Students' ability to thrive is dependent on their access to various forms of capital.

One thing people can do to support today's college students is to expand our own understandings of who college students are and work to support them in ways that adopt asset-based approaches to learning and development. Yosso's (2005) model of community cultural wealth critiques Bordieu's work for promoting a deficit ideology that "communities of color are culturally deprived while predominantly white communities are culturally rich" (Patton et al., 2016, p. 254). The same critique could be said to apply to low-income and underserved communities. Yosso outlines six types of community cultural wealth. These include *aspirational capital*, or an individual's capacity to remain hopeful and optimistic despite the presence of obstacles. This can be seen in Talia's assertion that "it is not a sign of weakness to ask for help, but shows determination, readiness, and strength to better oneself" (p. 172). *Linguistic capital* refers to the ability to communicate in one or more languages, as well as to use a variety of communication forms, such as storytelling and oral history. Dr. Rankin exhibits this in his use of "absorb-do-connect" activities in his classes where students are invited to go beyond rote learning.

Familial capital refers to the various forms of knowledge individuals gain through interaction with immediate and extended family, as well as concepts such as kinship and pedagogies of home. The parents' narrative is a wonderful example of the joys and challenges of familial relationships. *Navigational capital* refers to how students traverse diverse institutional settings, especially those that may be oppressive, and allows for "individual agency within institutional constraints" (Yosso, 2005, p. 80). As Wall describes, this may include asking questions about power such as "who has the influence to make change? Who can make their college and university experience better?" (p. 177). Yosso includes *social capital* and defines it as "networks of people and community resources" (p. 79) that serve as support networks for students. Finally, Yosso describes *resistant capital*, which refers to the myriad ways students work to counteract oppressive systems and structures and consists of "knowledge and skills fostered through oppositional behavior that challenges inequality" (p. 80). Wall asseverates: "University mission statements are seen as hollow promises...are the systems that are in place to assist students in being successful on campus not meeting their needs?" (p. 177). An important way to foster success for today's students is to use asset-based approaches to community and support students in accessing and developing each of these forms of capital.

Involvement Theory and Well-Being

The college student involvement literature points to the importance of building positive peer interactions through the integration of cocurricular and traditional learning activities (Astin, 1993; Padgett, Johnson, & Pascarella, 2012). Astin's

Student Involvement Theory (1993) purports that the quality of effort that students devote to educationally purposeful activities is directly related to student success in college. Student success has been broadly defined to include academic achievement; engagement in educational activities; development of knowledge, skills, and competencies; satisfaction; persistence; attainment of educational objectives; and post-college performance (Braxton et al., 2013; Kuh, 2008). Consider Talia Bailey's awareness of the positive effects of her campus involvement and leadership when she said, "[H]aving opportunities for student leadership (such as officer positions for clubs and volunteering opportunities) encourages students to achieve higher-level thinking, assess their critical problem-solving skills, and be creative with outside the box thinking" (p. 172). While not all students are as attuned to the benefits of involvement as Bailey, it stands that curricular and cocurricular campus involvement is a catalyst to student learning and development, and that college student educators play a significant role in the design, quality, and accessibility of those offerings.

One of the underexamined aspects of involvement theory is the effects of different types of involvement on student well-being. Well-being has numerous definitions but in a college context generally refers to building a life of vitality, purpose, resilience, and engagement. In its *Healthways Well-Being Five* research, Gallup (2014) defines well-being as "the interaction and interdependency between many aspects of life such as finding fulfillment in daily work and interactions, having strong social relationships and access to the resources people need, feeling financially secure, being physically healthy, and taking part in a true community" (p. 13). They suggest that well-being is an additive process where students who thrive in multiple categories are more likely to flourish than those who do not. At the time of the Gallup study, a majority of college graduates surveyed reported that they were thriving in only one or two of the interrelated elements of well-being. More than half (54%) of college graduates reported thriving in the purpose dimension of well-being, indicating that they were happy with their daily work and learn something new every day.

A dedication to student well-being is seen in the parents' essay about the ways they addressed a variety of well-being dimensions for each of their children. They ensured their children had access to financial resources. College students and recent graduates consistently score lowest on measures financial and physical well-being when compared to other aspects of well-being. In fact, Gallup data reveal that student loan debt is a strong hindrance to well-being where "the higher the loan amount, the worse the well-being" (p. 15). The parents emphasize the importance of strong social and community relationships in their description of how they support the students working on their farm. They recall, "[W]e cook dinners; we tell stories; we take them fishing and to ball games; we let them talk" (p. 170). At a time when social distancing has led to increased isolation and rising rates of anxiety and depression, attention to the relational aspects of well-being is paramount.

Another essential aspect of college student well-being is resilience, or how people deal with and learn to overcome the challenges and setbacks that life offers. Recent research indicates that people who have experienced some adversity in the form of negative or life-changing moments are ultimately happier and less stressed than those who have not had significant adverse experiences (Seery, Holman, & Silver, 2010). This does not imply that we should manufacture traumatic events for students, but rather that educators can help students develop the ability to cope, which includes their ability to manage their emotions, thoughts, and behaviors. Coping or failing forward may foster subsequent resilience, with resulting advantages for mental health and well-being (2010). Consider the parents' reaction to their third son's lack of thriving in college. They acknowledged his struggles and theirs, finally concluding, "It took a bumpy adjustment period, but he has a good steady job now that didn't require the degree he never really wanted, but we did" (p. 169).

Acknowledging that the bumpy road of life is not a permanent condition, building coping skills and resilience, and realizing that thriving and life purpose look different for every individual is a vital part of fostering student success.

Call to Action: Developing Liberatory Learning

The college students of today are the leaders, innovators, and problem-solvers of tomorrow. How we choose to support them will shape the future we inhabit. For this author, the way forward in supporting student success lies in acknowledging the many forces that shape and oppress our students and using this knowledge to counteract these forces and create more emancipatory forms of education. Liberatory learning refers to pedagogy, which helps students "break out of oppressive ways of thinking and acting that seem habitual but that have been imposed by the dominant culture" so that students can "create forms of thinking and living that are more democratic, harmonious, and true to their own experiences" (Brookfield, 1995, p. 209). Each of the stakeholders who contributed essays to this section holds vastly different intersectional identities. None of them makes claims that student success looks the same for all people. Each of them has found ways to successfully navigate the labyrinth of challenges that is higher education.

One possible road map to emancipation is Harro's (2013) Cycle of Liberation, which they designed after analyzing patterns of events common to every successful critical transformation effort. Their model depicts seven stages of change, though people can enter and exit the model at any point, and most processes of transformation take many cycles through the model. Working to end oppression is sadly never completely done. Harro defines liberation as *critical transformation* or being able to name and address the systemic structures and forces that contribute to oppression.

Harro believes that most people enter the Cycle of Liberation as a result of a "waking up" experience or critical incident that causes one to look at oneself and the world in new ways. We see this in this section's stakeholder essays in several ways. Talia Bailey's wake-up call is to advocate for mental health support on campus. Dr. Rankin realizes that faculty presence is the key to student learning and retention. Vernon Wall tries to wake up educators about the changing demographics and experiences of today's college students. The parents of four college students wake up to the realization that each of their children has unique gifts and challenges.

The next phases, "getting ready" and "reaching out," involve consciously dismantling and re-building aspects of ourselves based on our new views and perspectives. Harro states that "once we know something, we can't not know it anymore" (p. 620). Important processes at this stage include introspection, education, and consciousness-raising. While these processes serve to empower the self, they must be accompanied by processes of dismantling our stereotypes, ignorance, discriminatory or privileged attitudes, and behaviors that limit ourselves and others, such as collusion and oppressive language and actions. Part of this process is building a set of tools to use throughout the process, as well as seeking inspiration and connections in our journeys. We see this in Talia Bailey's use of counseling services and in Dr. Rankin's commitment to faculty development. We see it in the parents of college-aged children not adopting a cookie-cutter approach to challenging and supporting their children. We see it in Vernon Wall's reminder that so much of education is built on an outdated view of who is coming to college.

Social change never happens in isolation. The next stages of "building community" and "coalescing" require sustained dialogue with others. Building an inclusive university community involves dialoguing with people who are like us (who share the same social identities, or similar commitments to a cause) and with people who are different from us. The latter part is much harder and may require questioning assumptions, rules, roles, and structures. Harro says, "[W]e will never be able to focus on the real challenge – changing the system – until the barriers and boundaries that divide us are minimized." It is a radical act to spend time exploring our differences and deeply listening to those with whom we might initially disagree. Next, changemakers may join with allies to move into action by interrupting and confronting oppressive systems. This can include educating, fundraising, lobbying, conducting action research, working on policy, activism, and allyship. Action and activism done with preparation, thoughtful intention, and diverse coalitions can be much more powerful than activism alone.

The final stages are "creating and maintaining change." For Harro, creating change refers to the process of critically transforming institutions and creating a new culture. This stage asks participants to demonstrate leadership, question assumptions, take risks, share power, influence policy, and guide change. Educators have a choice "either to work in ways that legitimize and reinforce the status quo or in ways that liberate and transform the possibilities people see in their lives" (Brookfield, 1995, p. 209). Each of the essays included in this section addressed aspects of changemaking. Talia Bailey undergoes a transformation through intentional involvement in campus leadership and engagement opportunities. Dr. Rankin transforms the way he teaches to meet students where they are. Vernon Wall works at the systems and policy level to enact change.

To move toward transformation and liberation, let us return to the wisdom of college student Talia Bailey who reminds us so clearly what it is all about. She reflects, "[C]ollege can be intimidating, tiresome, stressful, and it can be difficult to find the motivation to keep going, but it is also a fun and diverse experience that helps us grow in ways we never thought possible" (p. 173). So, what can we do to support today's college students? We can support and challenge them to realize dreams they never thought possible.

References

Astin, A. W. (1993). *What matters in college? Four critical years revisited*. Jossey Bass.

Bandura, A. (1997). *Self-efficacy: The exercise of control*. W. H. Freeman.

Bourdieu, P. (1997). The forms of capital. In A. H. Halsey, H. Lauder, P. Brown, & A. Stuart Wells (Eds.), *Education, culture, economy, society* (pp. 46–58). Oxford University Press.

Braxton, J. M., Doyle, W. R., Hartley, H. V., Hirschy, A. S., Jones, W. A., & McLendon, M. K. (2013). *Rethinking college student retention*. Jossey-Bass.

Brookfield, S. D. (1995). *Becoming a critically reflective teacher*. Jossey-Bass.

Dweck, C. (2006). *Mindset: The new psychology of success*. Ballantine Books.

Gallup and Purdue University. (2014). *Great jobs great lives: The 2014 Gallup-Purdue index Report*. Retrieved on April 15, 2022 from https://www.gallup.com/services/176768/2014-gallup-purdue-index-report.aspx

Garrison, D. R., Anderson, T., & Archer, W. (2000). Critical inquiry in a text-based environment: Computer conferencing in higher education. *The Internet and Higher Education, 2*(2–3), 1–19.

Harro, B. (2013). The cycle of liberation. In M. Adams, W. J. Blumenfeld, R. Castaneda, H. W. Hackman, M. L. Peters, X. Zuniga (Eds.), *Readings for diversity of social justice,* 3rd ed. (618–625). Routledge.

Horton, W. (2012). *E-learning by design*. John Wiley & Sons.

Kuh, G. D. (2008). *High-impact educational practices: What they are, who has access to them, and why they matter*. Association of American Colleges & Universities.

Linder, C., & Myers, J. S. (2018). Institutional betrayal as a motivator for campus sexual assault activism. *NASPA Journal About Women in Higher Education, 11*(1), 1–16. doi:10.1080/19407882.2017.1385489

Padgett, R. D., Johnson, M. P., & Pascarella, E. T. (2012). First-generation undergraduate students and the impacts of the first year of college: Additional evidence. *Journal of College Student Development, 53*(2), 243–266.

Patton, L. D., Renn, K. A., Guido, F. M., Quaye, S. J., & Forney, D. S. (2016). *Student development in college* (3rd ed.). John Wiley & Sons.

Putnam, R. D. (2000). *Bowling alone: The collapse of America's social capital*. Simon & Schuster.

Ryan, R. M., & Deci, E. L. (2020). Intrinsic and extrinsic motivation from a self-determination theory perspective: Definitions, theory, practices, and future directions. *Contemporary Educational Psychology*, 61. doi: 10.1016/j.cedpsych.2020.101860.

Sanford, N. (1967). *Where colleges fail: The study of the student as a person.* Jossey-Bass

Schlossberg, N. K. (1989). Marginality and mattering: Key issues in building community. In D. C. Roberts (ed.), Designing campus activities to foster a sense of community. *New directions for students services, 48,* 5–15. Jossey-Bass.

Seery, M. D., Holman, E. A., & Silver, R. C. (2010). Whatever does not kill us: Cumulative lifetime adversity, vulnerability, and resilience. *Journal of Personality and Social Psychology, 99*(6), 1025–1041. doi:10.1037/a0021344

Yosso, T. (2005). Whose culture has capital? A critical race theory discussion of community cultural wealth. *Race, Ethnicity, & Education, 8*(1), 69–91.

CONCLUSION

Needham Yancey Gulley

Yancey Gulley (he/him/his) is an associate professor in the Higher Education Student Affairs program at Western Carolina University. His first co-edited book is *Using the CAS Professional Standards: Diverse Examples of Practice*. He is focused on scholarship that highlights diversity in higher education regarding both students and institutions.

Many in the academy, especially those familiar with marketing, are used to seeing campus advertisements that include precisely staged photographs of students in classrooms and labs or laying on blankets reading books in an oak-filled quad. Mostly the images look the same across institutions as marketing professionals take the "Three and a Tree" image that showcases carefully curated diversity of students framed in precise ways that highlight the idyllic nature of the institution. Yet, these images do not show student or institutional diversity with any depth and are more cliché than reality (160over90, 2012). A new collaboration between the Sedlin/Harring-Smith Foundation and Getty Images is using new photographs of college students to combat perpetuating outdated stereotypes of who today's college students are through visual imaging. Noting that our perceptions of what is possible and where we belong are greatly influenced by the representations we encounter, the project is strategically troubling the view our culture perpetuates about who attends college and how and why we think that way.

> Long before many people enroll in college, they see a version of it on glowing screens. Movies, television shows, and photographs flood our eyeballs with images of college students, shaping our understanding of whom

DOI: 10.4324/9780429319471-20

higher education serves. The more folks we see who look like us, the more we might believe that we, too, belong in college....

But all those fresh-faced kids on tree-shaded quads are, in fact, the minority.... Now, more than ever, some higher-education experts say, the world needs to see more images of students who fit a different description.

(Hoover, 2020, para. 1, 6)

The New College Majority Photo Series is designed to highlight the demographics of today's college students. Leveraging the massive image repository of Getty Images and using stock image sites such as iStock, new images are being labeled and curated that depict the diversity of students today, such as mothers in college balancing duties, homeless students living in their cars, students attending college with COVID-19 protocols in place, and veteran students engaging on campus. The hope is that these images will help expand the public idea of the college student today, moving us to a more accurate representation that ultimately influences our perceptions of who they are and who they can become.

Private foundations and agencies are recognizing that there is a disconnect in who college students are and who we, as citizens, believe they are. Consequently, those groups are putting resources toward correcting this disconnect, highlighting the scope of the problem. It is not just the general public who has a skewed view of today's college students, it is the internal and external stakeholders of higher education too.

Chris Copes, one of the college students who provided an essay for this text, also highlighted that those going to college today are not the "traditional" student that many of us are used to thinking about, saying, "'[N]ontraditional' best describes many of today's college students" (p. 67). He emphasizes that those he attends college with come from various backgrounds and ages with responsibilities outside of college and enrolled in diverse types of institutions at ever-increasing rates. But these are not the only way he sees today's college students as outside the "traditional" trope. Chris noted,

We are nontraditional not only in the fact that not all of us are students straight out of high school who will graduate college in four years but also in the way that we buck at the idea of doing things the traditional way just because it is how things have always been done. Today's college students are about paving our own way to the future we want...even if it is not the most conventional way of doing things.

(p. 67)

By understanding who college students are and how they engage in higher education, we can support them in doing just that – paving their own way. However, if our baseline understanding of who college students are is misunderstood, it is no wonder that different groups who influence higher education think differently about student needs, opportunities, and the ways to support them.

By understanding how these different players understand students and their roles in supporting them, we have the potential to engage in productive conversations and collaborations aimed at student success. The opening chapters prepared readers to understand who students are demographically, illuminating their diversity while introducing the types of people who have a vested *interest in* and *impact on* higher education. With that foundation in mind, the real message of the book privileges the voices of stakeholders. Examining how these stakeholders discuss college students from their various positionalities illustrates the wide range of ideas that exist about college students and encourages the readers to see how individual roles influence those perspectives.

There are any number of ways to analyze and interpret the large number of perspectives and positionalities represented in this text. The essayists have given voice to their lived experiences and in some cases their expectations, hopes, and dreams. The scholars who offered analyses of contributions to each guiding question have provided a collective reading of the essays and highlighted intersections across contributions and in relation to relevant literature. None of this is exhaustive, but it offers guidance for readers as you consider your ways of meaning making in relation to the diversity of perspectives you found in the text. The analysis also offers something for you to agree with and/or push back on. Everyone who has contributed to this book has a framework from which they see the world, and that framework comes from a myriad of factors, such as their educational background, the various roles they inhabit (student, educator, parent, etc.), their economic class, race, and gender. You are invited to take the honest and opinion-oriented essays of contributors, the data and theoretical framing of the opening chapters, and the thoughtful dissection of essays in the various analyses to understand this information in your own way and from your own unique perspective. Later, I will provide some guiding questions to help you get started. For now, I offer some of my own initial thoughts, specifically on the essays from the stakeholders.

Examples of Collective Analysis

In this section, I provide an example of how readers might reflect on this book by showing examples from my own reading. I do so by looking at the text holistically and taking a group of essays from similar stakeholders to see what topics of similarity come up in those contributions. Then, I look to see if those same topics are discussed by other stakeholders, and in what ways. For the example, I start with essays by college students, as I think it is important to continually center their perspectives in all that we do.

In reviewing the stakeholder essays in this book as a whole, regardless of the question to which they were prompted to respond, several core elements can be identified. These thematic topics include areas of congruence and incongruence. As a way of highlighting student voices (and recognizing that students are the only stakeholders whose voice is present across all five prompts), I have identified mental health, peer support/connections, basic resources, and involvement as the primary common elements. The following is an exploration of those elements, giving special attention to how they were discussed by students and then looking at essay contributions by other types of contributors to see if they discussed those elements, and if so, how. What I found is that when non-students discussed these topics, those stakeholders were most frequently others internal to higher education (e.g., higher education professionals and faculty). Meanwhile, external stakeholders (those not enrolled in or employed within higher education) were mainly silent on these matters altogether. Next is a discussion of this analysis by the common elements identified earlier.

Mental Health

The college students who wrote essays for this book came from a range of backgrounds and were attending very different types of institutions. Yet, there were many things they discussed that showed up across their contributions. Several of the students spoke directly about needing to have a variety of supports while in college. Students frequently mentioned mental health concerns in their essays. Sarah Ali discussed this in her contribution, saying, "It might benefit students if a university could provide long-term psychological services throughout their academic career versus a more triage-based model of mental health care. However, many universities do not have the staff numbers to match the mental health needs of their student population. I believe an increase in counseling and psychological services would positively impact participating students" (p. 90). Here she hit on something that students frequently discuss but of which external stakeholders are likely not aware – the difficulty in getting quick and consistent mental health services on college campuses. On-campus counseling centers were overwhelmed prior to the onset of COVID-19, and there is every indication that they will be more so now (Abrams, 2020). Yet, another student contributor, Talia Bailey, noted that without the free mental health counseling services made available at her institution, she would not have been successful.

In her analysis of essays, Michelle Espino said, "Therapists and counselors should not be the only staff members addressing students' mental health concerns. Rather, counseling centers should be crafting relationships across campus that help students address academic anxiety, physical wellness, and racism (among other forms of oppression) that they may face" (p. 108). She acknowledged that many stakeholders have an opportunity to support the mental health of college students. But when I reflect on the essay contributions as a whole, I note some comments on this issue from students and those who work directly in education but a general lack of acknowledgment from stakeholders whose primary roles are external to the academy. The question we should be asking ourselves here is, "Why?" There are some instances of external partnerships working to address the need for mental health services for students, such as the College Mental Health Program (https://www.mcleanhospital.org/treatment/cmhp) out of McLean Hospital. Yet, I was surprised to see so little acknowledgment from external contributors when internal ones readily recognized these needs.

Peer Support/Connections

In their essays, students frequently mentioned the importance of peers to their college experience. They realized that the other students with whom they were engaged were important parts of their educational journey and that they could support each other. In fact, for some students, peer support was presented as the most important type. For example, Ximena Silva-Avila, a college student, said,

> It was not the institution but my peers who told me about internships that have turned out to be the most useful. It was my peers who held me as I sobbed when I felt lonely, validated my place at my institution, and told me which professors I should go speak to in order to get more support and encouragement. It was my peers who celebrated me when I won a prestigious national fellowship, not the university. It was my peers who challenged my way of thinking, albeit it was often in the context of a course we were taking. More importantly, it was my peers who showed me I did not have to think I was alone because I was not alone. It has been my peers who have taught me to be a better person and see the world in such a positive and supportive light that has been invaluable in my career thus far.
>
> (p. 152)

As a first-generation college student, Ximena credits her peers for helping her matriculate much more than they acknowledge the work of the institution. The student-to-student relationship is often paramount to success. As Lee and Harris (2020) found, this relationship is particularly crucial for the success of low-income, first-generation, and working-class students.

The importance of peer-to-peer support was echoed by internal stakeholders like Roslyn Gowens who noted the impact of social media and technology in allowing peers to stay connected more easily. I would add that this technology also widens the peer support network beyond one's geographic community or institution of higher education. Mac Mayfield, a high school student also indicated the important part that peer-to-peer mentoring can have on student success. Yet, the essays from external stakeholders barely mentioned student peer-to-peer relationships in their essays. Given that they were so frequently discussed as integral to the college student experience by the students and internal stakeholders (not to mention the literature discussed in the analysis chapters), the question becomes, "Why?"

Basic Resources

Among student essayists, there was a theme of acknowledging that basic needs must be met for them to find success in college. Some of the internal stakeholders also discussed aspects of basic needs that must be taken care of for students to be successful. These needs ranged from those highlighted by Maslow's hierarchy of needs (1943) to extensions of that like funding for a college education. One student contributor who is also a self-identified DREAMer really brought home the idea that students need assistance paying for college as a starting place to attendance but also shared that there are many expenses other than tuition and fees that students have a difficult time meeting without support. Scholarships (not loans) are necessary for many students to attend a college or university and living expenses must be included in those awards. Opportunities for this do exist, as outlined by Executive Vice President for Academic and Student Affairs Carolina Angelo, who discusses this at length in her essay. Another student, Sarah Ali, discussed a variety of needs students have but rooted them all in the necessity for the basic life needs to be met before anything else can happen. She said, "I believe the needs of college students are directly correlated to their surrounding environment. In order for a student to succeed in college, their basic human needs must be met. This includes housing stability, well-being, food security, and a stress-free zone to study" (p. 89). For students to learn, grow, and develop, they must be challenged through cognitive dissonance, and that is not possible without a strong foundation.

Directly related to this conversation is the question posed by essayist Vice Chancellor for Student Affairs Willie Banks, who asked, "If our students are struggling at the bottom of Maslow's hierarchy of needs, how can they thrive in their educational pursuits" (p. 117)? When analyzing essays, Julie Owen (reflecting specifically on a contribution from Vernon Wall, 2020–2021 president of ACPA College Student Educators International) noted there are great disparities in access to basic needs of college students based on generational history, experiences, and wealth. So, the fact that there are basic needs for students that need to be met also becomes an issue of equity and justice. But these issues were barely discussed in many of the essays provided by contributors, specifically external ones, so we are left to, again, ask, "Why?" As Michelle Espino indicated in her analysis chapter, the reason could be that others assume that the basic needs of students are already met. Though we know from many scholars that this is not the case. Take for example the work of Hallett, Crutchfield, and Maguire (2019) on addressing homelessness and housing insecurity in higher education. Institutions are working hard to address this issue and others; for example, Long Beach City College, a community college in Long Beach, California, has started an exploratory program allowing underhoused students to live in their cars in a parking deck on campus (Weissman, 2021). What more could be done if all stakeholders came together?

Involvement

Student contributors to this text indicated that students benefit from engaging in a variety of activities outside of the classroom or alongside their coursework while in college. Talia Bailey, a college student contributor to this book, really spoke about the power of being involved on campus to assist in student retention and graduation. Yet, while she focuses on the power of involvement outside of the curriculum like leadership in clubs and student organizations, she also notes that cocurricular engagement is incredibly beneficial, saying, "Employer opportunities, such as co-ops, internships, and career fairs, that benefit the future of students can encourage students to keep striving in their studies because they can visualize themselves in the workplace" (p. 172). This is an incredibly important point for many students who are engaged in higher education today. As this book has pointed out, many students do not attend full-time or in residential capacities. Many have outside responsibilities that keep them from engaging in clubs and organizations. But that does not mean that they do not want to be involved, but that their engagement looks different. Institutions need to adjust.

Other institutions might look to community and technical colleges for guidance on how to frame involvement in curricular ways that engage students not only within the institution but also with the community of employers who will want to hire them. Pointing out the use of apprenticeship as a form of education since the Middle Ages, Caroline Angelo, Executive Vice President for Academic and Student Affairs at Atlanta Technical College, speaks to the power of similar on-the-job learning as central to the purpose of education in these systems. In her essay, she even points out that such opportunities are not only good for students, but they are also good for communities and economies. She notes the synergy present in this type of involvement, saying, "This focus on apprenticeships at high levels of government and education represents a significant opportunity for the unemployed, underemployed, and undecided to earn a college credential and find rewarding employment" (p. 143). Lerman (2010), writing for the Urban Institute, made a distinct argument that seeing apprenticeships as opportunities for student engagement can have a positive impact on retention and graduation rates in community colleges. Yet, very few contributors to this text framed involvement or engagement in these ways. Why? Maybe because, as previously discussed, many stakeholders have a false idea of the students who are engaged in higher education, even though the data tells us they are more like those historically served by community colleges than many care to admit or recognize during their decision-making.

Other Possibilities

There are, of course, other ways to consider and engage with the information in this book. Here are two others to get you started:

1. Review the text to see what alignment or misalignment the information here has with the Association of American Colleges and Universities' High-Impact Practices (Kuh, 2008).
2. Analyze the information in this text in light of the general standards and learning outcomes and domains from the Council for the Advancement of Standards in Higher Education (2019).

Concluding Questions for Consideration

With so much information provided in this text, I wanted to provide readers with a potential guide for considering how their own experiences, perceptions, and positionalities might influence how they think about today's college students. In the introduction, I suggested readers pause and take time to answer the five guiding questions of this text for themselves, indicating that those responses would be useful later. Now I offer a new set of questions, some of which ask you to reflect on the original answers you provided. These guiding questions were created with the intention of getting readers to think deeply about the perspectives of multiple stakeholders. For each question, I have provided a subquestion that encourages readers who are willing to take an even deeper look at the content in relation to their own ideas and beliefs. Thoughtfully consider these questions and your responses.

1. Describe who you generally think of as being a college student. What age are they? Where do they attend? What happens in their lives outside of the classroom?
   a. In looking at the data presented in this book and elsewhere, is your image accurate for the majority of those attending college?
   b. For a more critical examination, consider how your responses to question one are reflective of aspects of identity such as race, gender, ability, and economic status.
2. When reading Chapter 2, what data struck you as most shocking, or which piece of information gave you the biggest "light bulb moment"?
   a. Consider why this particular tidbit was interesting for you. Did it confirm something you already knew but rarely see articulated, or was it information that was counter to your concepts of higher education?
   b. For a more critical examination, think about who has access to that information and which stakeholders do not have access, as well as who might want to keep others unaware of this fact.

3. When reading Chapter 3, what discussions of diversity made you question some of your reactions to the data presented in Chapter 2?
   a. How might your feelings, attitudes, and behaviors toward diversity be shaped by your everyday lived experiences from/within such a position?
   b. For a more critical examination, think about how your perceptions of diversity might be different from other stakeholders in higher education. What might cause the difference in conceptualizations?
4. When reading Chapter 4, which aspects of the various higher education stakeholders did you identify with?
   a. What in your past has made those perspectives accessible to you and why?
   b. For a more critical examination think about the kinds of stakeholders you consider most different than you. What are their motivations? What good ideas do they have that align with yours? How might you form a relationship with one stakeholder outside of your worldview?
5. Look back to how you responded to the following question when presented in Chapter 1. Who are today's college students?
   a. After reading this text, how has your answer been affirmed and/or challenged?
   b. For a more critical examination, consider what voice presented in this text gave you the most challenge in regard to your understanding of who you considered to be today's college students. What has kept your conceptualization of today's college students rooted in your own understanding, and what will it take to expand it?
6. Look back at how you responded to the following question presented in Chapter 1. What are the needs of today's college students?
   a. After reading this text, how has your answer been affirmed and/or challenged?
   b. For a more critical examination, consider what voice presented in this text gave you the most challenge in regard to your understanding of the needs of today's college students. How might you increase your capacity to see beyond your view?
7. Look back at how you responded to the following question presented in Chapter 1. What are the most significant challenges of today's college students?
   a. After reading this text, how has your answer been affirmed and/or challenged?
   b. For a more critical examination, consider what voice presented in this text gave you the most challenge in regard to your understanding of the challenges for today's college students. Are those understandings rooted in your own challenges, or are they informed by other insights? How? Why?

8. Look back at how you responded to the following question presented in Chapter 1. What are the most significant opportunities for today's college students?

   a. After reading this text, how has your answer been affirmed and/or challenged?

   b. For a more critical examination, consider what voice presented in this text gave you the most challenge in regard to your understanding of the opportunities for today's college students. Are these opportunities equitably available to all college-seeking populations? Why or why not?

9. Look back at how you responded to the following question presented in Chapter 1. What can you do to support today's college students?

   a. After reading this text, how has your answer been affirmed and/or challenged?

   b. For a more critical examination, consider what voice presented in this text gave you the most challenge in regard to your understanding of how you might support today's college students. What are you not doing that you could be doing? How might you engage other stakeholders in supporting students in areas in which you are not equipped?

10. Given that this text cannot cover all voices and perspectives, which ones are missing?

    a. How might you go about engaging those stakeholders in conversations to better understand their motivations, conceptualizations, and contributions?

    b. For a more critical examination, what scholarship or experiences might you engage in to further your understanding and that of others related to the themes presented in this text?

Conclusion

The idea for this book came out of years of hearing disagreements about who college students are and talking with students for many years who did not understand why other stakeholders made certain decisions that, to students, seemed antithetical to their experience. There exists a lack of recognition of the multiple positionalities from which stakeholders view higher education. So many people care about higher education but have a difficult time finding solutions to the problems that the system faces due to a lack of really hearing and valuing the perspectives of others. Now, as I look back at this text and the many contributions people made to it, I realize that I was, myself, searching for answers in creating an outlet for exploration of diverse voices. Maybe I was even looking for who had the magic answer to the questions that face the systems of higher education about which so many of us care. What has become incredibly apparent to me is that the answer to the questions, "Who knows today's college students, who knows what they need, who knows what their challenges are, who knows what their opportunities are, and what can we individually and collectively do support them?" are not singular. As my colleague/friend (and contributor to this text) Laura Dean, continually reminds me when viewing multiple perspectives, there does not have to be one answer, much in the world is a both/and proposition. The reality (for me, at least), is that the answer to those questions is held by none of us and, yet, all of us. We all have pieces of the puzzle, but we seem to be unwilling to accept that our piece might not fit where and how we think it should and that someone else might have part of the puzzle that we need. If you have ever put together a complicated puzzle with a group of people (I, myself, have only done this a handful of times), it is often the case that everyone looks at the picture on the box and starts grabbing puzzle pieces with colors or images that make up certain aspects of the overall image. Everyone around the table is trying to build the whole thing, to get it "right," yet we are all hoarding pieces and cannot seem to grasp that someone across the table might have the key to finishing our own contributions to the whole. When building a puzzle over holiday, I often do not even know what sections other folx are working on as I try to create whatever part of the whole I have decided to focus on at the moment. The communication is poor and the motivations for actual completion are varied – some of us want to do a bit and go swimming, others want to sit for hours ruminating over this and the politics of the day at the same time, others are very caring of the people around the table but could care less about the puzzle itself, others just do not have the attention span or the back muscles to sit for three hours putting together a fragmented image of the Mona Lisa, which only gives a small glint of pleasure and a wry smile back when you complete it anyway. If we communicated about our perspectives, our ways of knowing and seeing, our motivations, our constraints, and really focused on the reality of the situation, we could be much more effective in the overall task. Or, at least, we could know who was most likely consciously or unconsciously hoarding the one piece that we need to complete our section of the whole and negotiate to engage it.

I hope that this book helps all of us who care about college students (past, present, and future) and who have control of various pieces of the puzzle that is the very complicated and laborious system we call higher education to pause, check the reality of our situation, and work to understand the pieces and those who contribute to the whole. If we do that, we can maybe resolve the both/and proposition out of an either/or reality to create an opportunity for all. That is a puzzle worth building.

Postscript

Over the course of the past two years as I was finalizing this book, terms like "unprecedented times," "social reckoning," "cultural revolution," and "political unrest" have been ever-present in our everyday lives. I have worked with students wrestling with the racist foundations of the academy and heard them announce that nothing like the current racial tensions in the United States and North America has happened before. Yet, this is not the first time in history that citizens and college students spoke up against racism and demanded action; we can look to revolutions against the Jim Crow South or the work of the Rainbow Coalition in the 1960s. Similarly, I have seen the world in a state of panic over a virus that was basically ignored when it began because it only impacted nondominant populations, and our institutions of higher education escaped the initial waves of illness because the general populations that attended them were from the more privileged elite. This was not unprecedented – some of us survived the AIDS crisis while most leaders ignored it. In recent years, there has also been a huge cry to adjust how higher education operates. Some days the academy is too liberal, and other days, we are accused of being too slow to change. One day we are supposed to be cost free and the next we should raise tuition prices as state legislatures drastically cut funding. Again, not new. This all seems a bit like history repeating. All of this false rhetoric of the "new" problems shields us from having to look at what has been changing (or not) all along.

In terms of higher education and the scope of this book – similar patterns emerge. What has been changing is our students and who we serve. What has not changed is the system of higher education, our funding trends, or our regulatory oversight – at least not in ways that acknowledge the shift in our students. We continue to operate in the old ways. If we take time to discuss with each other what has really been happening on our campus and across our institutional profiles; if we stop playing pundit ping-pong with those stakeholders we disagree with and, instead, hear them out and find their motivations and our own; if we ask our students what they need instead of telling them who they should be; if we do these things and more, we have the potential to build a new vision and not just put together an image that looks just like the puzzle lid and instead create something truly unique.

References

160over90 (2012). *Three and a tree: How to take down bad university marketing one cliché at a time.* Author.

Abrams, Z. (2020). A crunch at college counseling centers. *Monitor on Psychology, 51*(6). Retrieved on November 9, 2021, from https://www.apa.org/monitor/2020/09/crunch-college-counseling

Council for the Advancement of Standards in Higher Education (2019). *CAS profession standards for higher education* (10th ed.). Washington, DC: Author.

Hallett, R. E., Crutchfield, R. M., & Maguire, J. J. (2019). *Addressing homelessness and housing insecurity in higher education: strategies for educational leaders.* Teachers College Press.

Hoover, E. (2020, November 1). *What does a college student look like? Stock images from the quad are getting an update.* The Chronicle of Higher Education. Retrieved on April 15, 2022, from https://www.chronicle.com/article/what-does-a-college-student-look-like-stock-images-from-the-quad-are-getting-an-update?cid=gen_sign_in

Kuh, G. (2008). *High-impact educational practices: What they are, who has access to them, and why they matter.* Association of American Colleges and Universities.

Lee, E. M., & Harris, J. (2020). Counterspaces, counterstructures: Low-income, first-generation, and working-class students' peer support at selective colleges. *Sociological Forum, 35*(4), 1135–1156.

Lerman, R. I. (2010). Expanding apprenticeship: A way to enhance skills and careers. *Urban Institute.* Retrieved on April 15, 2022, from https://www.urban.org/sites/default/files/publication/29691/901384-Expanding-Apprenticeship-A-Way-to-Enhance-Skills-and-Careers.PDF

Maslow, A. H. (1943). A theory of motivation. *Psychological Review, 50*, 370–396.

Weissman, S. (2021, November 5). Community college opens parking garage to unhoused students. *Inside HigherEd.* Retrieved on April 15, 2022, from https://www.insidehighered.com/quicktakes/2021/11/05/community-college-opens-parking-garage-unhoused-students

INDEX

Page numbers in **bold** indicate tables, page numbers in *italics* indicate figures and page numbers followed by n indicate notes.

Taylor & Francis eBooks

www.taylorfrancis.com

A single destination for eBooks from Taylor & Francis
with increased functionality and an improved user
experience to meet the needs of our customers.

90,000+ eBooks of award-winning academic content in
Humanities, Social Science, Science, Technology, Engineering,
and Medical written by a global network of editors and authors.

TAYLOR & FRANCIS EBOOKS OFFERS:

A streamlined
experience for
our library
customers

A single point
of discovery
for all of our
eBook content

Improved
search and
discovery of
content at both
book and
chapter level

REQUEST A FREE TRIAL
support@taylorfrancis.com

 Routledge
Taylor & Francis Group

 CRC Press
Taylor & Francis Group